BROOKLANDS
BOOKS

Cadillac Automobiles 1949-1959

Compiled by
R.M. Clarke

ISBN 1 869826 795

Distributed by
Brooklands Book Distribution Ltd.
'Holmerise', Seven Hills Road,
Cobham, Surrey, England

Printed in Hong Kong

BROOKLANDS ROAD TEST SERIES

AC Ace & Aceca 1953-1983
Alfa Romeo Alfasud 1972-1984
Alfa Romeo Alfetta Coupes GT. GTV. GTV6 1974-1987
Alfa Romeo Giulia Berlinas 1962-1976
Alfa Romeo Giulia Coupes 1963-1976
Alfa Romeo Spider 1966-1987
Allard Gold Portfolio 1937-1958
Alvis Gold Portfolio 1919-1969
American Motors Muscle Cars 1966-1970
Aston Martin Gold Portfolio 1972-1985
Austin Seven 1922-1982
Austin A30 & A35 1951-1962
Austin Healey 3000 1959-1967
Austin Healey 100 & 3000 Col No.1
Austin Healey 'Frogeye' Sprite Col No.1 1958-1961
Austin Healey Sprite 1958-1971
Avanti 1962-1983
BMW Six Cylinder Coupes 1969-1975
BMW 1600 Col. 1 1966-1981
BMW 2002 1968-1976
Bristol Cars Gold Portfolio 1946-1985
Buick Automobiles 1947-1960
Buick Muscle Cars 1965-1970
Buick Riviera 1963-1978
Cadillac Automobiles 1949-1959
Cadillac Automobiles 1960-1969
Cadillac Eldorado 1967-1978
High Performance Capris Gold Portfolio 1969-1987
Chevrolet Camaro & Z-28 1973-1981
High Performance Camaros 1982-1988
Chevrolet Camaro Col No.1 1967-1973
Camaro Muscle Cars 1966-1972
Chevrolet 1955-1957
Chevrolet Impala & SS 1958-1971
Chevrolet Muscle Cars 1966-1971
Chevelle and SS 1964-1972
Chevy EL Camino & SS 1959-1987
Chevy II Nova & SS 1962-1973
Chrysler 300 1955-1970
Citroen Traction Avant Gold Portfolio 1934-1957
Citroen DS & ID 1955-1975
Citroen 2CV 1949-1988
Shelby Cobra Gold Portfolio 1962-1969
Cobras & Replicas 1962-1983
Corvair 1959-1968
Chevrolet Corvette Gold Portfolio 1953 1962
Corvette Stingray Gold Portfolio 1963-1967
High Performance Corvettes 1983-1989
Datsun 240Z 1970-1973
Datsun 280Z & ZX 1975-1983
De Tomaso Collection No.1 1962-1981
Dodge Charger 1966-1974
Dodge Muscle Cars 1967-1970
Excalibur Collection No.1 1952-1981
Ferrari Cars 1946-1956
Ferrari Cars 1973-1977
Ferrari Dino 1965-1974
Ferrari Dino 308 1974-1979
Ferrari 308 & Mondial 1980-1984
Ferrair Collection No.1 1960-1970
Fiat-Bertone X1/9 1973-1988
Fiat Pininfarina 124 + 2000 Spider 1968-1985
Ford Automobiles 1949-1959
Ford GT40 Gold Portfolio 1964-1987
Ford Fairlane 1955-1970
Ford Falcon 1960-1970
High Perfomance Mustangs 1982-1988
Ford Cortina 1600E & GT 1967-1970
Ford RS Escorts 1968-1980
High Performance Escorts Mk1 1968-1974
High Performance Escorts Mk II 1975-1980
Honda CRX 1983-1987
Hudson & Railton 1936-1940
Jaguar Cars 1957-1961
Jaguar Cars 1961-1964
Jaguar Mk2 1959-1969
Jaguar E-Type Gold Portfolio 1961-1971
Jaguar E-Type 1966-1971
Jaguar E-Type V-12 1971-1975
Jaguar XKE Collection No.1 1961-1974
Jaguar XJ6 1968-1972
Jaguar XJ6 Series II 1973-1979
Jaguar XJ6 & XJ12 Series III 1979-1985
Jaguar XJ12 1972-1980
Jaguar XJS Gold Portfolio 1975-1988
Jaguar XK120.XK140.XK150 Gold Portfolio 1948-1960
Jeep CJ5 & CJ6 1960-1976
Jeep CJ5 & CJ7 1976-1986
Jensen Cars 1946-1967
Jensen Cars 1967-1979
Jensen Interceptor Gold Portfolio 1966-1986
Jensen Healey 1972-1976
Lamborghini Cars 1964-1970
Lamborghini Cars 1970-1975
Lamborghini Countach Col No.1 1971-1982
Lamborghini Countach & Urraco 1974-1980
Lamborghini Countach & Jalpa 1980-1985
Lancia Stratos 1972-1985
Land Rover 1948-1973 - A Collection
Land Rover Series II & IIa 1958-1971
Land Rover Series III 1971-1985
Land Rover 90 & 110 1983-1989
Lincoln Gold Portfolio 1949-1960
Lincoln Continental 1961-1969
Lotus and Caterham Seven Gold Portfolio 1957-1989
Lotus Elan Gold Portfolio 1962-1974
Lotus Elan Collection No.2 1963-1972
Lotus Elite 1957-1964
Lotus Elite & Eclat 1974-1982
Lotus Turbo Esprit 1980-1986
Lotus Europa 1966-1975
Lotus Europa Collection No.1 1966-1974
Lotus Seven Collection No.1 1957-1982
Marcos Cars 1960-1988
Maserati 1965-1970
Maserati 1970-1975
Mazda RX-7 Collection No.1 1978-1981
Mercedes 190 & 300SL 1954-1963

Mercedes 230/250/280SL 1963-1971
Mercedes Benz SLs & SLCs Gold Portfolio 1971-1989
Mercedes Benz Cars 1949-1954
Mercedes Benz Cars 1954-1957
Mercedes Benz Cars 1957-1961
Mercedes Benz Compeition Cars 1950-1957
Mercury Muscle Cars 1966-1971
Metropolitan 1954-1962
MG TC 1945-1949
MG TD 1949-1953
MG TF 1953-1955
MG Cars 1959-1962
MGA Roadsters 1955-1962
MGA Collection No.1 1955-1982
MGB Roadsters 1962-1980
MGB GT 1965-1980
MG Midget 1961-1980
Mini Moke 1964-1989
Mini Muscle Cars 1961-1979
Mopar Muscle Cars 1964-1967
Mopar Muscle Cars 1968-1971
Morgan Three-Wheeler Gold Portfolio 1910-1952
Morgan Cars 1960-1970
Morgan Cars Gold Portfolio 1968-1989
Morris Minor Collection No.1
Mustang Muscle Cars 1967-1971
Oldsmobile Automobiles 1955-1963
Old's Cutlass & 4-4-2 1964-1972
Oldsmobile Muscle Cars 1964-1971
Oldsmobile Toronado 1966-1978
Opel GT 1968-1973
Packard Gold Portfolio 1946-1958
Pantera Gold Portfolio 1970-1989
Plymouth Barracuda 1964-1974
Plymouth Muscle Cars 1966-1971
Pontiac Tempest & GTO 1961-1965
Pontiac GTO 1964-1970
Pontiac Firebird 1967-1973
Pontiac Firebird and Trans-Am 1973-1981
High Performance Firebirds 1982-1988
Pontiac Fiero 1984-1988
Pontiac Muscle Cars 1966-1972
Porsche 356 1952-1965
Porsche Cars in the 60's
Porsche Cars 1960-1964
Porsche Cars 1964-1968
Porsche Cars 1968-1972
Porsche Cars 1972-1975
Porsche Turbo Collection No.1 1975-1980
Porsche 911 1965-1969
Porsche 911 1970-1972
Porsche 911 1973-1977
Porsche 911 Carrera 1973-1977
Porsche 911 Turbo 1975-1984
Porsche 911 SC 1978-1983
Porsche 914 Gold Portfolio 1969-1976
Porsche 914 Collection No.1 1969-1983
Porsche 924 Gold Portfolio 1975-1988
Porsche 928 1977-1989
Porsche 944 1981-1985
Range Rover Gold Portfolio 1970-1988
Reliant Scimitar 1964-1986
Riley 11/2 & 21/2 Litre Gold Portfolio 1945-1955
Rolls Royce Silver Cloud 1955-1965
Rolls Royce Silver Shadow 1965-1981
Rover P4 1949-1959
Rover P4 1955-1964
Rover 3 & 3.5 Litre 1958-1973
Rover 2000 + 2200 1963-1977
Rover 3500 1968-1977
Rover 3500 & Vitesse 1976-1986
Saab Sonett Collection No.1 1966-1974
Saab Turbo 1976-1983
Shelby Mustang Muscle Cars 1965-1970
Stubebaker Gold Portfolio 1947-1966
Stubebaker Hawks & Larks 1956-1964
Sunbeam Tiger & Alpine Gold Portfolio 1959-1967
Thunderbird 1955-1957
Thunderbird 1958-1963
Thunderbird 1964-1976
Toyota MR2 1984-1988
Triumph 2000. 2.5. 2500 1963-1977
Triumph GT6 1966-1974
Triumph Spitfire 1962-1980
Triumph Spitfire Col No.1 1962-1982
Triumph Stag 1970-1980
Triumph Stag Collection No.1 1970-1984
Triumph TR2 & TR3 1952-60
Triumph TR4-TR5-TR250 1961-1968
Triumph TR6 1969-1976
Triumph TR6 Collection No.1 1969-1983
Triumph TR7 & TR8 1975-1982
Triumph Vitesse & Herald 1959-1971
TVR Gold Portfolio 1959-1988
Volkswagen Cars 1936-1956
VW Beetle Collection No.1 1970-1982
VW Golf GTi 1976-1986
VW Karmann Ghia 1955-1982
VW Kubelwagen 1940-1975
VW Scirocco 1974-1981
VW Bus. Camper. Van 1954-1967
VW Bus. Camper. Van 1968-1979
VW Bus. Camper. Van 1979-1989
Volvo 120 1956-1970
Volvo 1800 1960-1973

BROOKLANDS ROAD & TRACK SERIES

Road & Track on Alfa Romeo 1949-1963
Road & Track on Alfa Romeo 1964-1970
Road & Track on Alfa Romeo 1971-1976
Road & Track on Alfa Romeo 1977-1989
Road & Track on Aston Martin 1962-1984
Road & Track on Auburn Cord and Duesenburg 1952-1984
Road & Track on Audi & Auto Union 1952-1980
Road & Track on Audi 1980-1986
Road & Track on Austin Healey 1953-1970
Road & Track on BMW Cars 1966-1974
Road & Track on BMW Cars 1975-1978
Road & Track on BMW Cars 1979-1983

Road & Track on Cobra, Shelby & GT40 1962-1983
Road & Track on Corvette 1953-1967
Road & Track on Corvette 1968-1982
Road & Track on Corvette 1982-1986
Road & Track on Datsun Z 1970-1983
Road & Track on Ferrari 1950-1968
Road & Track on Ferrari 1968-1974
Road & Track on Ferrari 1975-1981
Road & Track on Ferrari 1981-1984
Road & Track on Fiat Sports Cars 1968-1987
Road & Track on Jaguar 1950-1960
Road & Track on Jaguar 1961-1968
Road & Track on Jaguar 1968-1974
Road & Track on Jaguar 1974-1982
Road & Track on Jaguar 1983-1989
Road & Track on Lamborghini 1964-1985
Road & Track on Lotus 1972-1981
Road & Track on Maserati 1952-1974
Road & Track on Maserati 1975-1983
Road & Track on Mazda RX7 1978-1986
Road & Track on Mercedes 1952-1962
Road & Track on Mercedes 1963-1970
Road & Track on Mercedes 1971-1979
Road & Track on Mercedes 1980-1987
Road & Track on MG Sports Cars 1949-1961
Road & Track on MG Sprots Cars 1962-1980
Road & Track on Mustang 1964-1977
Road & Track on Peugeot 1955-1986
Road & Track on Pontiac 1960-1983
Road & Track on Porsche 1961-1967
Road & Track on Porsche 1968-1971
Road & Track on Porsche 1972-1975
Road & Track on Porsche 1975-1978
Road & Track on Porsche 1979-1982
Road & Track on Porsche 1982-1985
Road & Track on Porsche 1985-1988
Road & Track on Rolls Royce & B'ley 1950-1965
Road & Track on Rolls Royce & B'ley 1966-1984
Road & Track on Saab 1955-1985
Road & Track on Toyota Sports & GT Cars 1966-1984
Road & Track on Triumph Sports Cars 1953-1967
Road & Track on Triumph Sports Cars 1967-1974
Road & Track on Triumph Sports Cars 1974-1982
Road & Track on Volkswagen 1951-1968
Road & Track on Volkswagen 1968-1978
Road & Track on Volkswagen 1978-1985
Road & Track on Volvo 1957-1974
Road & Track on Volvo 1975-1985
Road & Track - Henry Manney at Large and Abroad

BROOKLANDS CAR AND DRIVER SERIES

Car and Driver on BMW 1955-1977
Car and Driver on BMW 1977-1985
Car and Driver on Cobra, Shelby & Ford GT 40 1963-1984
Car and Driver on Corvette 1956-1967
Car and Driver on Corvette 1968-1977
Car and Driver on Corvette 1978-1982
Car and Driver on Corvette 1983-1988
Car and Driver on Datsun Z 1600 & 2000 1966-1984
Car and Driver on Ferrari 1955-1962
Car and Driver on Ferrari 1963-1975
Car and Driver on Ferrari 1976-1983
Car and Driver on Mopar 1956-1967
Car and Driver on Mopar 1968-1975
Car and Driver on Mustang 1964-1972
Car and Driver on Pontiac 1961-1975
Car and Driver on Porsche 1955-1962
Car and Driver on Porsche 1963-1970
Car and Driver on Porsche 1970-1976
Car and Driver on Porsche 1977-1981
Car and Driver on Porsche 1982-1986
Car and Driver on Saab 1956-1985
Car and Driver on Volvo 1955-1986

BROOKLANDS PRACTICAL CLASSICS SERIES

PC on Austin A40 Restoration
PC on Land Rover Restoration
PC on Metalworking in Restoration
PC on Midget/Sprite Restoration
PC on Mini Cooper Restoration
PC on MGB Restoration
PC on Morris Minor Restoration
PC on Sunbeam Rapier Restoration
PC on Triumph Herald/Vitesse
PC on Triumph Spitfire Restoration
PC on VW Beetle Restoration
PC on 1930s Car Restoration

BROOKLANDS MOTOR & THOROGHBRED & CLASSIC CAR SERIES

Motor & T & CC on Ferrari 1966-1976
Motor & T & CC on Ferrari 1976-1984
Motor & T & CC on Lotus 1979-1983

BROOKLANDS MILITARY VEHICLES SERIES

Allied Mil. Vehicles No.1 1942-1945
Allied Mil. Vehicles No.2 1941-1946
Dodge Mil. Vehicles Col. 1 1940-1945
Military Jeeps 1941-1945
Off Road Jeeps 1944-1971
Hail to the Jeep
US Military Vehicles 1941-1945
US Army Military Vehicles WW2-TM9-2800

BROOKLANDS HOT ROD RESTORATION SERIES

Auto Restoration Tips & Techniques
Basic Bodywork Tips & Techniques
Basic Painting Tips & Techniques
Camaro Restoration Tips & Techniques
Custom Painting Tips & Techniques
Engine Swapping Tips & Techniques
How to Build a Street Rod
Mustang Restoration Tips & Techniques
Performance Tuning - Chevrolets of the '60s
Performance Tuning - Ford of the '60s
Performance Tuning - Mopars of the '60s
Performance Tuning - Pontiacs of the '60s

BROOKLANDS BOOKS

CONTENTS

5	The High-Compression Cadillacs Road Test	*Motor*	March	2	1949
8	The 1949 Cadillac — Car of the Year	*Motor Trend*	Nov.		1949
10	The Cadillac V-8 S.62 Road Test	*Motor*	March	22	1950
14	Cadillac Motor Trial	*Motor Trend*	Nov.		1951
17	Cadillac Series 62 Saloon Road Test	*Autocar*	Nov.	9	1951
20	Road Testing the 50th Anniversary Cadillac	*Motor Trend*	Sept.		1952
24	Testing the Cadillac Series 62	*Science and Mechanics*	Oct.		1952
27	Cadillac — Car of the Year	*Motor Trend*	Feb.		1953
31	Sectioned Cadillac	*Hop Up*	May		1953
34	Cadillac — America's Favorite Luxury Car	*Motor Trend*	May		1953
38	Cadillac: El Camino, Park Avenue & La Espada	*Motor Life*	April		1954
39	Cadillac 62 Sedan	*Motor Life*	August		1954
41	Full Details: '55 Cadillac	*Motor Trend*	Jan.		1955
43	Better than the Best	*Modern Motor*	Sept.		1955
44	Cadillac Fleetwood 60 Special Road Test	*Motor Life*	May		1955
46	Cadillac Specials	*Car Life*	May		1955
47	The Eldorado Brougham — new for 1956	*Motor Life*	Sept.		1955
48	Caddie Coupé	*Wheels*	Nov.		1955
49	The 1956 Cadillac	*Motor Life*	Dec.		1955
50	A Barris Bonanza	*Motor Trend*	Dec.		1955
52	1956 Cadillac — Consumer Analysis	*Car Life*	June		1956
54	The Cadillac 60 Special Road Test	*Motorsport*	May		1956
57	The 1957 Cadillac	*Motor Life*	Dec.		1956
58	Cadillac Engineering	*Motor Life*	Dec.		1956
59	Eldorado Brougham for '57	*Motor Life*	Feb.		1957
60	1957 Cadillac — Consumer Analysis	*Car Life*	May		1957
64	Cadillac Road Test	*Motor Life*	May		1957
66	Cadillac 60 Special Road Test	*Motor Trend*	June		1957
68	Cadillac	*Motor Trend*	Jan.		1958
70	1958 Cadillac — Consumer Analysis	*Car Life*	May		1958
74	Cadillac Road Test	*Motor Life*	July		1958
76	1958 Cadillac — Analysis & Opinions	*Popular Mechanics*	July		1958
79	Americans for 1959	*Motor*	Oct.	1	1958
80	The 1959 Cadillac	*Motor Life*	Nov.		1958
82	1959 Cadillac — Consumer Analysis	*Car Life*	May		1959
86	Cadillac and Imperial — Comparison Test	*Motor Life*	May		1959
88	Elegant Eldorado	*Motor Trend*	Sept.		1959
90	Cadillac Eldorado Brougham — Drivers Report	*Motor Life*	Oct.		1959
92	1959 Cadillac Eldorado Biarritz	*Special Interest Autos*	August		1985

BROOKLANDS BOOKS

ACKNOWLEDGEMENTS

The compiling of this book has been a very enjoyable nostalgic trip back to my late teens. In 1951 I paid my first visit to North America and landed in Galveston, Texas with $50 in my pocket and an unquenchable appetite to see all.

Seven months later, after hitch-hiking through 31 states and a number of Canadian provinces I headed back to Europe. In that brief period I spent a great deal of time being an automobile passenger in an impressive variety of vehicles. The search for these historic stories brought back memories of journies in Henry Js and Hudsons, in Mercurys and Macks, in practical pick-ups and of course when luck smiled on me in comfortable Cadillacs.

The inspiration for this book came from A.B. Lafri of Karlskrona, Sweden and our thanks go to him for his valuable suggestions. Our main thanks however must be directed to the authors and publishers of the articles that are reprinted here for allowing us to include their interesting and copyright road tests and other pieces in this reference series.

We are indebted in this instance to the management of Autocar, Car Life, Hop Up, Modern Motor, Motor, Motor Life, Motorsport, Motor Trend, Popular Mechanics, Science and Mechanics, Special Interest Autos and Wheels for their generosity and on-going support.

R.M. Clarke

BIGGEST AND BEST.—Heading the Cadillac range is the Model 75, a long-wheelbase car available with 7- or 9-seater coachwork which retains such conventional features as rubber-covered running-boards.

The High-compression Cadillacs

America's Quality Car Redesigned to Incorporate a New Overhead-valve V8 Engine Developing 160 b.h.p.

PIONEERS in the production of new engines strong enough to withstand eventual use with ultra-high-compression ratios and promised high-octane fuels are General Motors Corporation. Since the London Motor Exhibition in October all cars in their most expensive range, the Cadillacs, have been redesigned to incorporate an overhead-valve V8 engine, which also appears in substantially modified form in certain Oldsmobile models.

A sectioned view of this engine has already appeared in "The Motor," and the arrival of fuller specifications makes it clear that it incorporates a great many characteristically modern features. It has been designed to meet present-day needs for fuel economy without sacrifice of performance, and to be light and compact with a view to installation in low cars.

Space saving has its root in the cylinder dimensions of the 90-degree V8 engine, the cylinders of which have a stroke-bore ratio of 0.95 instead of the 1.28 of the unit hitherto produced. In conjunction with this change in cylinder shape, connecting rods have been shortened to $6\frac{5}{8}$ ins. and the overall piston length to $3\frac{1}{8}$ ins., piston skirts being cut away on the non-thrust carrying faces to provide clearance for the crankshaft counterbalance weights.

The wedge form of the combustion chambers is evident in the sectioned drawing of the engine, and the location of the sparking plug gives the flame spread from a large towards a smaller volume, which makes for smooth running. For the U.S. market, a compression ratio of 7.5 to 1 is used, giving the notably high brake mean effective pressure of 142 lb. per sq. in. on the high-octane premium-price fuels now available. Future models will probably have an even higher compression ratio, but cars exported to countries where only low-grade fuel is supplied have the compression ratio lowered to 6.7 to 1.

Carburation is by a $1\frac{1}{4}$-in. twin-choke Carter down-draught unit, drawing air via an oil-bath filter and equipped with an

TWO-PEDAL.—Fitting of the optional Hydra-Matic 4-speed fully automatic transmission eliminates the clutch pedal, leaving only the dip switch to be operated by the driver's left foot.

CONTINUITY.—Running-boards which appear only on long-wheelbase models are blended into the line of protective chrome strips on front mudguards and rear-wheel covers.

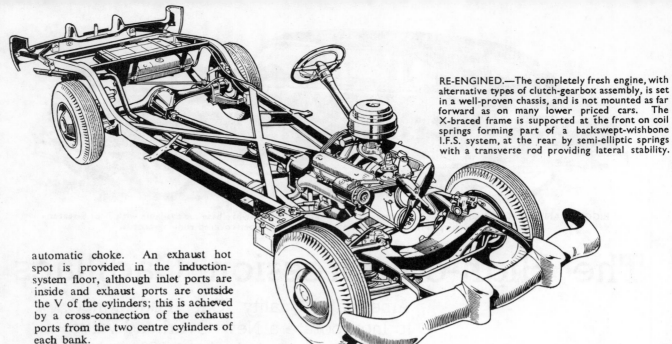

RE-ENGINED.—The completely fresh engine, with alternative types of clutch-gearbox assembly, is set in a well-proven chassis, and is not mounted as far forward as on many lower priced cars. The X-braced frame is supported at the front on coil springs forming part of a backswept-wishbone I.F.S. system, at the rear by semi-elliptic springs with a transverse rod providing lateral stability.

automatic choke. An exhaust hot spot is provided in the induction-system floor, although inlet ports are inside and exhaust ports are outside the V of the cylinders; this is achieved by a cross-connection of the exhaust ports from the two centre cylinders of each bank.

Rigidity is a characteristic of the new engine, the crankshaft with its $2\frac{1}{4}$-in.-diameter crankpins being supported in five main bearings of $2\frac{1}{2}$-in. diameter. Crankcase and cylinder blocks form a single casting, in which the gear-driven five-bearing camshaft runs.

Alternative transmissions are offered by Cadillac, the orthodox one being a combination of $10\frac{1}{2}$-in. single-dry-plate clutch and three-speed synchromesh gearbox. For those who prefer two-pedal control, there is the General Motors Hydra-Matic transmission available.

Automatic Transmission

Part one of this automatic transmission takes the form of a fluid coupling, a species of automatic clutch which has long been known in this country as the " fluid flywheel." An interesting detail is that, although such a coupling is often expected to cushion the transmission, in this application it is supplemented by a torsionally springy coupling, such as is usually incorporated in the centre of a modern dry-plate clutch.

Part two of the Hydra-Matic transmission is a four-speed epicyclic gearbox. Three gear trains are provided, two of which, when used separately or together, provide the three indirect gears or can be locked solid for direct drive, the remaining gear train being for reversing. The operation of the gearbox is in automatic response to speed and load, so that on gentle running the engine revs. are kept low, but with hard use of the throttle the engine is allowed to attain the speed at which its full power is developed. To quote an example, on full-throttle acceleration the upward change from third to

PLAINER PLUMBING.—The number of flexible hoses in the main cooling water circuit is cut down to two, by this neat assembly of pump, thermostatic by-pass, and cross-pipes inter-linking the cylinder blocks and heads.

top gear will only take place when a speed of approximately 65 m.p.h. is attained, and third gear will be re-engaged if a gradient slows the car below 60 m.p.h. On very light throttle, however, top gear will come into action so soon as the car speed exceeds 18 m.p.h., and be held until the speed has sunk as low as 14 m.p.h. unless the throttle is opened.

The chassis in which this power unit is installed may be regarded as very typical of good modern U.S. practice without being in any sense revolutionary. It is X-braced and has channel-section longerons of $6\frac{5}{8}$ ins. maximum depth, the whole being downswept between the axles to give a low floor level. Exhaust piping and the propeller shaft pass through the X-bracing structure,

RAKISH.—The combination of two-door coupé body and series 62 chassis make one of America's fastest production cars.

Model	Series 61, 62, 60S	Series 75
Engine Dimensions:		
Cylinders	V8	V8
Bore	97 mm.	97 mm.
Stroke	92 mm.	92 mm.
Cubic capacity	5,440 c.c.	5,440 c.c.
Piston area	91.3 sq. ins.	91.3 sq. ins.
Valves	Pushrod, o.h.v.	Pushrod, o.h.v.
Compression ratio	7.5 to 1	7.5 to 1
Engine Performance:		
Max. b.h.p.	160	160
at	3,800 r.p.m.	3,800 r.p.m.
Max. b.m.e.p.	142 lb./sq. in.	142 lb./sq. in.
at	1,800 r.p.m.	1,800 r.p.m.
B.h.p. per sq. in. piston area	1.75	1.75
Peak piston speed, ft. per min.	2,290	2,290
Engine Details:		
Carburetter	Carter 1¼ in. dual d/d.	Carter 1¼ in. dual d/d.
Ignition	Delco-Remy coil	Delco-Remy coil
Plugs: make and type	14 mm. AC, type 48	14 mm. AC, type 48
Fuel pump	Mechanical	Mechanical
Fuel capacity	16½ gallons	16½ gallons
Oil capacity	8½ pints	8½ pints
Cooling system	Pump and fan	Pump and fan
Water capacity	3¾ gallons	3¾ gallons
Electrical system	Delco-Remy, 6 volt	Delco-Remy, 6 volt
Battery capacity	115 amp.-hours.	115 amp.-hours
Transmission:		
Clutch	Fluid coupling or Long single dry plate 10½ in. dia.	Fluid coupling or Long single dry plate 11 in. dia.
Gear ratios with hydra-matic transmission:		
Top	3.86	3.77
3rd	4.87	5.47
2nd	8.85	9.93
1st	12.83	14.40
Rev.	14.46	16.23
Gear ratios with synchro-mesh gearbox:		
Top	3.77	4.27

Model	Series 61, 62, 60S	Series 75
Transmission—contd.:		
2nd	5.76	6.63
1st	9.00	10.20
Rev.	9.00	10.20
Prop. shaft	Open	Open
Final drive	Hypoid bevel	Hypoid bevel
Chassis Details:		
Brakes	Bendix hydraulic	Bendix hydraulic
Brake drum diameter	12 ins.	12 ins.
Friction lining area	220 sq. ins.	233 sq. ins.
Suspension:		
Front	Coil and wishbone, i.f.s.	Coil and wishbone, i.f.s.
Rear	Semi-elliptic leaf	Semi-elliptic leaf
Shock absorbers	Piston type, Delco	Piston type, Delco
Wheel type	Steel disc	Steel disc
Tyre size	8.20 × 15	7.50 × 16
Steering gear	Saginaw recirculating ball	Saginaw recirculating ball
Dimensions:		
Wheelbase	10 ft. 6 ins.	11 ft. 4¼ ins.
Track:		
Front	4 ft. 11 ins.	4 ft. 10½ ins
Rear	5 ft. 3 ins.	5 ft. 2½ ins.
Overall length	17 ft. 11 ins.	18 ft. 9¾ ins.
Overall width	6 ft. 7 ins.	6 ft. 10¼ ins.
Overall height	5 ft. 3¾ ins.	5 ft. 8½ ins.
Ground clearance	7¾ ins.	8¼ ins.
Turning circle	46¾ ft. (over bumpers)	49 ft. (over bumpers)
Dry weight	36 cwt.	41¾ cwt.
Performance Data (Hydra-matic transmission):		
Piston area, sq. ins. per ton	50.6	43.7
Brake lining area, sq. ins. per ton	122	112
Top gear m.p.h. per 1,000 r.p.m.	25.2	23.25
Top gear m.p.h. at 2,500 ft./min. piston speed	104	96.5
Litres per ton-mile, dry	3,600	3,360

the shaft being a single tubular unit taking drive from a rear extension of the gearbox to the hypoid axle.

Front suspension is independent, by coil springs and unequal backswept wishbones, and there is an anti-roll torsion bar. At the rear, 2-in.-wide semi-elliptic leaf springs take the drive and braking loads, but a transverse rod is provided to give lateral location of the chassis.

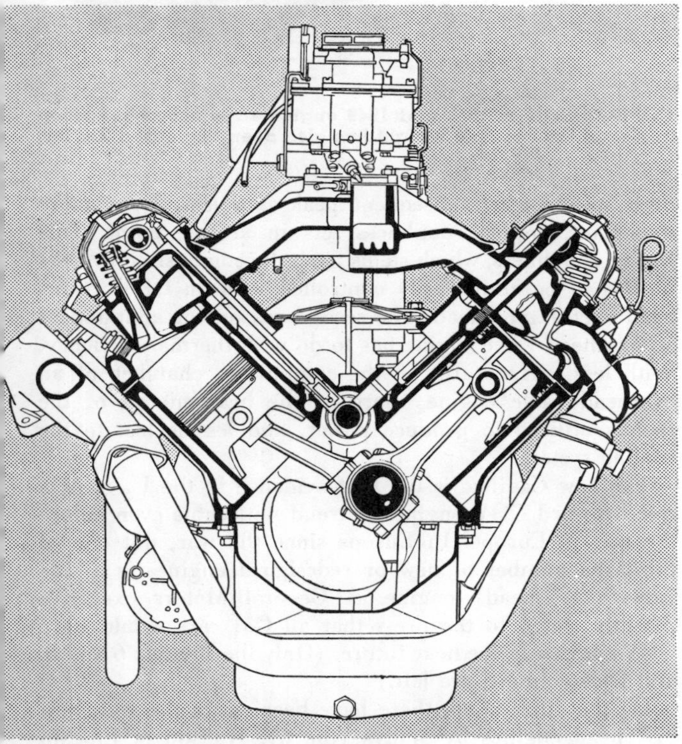

POWER SECTION.—Economy is the main claim for the new engine, high compression ratios being acceptable with the carefully designed combustion chamber, in which are overhead valves operated by hydraulic tappets, pushrods and rockers. Lighter than the side-valve V-8 it supersedes, the new engine is of enlarged cylinder bore and shortened piston stroke. Cross passages interlink the exhaust systems to provide a hot-spot beneath the dual downdraught carburetter.

All springs are damped by Delco shock absorbers of double-acting hydraulic pattern. Bendix hydraulic brakes operate in 12-in.-diameter steel-faced cast-iron drums, and 56 per cent. of braking effort is applied to the front wheels, braking areas being generous by U.S. standards.

Coachwork styles are based upon two-door coupé, four-door sedan and two-door convertible bodies for the normal-wheelbase chassis, plus bodies seating five, seven or nine people for mounting on the long 75-series chassis. There are, however, quite wide variations in interior and exterior finish details as between the 61, 62 and 60S series cars, which cater for either conservative or advanced tastes. All bodies are of Fisher steel construction, equipped with such items as lamps which light up automatically when doors or luggage locker are opened. On certain models, hydraulic push-button control is applied to windows, front-seat adjustment and folding coupé top.

Perhaps the most striking recognition feature of recent Cadillac models, including those with the now-obsolete side-valve engine, is the tail-fin motif on each rear mudguard. Tail lamps are formed in these fins, and one lamp hinges up to reveal the fuel filler. Visible modifications on the 1949 o.h.v. models are a slightly lengthened bonnet and a new, low, full-width radiator grille.

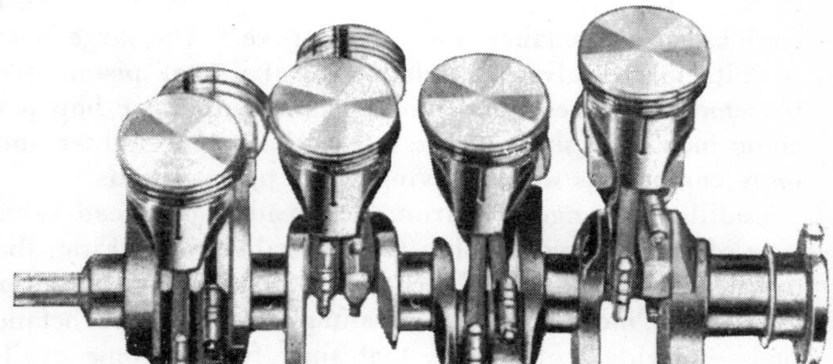

MECHANISM.—Visible in this photograph are the sturdy 4-throw 5-bearing crankshaft, the side-by-side big end bearings, and the slipper pistons whose skirts are cut away to clear the crankshaft counterweights at bottom dead centre.

CAR OF THE YEAR

THE 1949 CADILLAC

by John Bond

NOTE: In this article, automotive enthusiast John Bond was asked to describe his idea of the most advanced of the 1949 models. Before making his selection, he considered all models, ranging from the Jeepster through the Lincoln, and gave serious thought to the engine, appearance, and handling characteristics. His final choice may be subject to controversy, but definitely has merit.—Editor

CHOOSING an outstanding "car of the year" for certain years past may be difficult, but for 1949 the selection is narrowed down to three most worthy of consideration: Ford, Oldsmobile, and Cadillac.

While the Ford has an entirely new chassis and body, plus many mechanical changes, it offers nothing new or outstanding from an engineering viewpoint, since it now falls in line with conventional design practice established by competitors before the war.

The Cadillac was chosen in preference to the Olds because, while both have outstanding new V-8 engines which are similar, they are not by any means the same. The Cadillac, with 10 per cent more piston displacement than the Olds, develops 18.5 per cent more bhp and weighs a few pounds less.

This new engine by Cadillac is not the so-called Kettering engine, which was a small six of 180 cubic inches. The Kettering six was a square engine (equal bore and stroke), had seven main bearings, used a simple combustion chamber shape about like the last Buick Six of 1930, looked externally very similar to the current 216.5 cubic inch Chevrolet, and was even heavier than the Chevrolet. While the Cadillac was developed concurrently with the GM Research 12.5 to 1 compression engine, it is considerably different.

The 1949 Cadillac powerplant, with a cylinder bore of 3.8125 inches and a stroke of only 3.625 inches, is unique in that this gives it a stroke-bore ratio of 0.95:1. (Most engines have a smaller bore than stroke.) The large bore permits large valves in relation to the total piston displacement with resultant good specific output, or bhp per cubic inch. The short stroke makes the engine lighter and more compact as well as giving lower piston speeds.

Cadillac's change-over from "L" head to overhead valve type of design accomplishes two desirable goals. First, the overhead valve engine is recognized as a definite must for getting the most potential advantage from higher octane fuels—provided, of course, that such fuels become available at economic prices. It is not possible to increase compression ratio in "L" head engines to much over 8:1, even with better fuel, because volumetric efficiency falls off at

1948 OUTLINE

COMPARISON of 1948 and 1949 engine sizes shows reduction in size of later model. Weight has also been decreased 220 lbs.

high speeds with consequent peak bhp loss. Even more important, engine roughness sets in at this point. This engine roughness, which stems from the combustion process itself, can be more easily controlled with an OHV (overhead valve) type head. The second reason for adaption of an overhead valve engine has to do with thermal efficiency. With less surface area in the combustion chamber of an overhead valve engine, more of the heat energy of the fuel is utilized to produce power, and less is lost to the cooling system.

The new Cadillac is the first evidence in the U. S. of a trend toward OHV engines, a trend noticeable even before the war in Europe. In Europe since the war, not one of the large number of new or redesigned engines is a side valve ("L" head) engine. A General Motors executive recently stated to the press that all GM cars would have OHV engines in the near future. (Only the Pontiac 6 and 8, and Oldsmobile 6 are left.)

On the other hand, there have been, since the war, new "L" head engines by Willys (the 6), Hudson 6, Lincoln V-8, and redesigns by Ford (6 and 8) and Packard. Hudson's President E. A. Barit recently made the statement that they could go to 9.2:1 compression ratios with only minor changes to their present "L" head designs. Such

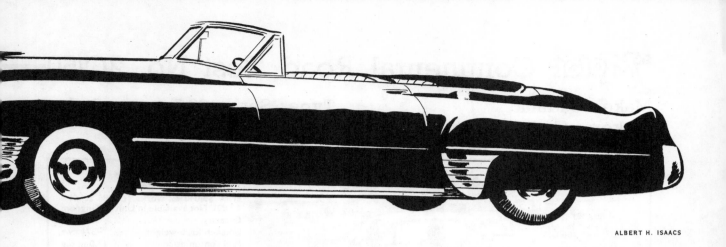

ALBERT H. ISAACS

a statement is somewhat premature from the standpoint that fuels requiring compression ratios beyond the practical range of "L" head engines are probably a long way off. The cost of producing 100 octane gasoline is not only very high, but it is a waste of our dwindling petroleum reserves.

Aside from the technical considerations already discussed, perhaps the only real test of the worth of a new car or engine is the net gain or loss to the purchaser. With an increase of 10 bhp, the Cadillac now develops 160 bhp with the engine stripped, or 133 bhp "as installed," with

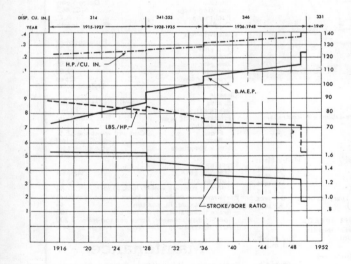

TRENDS in design characteristics of Cadillac V-8 engines

all accessories. This increase in power, together with a very noteworthy decrease in engine weight of 220 pounds (including saving in cooling system), results in a noticeable improvement in acceleration performance. The increase in compression ratio, though only from 7.25 to 7.50, is an automatic guarantee of reduced fuel consumption. Actually, as a result of reduced engine friction and improved thermal efficiency, the average user should get about two miles per gallon better mileage with the new model.

Perhaps an even more important advantage of the new OHV Cadillac engine to its owner is its increased durability.

Cadillac engineers have done a thorough job of development work toward improved stamina in every part of the engine. To give just one example, in a paper read before the Society of Automotive Engineers describing the new engine, photographs were shown of engine bearings after test runs at 4250 rpm or an equivalent of 108 mph. (Of course, the car will not actually travel that fast on the road.) The 1948 engine, with 4.50 inch stroke, was run 131 hours at this speed. The bearings could be described as being in fair condition, and good for many more hours of running. However, they would certainly be replaced if encountered by a competent mechanic in the field. On the other hand, the bearings from the new short stroke engine were in perfect condition after 541 hours at the same speed, or more than four times the test period on the long stroke engine.

Automobile engines are not subject to the annual external sheet metal changes for the benefit of providing a new-appearing model. The new Cadillac OHV powerplant is brand new, and can normally be expected to be continued with little change for a period of at least seven years. By looking ahead, Cadillac engineers have designed an engine which can easily and economically have its compression ratio increased to anything up to 12:1, with assurance to the owner that he can take full advantage of future fuels, with no harmful effects.

Finally, it is encouraging to see a new model offered with no readily visible styling changes, thus reversing the usual "face-lifting" trend, along with using the original model engine.

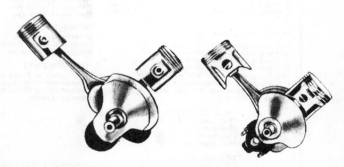

THOMAS J. MEDLEY

COMPARISON of 1948 and 1949 crankshaft and piston assemblies—major factor in weight reduction and added acceleration

Make: Cadillac   **Type:** Series 62 Touring Sedan
Makers: Cadillac Motor Car Division,
Ceneral Motors Corpn., Detroit, Mich., U.S.A.

Dimensions and Seating

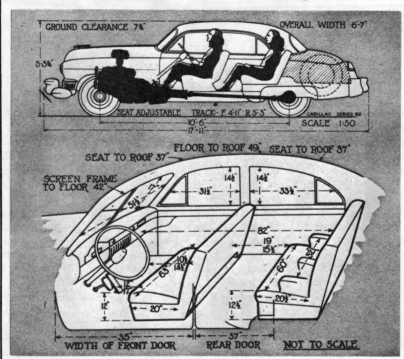

In Brief

Price $3,040 ex works (£1,086 at £1 = $2.80). Not available in United Kingdom.

Capacity	...	5,420 c.c.
Unladen kerb weight	...	37¼ cwt.
Fuel consumption	...	17.0 m.p.g.
Maximum speed	...	99.7 m.p.h.
Maximum speed on 1 in 20 gradient	...	84 m.p.h.

Acceleration,
10–30 m.p.h. in Hydra-Matic 3.6 secs.
0–50 m.p.h. through gears 11.6 secs.
Gearing 25.2 m.p.h. in top at 1,000 r.p.m.
104 m.p.h. at 2,500 ft. per min. piston speed.

Specification

Engine

Cylinders	...	V.8
Bore ...	...	96.84 mm.
Stroke ...	...	92.07 mm.
Cubic capacity ...	...	5,420 c.c.
Piston area ...	...	91.3 sq. in.
Valves ...	Push rod o.h.v.
Compression ratio ...	...	7.5/1
Max. power ...	...	160 b.h.p.
at ...	...	3,800 r.p.m.
Piston speed at max. b.h.p.	2,290 ft. per min.
Carburetter	...	Carter
Ignition ...	Delco-Remy
Sparking plugs ...	A.C. 46.5
Fuel pump ...	...	A.C.
Oil filter	Floating intake

Transmission

Clutch	Fluid coupling
Top gear ...	...	3.77
3rd gear ...	...	4.87
2nd gear ...	...	8.85
1st gear ...	...	12.83
Propeller shaft ...	...	Open
Final drive ...	...	Hypoid bevel

Chassis

Brakes ...	Bendix hydraulic servo
Brake drum diameter ...	...	12 ins.
Friction lining area ...	220 sq. in.
Suspension:		
Front ...	Coil and wishbone I.F.S.
Rear ...	Semi-elliptic leaf
Shock absorbers ...	Delco telescopic
Tyres ...	...	8.00 x 15

Steering

Steering gear	...	Saginaw
Turning circle ...	...	45 ft.
Turns of steering wheel, lock to lock	...	4¼

Performance factors (at laden weight as tested)
Piston area, sq. in. per ton ... 45
Brake lining area, sq. in. per ton ... 108
Specific displacement, litres per ton-mile 3,200
Fully described in "The Motor," March 2, 1949.

Test Conditions

Dry, cold, little wind, 80 octane fuel. Maximum speed recorded on Aeltre-Jabbeke Autostrada.

Test Data

ACCELERATION TIMES

	Top	Hydra-Matic
10–30 m.p.h.		3.6 secs.
20–40 m.p.h. } see text		4.6 secs.
30–50 m.p.h.		6.1 secs.
40–60 m.p.h.	12.0 secs. } part throttle	7.5 secs.
50–70 m.p.h.	14.0 secs. } part throttle	8.8 secs.
60–80 m.p.h.	16.2 secs. }	13.1 secs.

ACCELERATION TIMES Through Gears

0–30 m.p.h.	5.1 secs.
0–40 m.p.h.	7.8 secs.
0–50 m.p.h.	11.6 secs.
0–60 m.p.h.	15.8 secs.
0–70 m.p.h.	20.7 secs.
0–80 m.p.h.	31.7 secs.
Standing quarter-mile ...	20.0 secs.

MAXIMUM SPEEDS

Flying Quarter-mile

Mean of four opposite runs ...	99.7 m.p.h.
Best time equals ...	101.1 m.p.h.

Speed in Gears

Max. speed in 3rd gear ...	66 m.p.h.
Max. speed in 2nd gear ...	30 m.p.h.
Max. speed in 1st gear ...	14 m.p.h.

FUEL CONSUMPTION

24.0 m.p.g. at constant 30 m.p.h.
23.5 m.p.g. at constant 40 m.p.h.
21.0 m.p.g. at constant 50 m.p.h.
18.0 m.p.g. at constant 60 m.p.h.
14.0 m.p.g. at constant 70 m.p.h.
11.5 m.p.g. at constant 80 m.p.h.
Overall consumption for 136 miles, 8 gallons, equals 17.0 m.p.g.

WEIGHT

Unladen kerb weight ...	37¼ cwt.
Front/rear weight distribution ...	52/48
Weight laden as tested ...	40¼ cwt.

INSTRUMENTS

Speedometer at 30 m.p.h.	accurate
Speedometer at 60 m.p.h.	3% fast
Speedometer at 80 m.p.h.	4% fast
Distance recorder	4% fast

HILL CLIMBING (at steady speeds)

Max. speed on 1 in 20 ...	84 m.p.h.
Max. speed on 1 in 15 ...	79 m.p.h.
Max. speed on 1 in 10 ...	70 m.p.h.
Max. speed on 1 in 5 ...	45 m.p.h.

BRAKES AT 30 m.p.h.

0.95 g. retardation (= 31.6 ft. stopping distance) with 90 lb. pedal pressure.
0.75 g. retardation (= 40 ft. stopping distance) with 50 lb. pedal pressure.
0.35 g. retardation (= 86 ft. stopping distance) with 25 lb. pedal pressure.

Maintenance

Fuel tank : 16½ gallons. **Sump :** 8½ pints. **Gearbox and differential :** 20 pints. **Rear axle :** 4 pints. **Radiator :** 29 pints (3 drain taps). **Chassis lubrication :** By grease gun every 1,000 miles to 22 points, plus 2 generator oil cups. **Ignition timing :** 32 deg. b.t.d.c. full advance. **Spark plug gap:** 0.033 in. **Contact breaker gap:** 0.0125. **Valve timing :** I.O. 19 B.T.D.C., I.C. 83° A.B.D.C., E.O. 53° B.B.D.C., E.C.49° A.T.D.C. **Tappet clearances :** Zero Lash tappets. **Front wheel toe-in :** 1/32 in. : 3/32 in. **Camber angle :** minus 3/8 in. : plus 3/8 in. **Castor angle :** minus ¾ in. : plus ¼ in. **Tyre pressures :** Front 24 lb., rear 24 lb. **Brake fluid :** Delco. **Battery :** Delco 6-volt 115 amp./hour at 20-hour rate. **Lamp bulbs :** 6 volt; Headlight 43-35 watt; parking and signal lamps 21-3 CP; stop and tail lamp 21-3 CP; instrument cluster 2 CP; dome light (except 6267) 15 CP; instrument panel clock light 2 CP; courtesy lamps 7523-33 1 CP; licence plate light 3 CP; trunk compartment light 2 CP; directional signal indicator 1 CP; glove compartment light 2 CP; beam indicator 1 CP.

Ref. US/55/50

-The CADILLAC V.8 S.62

High Performance, Extremely Quiet Running and Automatic Gear Changing are Prominent Features of One of America's Finest Cars

ALMOST invariably, cars road tested by "The Motor" are submitted by the manufacturers concerned or by their agents, but in the case of the Cadillac V.8 about to be reviewed this is not so. The car in question is the private property of a well-known American enthusiast, Briggs S. Cunningham, Esq., who for personal reasons has had it maintained in Europe and who was kind enough to make it available for road test purposes. The car tested had rather more than 7,000 miles on the odometer and during this period had received regular but strictly routine attention. For practical reasons it was necessary to take the maximum speed figures immediately before, and the acceleration and fuel consumption figures, directly after, a journey to Turin and it is therefore possible that the figures quoted in the accompanying data panel are slightly inferior to those that would have been recorded by a works-tuned car. Even as they stand they indicate performance of an extremely high order, and a one-way timed speed of over 100 m.p.h. has been recorded by only one other closed car during the whole of the post-war series of "The Motor" Road Tests. But, startling as some of the figures appear, it is in other respects that the latest V.8 Cadillac makes the greatest impact upon the European observer.

Cadillac lends a certain majesty which is not always present with this type. The figures for overall width, length and weight tell their own story, and they are matched by one of the largest engines in world production, with a capacity of 5.4 litres, and 160 b.h.p. at the moderate engine speed of 3,800 r.p.m. The engine is notable for a stroke/bore ratio under unity and the use of overhead valves in conjunction with a cylinder head design which permits a very high compression ratio, although on the car tested the figure is limited to 7.5 : 1 for use in conjunction with 80 octane fuel. This drives the car through a fluid flywheel and a four-speed epicyclic gear box in which the ratio employed is automatically chosen by a control which tastes both engine speed and throttle opening.

The Cadillac is a vehicle manifestly intended to cover long distances at a high cruising speed whilst demanding the absolute minimum of effort from the driver and imposing the smallest possible distraction upon the passengers. Outstanding overall silence both in respect of mechanical noise, and also the equally important and often neglected aspects of road noise and wind roar, is perhaps the major virtue which is noticed in ordinary

of the speed range, nearly 12 m.p.g. being available at a steady 80 m.p.h. and 14 m.p.g. at a level 70 m.p.h. On long runs on part throttle the car will achieve 17 m.p.g. overall but it is only fair to add that, if full use is made of the acceleration and hill climbing in English conditions, there is a considerable worsening of the consumption, which may drop to below 10 m.p.g.

Fully Automatic Transmission

Before analysing the acceleration times one must remark upon the characteristics of the transmission and the kind of performance which is offered on the road. To take an extreme case, the car can be held at rest on the brakes with the throttle wide open with 100 per cent. slip in the fluid flywheel. On releasing the brakes, the fluid flywheel will play the part of an ordinary clutch and the speed will rise to 14 m.p.h. in first gear after which a speed-responsive governor will feed hydraulic pressure to the second-gear band and in this ratio 30 m.p.h. will be achieved. At this speed, a corresponding mechanism engages third gear on which the speed will rise to 66 m.p.h., whereupon top gear is enjoyed. Provided the engine is working on full throttle, there will be downward gear changes at approximately the same speeds under conditions of steadily increasing gradient and hence it is, for example, impossible to use full throttle and top gear between 10 and 30 m.p.h., for the mere act of opening the throttle fully inevitably engages a low ratio in this condition. The driver has, however, some control over the gear situation. Firstly, on light throttle openings the higher ratios will be engaged at very considerably lower speeds and one may for instance accelerate between 40 and 60 m.p.h. in top on part throttle in 12 seconds as compared with the 7.5 seconds achieved with full throttle and the automatically engaged third speed. Additionally there is a mechanical control which bars the engagement of third and fourth speeds and thus, by moving a lever to a position marked

IMPRESSIVE SIGHT.—One of the largest cars in the world, the Cadillac S.62 has a well-balanced appearance which is here excellently depicted.

It will be remembered that the chassis design is conventional in the sense that it has an X-braced frame, a hypoid rear axle with semi-elliptic rear springs, independent front suspension using the conventional unequal length wishbones, and open coil springs. The full-width body of envelope form would have been considered entirely heterodox immediately after the war but although it is now sufficiently established as to cause little comment, the sheer scale effect of the

running and conversation in ordinary tones can be maintained at between 80 and 90 m.p.h. on a speedometer which is only 4 per cent. fast at these speeds.

The combination of high acceleration with a comfortable cruising speed of not much less than 100 m.p.h. naturally results in exceedingly high overall speeds, and 60 miles in the hour may be considered normal on reasonably straight roads.

As can be seen from the data panel, fuel economy is excellent in the upper part

"LO," the engine may be used as a brake either when approaching a corner on the flat or for descending a long mountainous gradient.

From the foregoing description it will be seen that one cannot set out the acceleration figures in the normal terms of times taken on top gear, third gear, etc.; one must rather regard the transmission as an entity in which the infinitely variable torque converter is approached through the medium of four automatically engaged steps. The advantages of such a transmission are self-evident for there is neither clutch pedal nor clutch and except for abnormal conditions such as engine braking or reverse there is no need to touch a gear lever.

These advantages are won at slight cost. There is a definite increase in engine noise and "fuss" on full throttle as a result of the engine running up into the upper part of the speed range although the gears themselves are exceedingly quiet and the engagement thereof almost imperceptible when changing up. The absence of synchronisation between engine and tail shaft speed when changing down can produce a jerk which would bring a reprimand to a professional driver and a feeling of shame to the experienced amateur if a modicum of skill is not exercised. Very high stopping power is obtained with abnormally low pedal effort, but this is derived from a substantial servo effort in the shoes themselves which in turn leads to somewhat abrupt braking at low speeds in traffic and to a loss of poise in the car as a whole if the brakes are applied hard at high road speeds.

For a car which weighs nearly two tons, the steering is remarkably light and the fact that the wheel needs nearly five turns between one full lock and the other must be related to the very big angle through which the front wheels are turned, and to the exceedingly large lock which makes the car easy to handle in traffic and far more simple to park than one would imagine upon a mere study of its dimensions. The car is obviously not designed to corner in sports fashion but it handles accurately on bends with the slow response characteristic of the under-

Cadillac Road
Test - - Contd.

TWO-PEDAL DRIVE.— This illustration shows the complete absence of clutch pedal characteristic of the Hydra-Matic transmission, also the rubber seal in the air conduit which gives de-misting to the driver's side windows in addition to the windscreen.

steering car which puts rapid high-speed manœuvring out of the question.

The suspension system has obviously been designed to cope with two extreme conditions. It gives almost complete freedom from body movement on really smooth roads, the slight and infrequent irregularities of which are absorbed almost without notice. By reason of the stiff chassis and body structure, and the very large wheel movement permitted, exceedingly rough roads can be attacked at speeds in the environ of 40 or 50 m.p.h. with, again, but little effect upon the overall stability, the state of the road surface chiefly being deduced by increase in noise. On the wavy surfaces typical of neglected British main roads, the car is somewhat less satisfactory and, between 70 and 80 m.p.h., body movement of considerable frequency and magnitude can be built up.

Carrying Capacity

The latest V.8 Cadillac is particularly suitable for long-distance motoring, not only for technical reasons but also because the body accommodation is suitable for this purpose. The rear luggage locker is

CLEAR SPACE.—By mounting the spare wheel vertically at the side of the luggage locker it may be removed without disturbing the large amount of luggage which can be stowed under lock and key

of exceptional capacity, and, as three persons could be comfortably carried for any required number of miles on the front seat, the whole of the rear of the body (which will also seat three if required) can be kept free for additional stowage of personal luggage. There is also a considerable flat area between the back of the rear seat and the rear window which can be used for carrying small parcels, and a locker in the facia panel which will serve as a receptacle for maps, guide books, and the like. Less commendable is the fact that if only two persons are aboard, a passenger on the front seat notices the lack of an armrest and definitely feels the need for sideways support whilst, on this particular model, the general equipment of the car may well be thought excessively austere. One ashtray is provided, and that available to the rear seat passengers only. There is no under-scuttle accommodation for small parcels and the dark brown finish of the facia panels and window cappings may be thought more suitable for a utility car than for a make which ranks as one of the world's best. Similarly, the cloth upholstery is far from first-class quality, and there is an entire absence of the attention to personal comforts varying from ladies' mirrors and powder cases to cocktail cabinets and picnic trays which are normal to the European car of the highest class.

In fairness it should be stated that the Cadillac range offers a progression from the Spartan to the Athenian taste, and that the particular car reviewed was among the lower priced of nine models. Viewed in this light the car offers astonishing value for money. It has a performance which few makes can rival, even fewer surpass, a general silence of running (including low wind noise) which many will consider unbeaten, and an ease in driving which must be a great asset when very long mileages are attempted.

Jewels by Van Cleef & Arpels

Wanted ...
By Almost Half
the People!

According to a recent widespread survey—almost half the motor car owners in the United States would own a Cadillac, if they had their unrestricted choice. Cadillac was, in fact, voted the favorite by more than *five to one* over any other motor car built in America—a degree of leadership that is probably without parallel in all our industrial history. We regret, sincerely, that all who expressed their desire to own a Cadillac cannot do so. But we believe, with equal sincerity, that a great many have needlessly denied themselves the pleasure. Cadillac's relatively modest price, its unusual operating economy and long life, make it a *far* more practical and sensible possession than many motorists realize. Why not visit your dealer soon— and see for yourself? You might be surprised to find you're closer to the "Standard of the World" than you ever imagined.

CADILLAC MOTOR CAR DIVISION ★ GENERAL MOTORS CORPORATION

Cadillac MOTOR TRIAL

BORGESON SAYS, HERE'S A CAR THAT GIVES REAL ECONOMY WHETHER YOU WANT IT OR NOT

by Griff Borgeson

THERE'S NO getting away from it— General Motors is the design and sales genius of today's auto industry. Chevy is tops in sales; Pontiac has fine performance along with quiet, tasteful styling; Olds is the answer for most people who want jackrabbit performance at a moderate price; Buick, brazen as a bird of paradise, is one of the most desired cars in the world. Finally, there's Cadillac, everybody's dreamboat, probably the most coveted, most sold, and therefore most successful luxury car in the industry's long history. To complete the picture, GM looks ahead to mass desires of next year and of a decade from now—there are enough experimental features in Le Sabre, stylewise and machinerywise, to create a dozen radically-superior passenger cars tomorrow. And there's the XP-300. GM is both a super-shrewd judge of public taste and a daring pioneer—a rare but fortunate combination.

We need never have put the Cadillac through a Motor Trial to have arrived at these conclusions. In New York or Dallas, Chicago or Beverly Hills, people who have "arrived" acquire Cadillacs almost automatically. The Caddie is the badge of success. The big question is, "Why should it be so? There are other cars, equally fine." That's the point: GM has hit the bull's eye of the luxury target at which it was aiming with a degree of accuracy that can only mean skill—not chance.

We of MOTOR TREND research—Walt Woron, Dick van Osten, and I—have been familiar with Cadillac excellence for a long time. It's a story stretching back to 1900 when that unsung genius, Henry M. Leland, originated the make. He had learned the art of making interchangeable parts at the old Samuel Colt's arms works back in the last century. He applied his knowledge to the building of cars and amazed the world in 1906 with a remarkable demonstration. Before the Royal Automobile Club in England, three Cadillacs were torn down, the parts scrambled, three cars reassembled and successfully road tested. This was the first step in bringing the automobile within the economic reach of the general population. It also implied workmanship of superior quality and established the Cadillac tradition of excellence which survives today.

With a vast backlog of reader requests for a Cadillac Motor Trial, we cleared through Detroit and were told to pick up any car we chose at the vast showrooms of the Cadillac Motor Car Division in downtown Los Angeles. Our selection was a Series 62 sedan, chosen because we feel this car to be the best buy of its line and therefore the car of the greatest popular appeal. The four-day shakedown we gave it covered nearly 1000 miles over our customary test course, including all shadings of metropolitan traffic, broad super-highways, narrow country roads, long stretches of washboard, twisting mountain highways, and the flat-out surface of a five-mile long top-speed strip on famous El Mirage dry lake.

FUEL CONSUMPTION: This was the most surprising feature of the entire Motor Trial. Its 331 cu. ins. of displacement makes the Cad engine one of the world's largest. In a luxury car, designed for definitely brilliant performance, one hardly expects to find a penny-pinching appetite for gas. But the Cadillac actually gives better gas mileage than many more utilitarian cars!

In moderately heavy traffic our highly accurate instruments showed figures as high as 21 mpg. At a steady 30 mph

14

our best figure was 24.4 mpg and at a steady 45 we once hit 24.0 mpg. The top reading at 60 was an astonishing 18.1 mpg! This sort of economy from a big-engined car weighing over two tons is a classic example of the new American trend toward powerplants of high efficiency—a trend which was kicked off by Cadillac and Olds back in '49 and which the competition is forced to match.

ACCELERATION: A two-ton, plus, machine is usually lacking in distinction as a form of rapid transit. That the opposite is the case with Cadillac is another outstanding feature of the 160-bhp-engined cars. Our test machine packed the sporty weight:power ratio of 27.6:1 and this, plus a smooth, fast-shifting Hydra-Matic transmission gave us acceleration times which, averaged, rank fourth among the cars tested by MOTOR TREND Research this year. Having all this urge at the tip of one's toe gives the feeling of being in complete control of any traffic condition. With such power on instant tap one is inclined to drive more relaxedly, less hurriedly, even more courteously—after all, you are the boss of the road.

ENGINE: Cadillac anticipated the advantages of the V-type engine back in 1914 and has built no other type since. In 1930 the first ohv, V-type engine was introduced in the first V-16, followed in '31 by their first V-12, also with ohv. This experience, which continued through most of the Thirties, furnished the factory with an immense amount of practical experience with ohv-type engines. No other manufacturer had the benefit of such extended know-how and it's not surprising that Cad, accompanied by Olds, introduced America's first ohv V-8s.

Porting of the Cad engine is highly rational, aside from in-line valve arrangement, and intake manifold feed sequence has been carefully, intelligently worked out. Another direction in which this engine

CAVERNOUS ACCOMMODATION for luggage is provided. Rear-seat radio speaker is visible above spare tire. Switch on instrument panel permits any degree of balance between front and rear speakers, adds to listening enjoyment

blazed a new trail was in bore:stroke ratios. Short-stroke engines had been played with decades before, but Cadillac startled America by following an already-established Continental trend and using, in a production engine, a stroke actually less than the diameter of the bore.

What this accomplishes is reduction of piston speed at any given rpm, making for reduced hp losses within the engine. Further effects are quicker revving, improved economy, lighter weight in relation to output, and more compact dimensions. The combined advantages of the short-stroke engine have sent competition scurrying to follow Cadillac's lead, but the purchaser of a '51 Cad can be confident that his engine is probably the best-developed and least "buggy" of any of the truly post-war powerplants.

The ohv Cad engine's reliability and punch have been convincingly demonstrated in the most demanding test of all, road racing. Cad-Allard cars have competed successfully all over the US with a remarkable record of success for the past two seasons. Such troubles as they've had have never—to our knowledge—been traceable to their trusty engines. One last word on this subject deals with the unusual silence of the engine, notable even when wound tight on the Clayton dynamometer. And starting from stone cold is always amazingly quick and easy.

TRANSMISSION: Cadillac's Hydra-Matic for '51 has been improved, many of the troubles which plagued owners of earlier models having been eliminated. The shift from first to second is very fast, slower from second to third, quick from third to fourth. Engine braking is fine in both LOW and DRIVE ranges and the changing of gears is perfectly silent. Second gear comes in at about 14 mph, third at 25, fourth at 60. Study of the acceleration times in the Table of Performance shows that gear ratios in LOW are so low as to hold no advantages for quick getaways. With the car's wt.:power ratio, getaway in DRIVE matches the dig of just about anything on the road.

BRAKES: These tend to be like a race

MODEL OF EFFICIENCY. The Cad engine is notable for many of its features; among them are short rocker arms, very friction-free porting, good exhaust-valve cooling, excellent location of spark plug in efficient combustion chamber

car's clutch: all off or all on. They lock with the greatest of ease, dissipating the heavy car's dynamic inertia between tires and pavement, rather than between brake drums and linings.

Many cars today use what is known as Hotchkiss drive, the alternative arrangement being torque tube drive. As the rear wheels turn or, because of braking, do not turn, the rear axle tends to do a lot of turning, too. A torque tube is a steel tube around the driveshaft which is anchored at both ends and which absorbs the twisting effort (torque) of the rear axle. Hotchkiss drive has the advantage of lighter unsprung weight and lower cost but, unless steadied by torque arms from rear axle to frame, throws all the twisting load upon the rear springs. In the modern American car, these springs are soft and can be twisted a long way.

Cadillac uses Hotchkiss drive and the

EASE OF control has been carefully engineered into car's interior. Phyllis Avedon demonstrates convenient, feather-light seat-adjustment control

Cadillac Motor Trial

loads imposed upon the rear springs and universal joint are severe. When braking hard, the rear axle winds up on the springs, reaches the limit, snaps back to normal. This produces the breaking of traction shown below: the distance between full traction marks is about four ft. Cadillac brakes are not among the best.

SKIPPING OF rear wheels was a defect revealed in strenuous 45 mph braking tests. White lines are 3 ft. 10 ins. apart, indicate centers of full-traction marks with poor traction between

HANDLING QUALITIES: Cadillac's chassis has been much improved in '51. While the suspension layout remains its same, orthodox self—coil spring independent suspension in front, half-elliptics in the rear—it now bristles with shock absorbers and stabilizer bars. Still, the ride is not what it should be. The Caddie leaves nothing to be desired as a town conveyance, but on the open road it's another matter. At an indicated 70 mph, the rear end begins to skip from side to side in a very disturbing manner, becoming more pronounced with increased speed. Steering is very positive on corners up to a certain point—depending upon the sharpness of the curve—where control simply slips away from you. Steady 60 mph gas mileage checks were attempted on a gently-curving, six-lane highway. But real control wasn't there, and we dropped to 45.

Like most cars with the comfortable advantage of enormous cross-section tires, the Cadillac wheel must be tugged on heavily in the turns. If you touch the soft, or raised, shoulder of an asphalt road while moving at any speed at all, the front wheels give a mighty sidewise twist. Street car tracks are also a menace, flip the front wheels aside.

While the Cad doesn't seem to heel unusually in turns, passengers complain of being rolled about, this generally to the hair-raising accompaniment of tire shriek. Washboard roads—hardly the Caddie's design element—are hard for car and passengers to take. Cad's steering has an unusually full swing from lock to lock, therefore has a small turning circle and is

deceptively, pleasantly easy to park and to handle in traffic.

BODY AND INTERIOR: A glaring defect of almost every car today—blinding dashboard reflections on windshield when the sun is high—has not been corrected in the Cad. Interior appointments of the test car satisfied our somewhat austere and very functional tastes. Body components are nicely fitted, but detail finish —edges of doors, for example—is poor by pre-war Cadillac standards. Speaking of doors, there are two ways of designing interior door locks: so that the inside door handle will or will not work against the locking pin placed in the window trim. We feel that a pin which locks inside *and* outside handles has marked safety value; but the test car was not so constructed.

The rear-view mirror is suspended ⅓ of the distance down the windshield, effectively blocking vision on turns and in intersections. Aside from this one danger spot, visibility for the driver of a '51 Cadillac is a close approach to perfection.

A center arm rest would help anchor the

STYLING IS combined with function in the case of Cad's tail-light-covered gas tank filler cap. Button reflector at base is push-release lock

front-seat passenger. While the rear-seat passenger rides in superb comfort, his level is low and his view forward is poor. Upholstery is of nice quality, nicely fitted, and the Nylon slip covers, available as extras, are finely tailored. The front seat is high, limits headroom but makes for fine visibility, and legroom fore and aft are excellently provided for. The Cad's body contours make the outside rear mirrors unusually useful, give a perfect view of conditions at the rear. Instruments are well-grouped and our only recommendation for instrument panel improvement is the trivial one of an ash tray handy to the driver, plus the already-mentioned relocation of the rear-view mirror.

GENERAL IMPRESSIONS: America's Dreamboat, badge of the successful man, is a truly remarkable car, exceedingly luxurious, well-suited to town driving or highway cruising. It has all the acceleration you'll ever need in a utility, as opposed to a sports machine. Its dimensions and handling qualities are not intended to

satisfy the automotive acrobat or the devotees of maximum control. The Cad has a lot in common with a dry lakes hot rod in that it's at its best on the straightaway. Its tires protest against low-speed cornering and control vanishes early when cornering at speed. Rear end wander suggests staying below 70 mph on the straightaway and cornering behavior suggests staying below 55 when the highway begins to wind. Opening the car up to top speed should be reserved for absolute emergencies.

Cadillac is not the ultimate automobile. It is outstanding for style, elegance, silence, economy, and a fine engine. Its greatest shortcoming in our eyes is that it is not more securely glued to the road. This is the point of view not of the sporting enthusiast, but of the safety-minded critic of design in terms of function—the job to be done. Cadillac is good, aims at being the best. Being one of US' costliest cars, it should stand at the top in design.

TREND TRIALS NO.: Our uniform evaluation of a car, *as a buy*, gives a figure of 41.6, remarkably good for a car in this price class, better than some cars in the next lower-priced class. Responsible for this low figure are Cadillac's low fuel consumption and very low depreciation rate. As an investment, this is a good deal.

TABLE OF PERFORMANCE

DYNAMOMETER TEST

1200 rpm (full load) 20.5 mph		58 road hp
2000 rpm (full load) 35.5 mph		82 road hp
3100 rpm (full load) 82.0 mph	(max.)	92 road hp

ACCELERATION TRIALS (SECONDS)

	Low	Drive
Standing start ¼ mile	:21.22	:21.36
0-30 mph	: 5.79	: 5.66
0-60 mph	:17.00	:16.62
10-60 mph	:18.00	:16.34
30-60 mph	———	:13.77

TOP SPEED (MPH)

Fastest one-way run	97.08
Average of four runs	95.44

FUEL CONSUMPTION (MPG)

At a steady 30 mph	21.9
At a steady 45 mph	20.8
At a steady 60 mph	16.4
Through light traffic	17.8
Through medium traffic	15.8
Through heavy traffic	13.2

BRAKE CHECK

Stopping distance at 30 mph	45 ft. 4 ins.
Stopping distance at 45 mph	101 ft. 6 ins.
Stopping distance at 60 mph	226 ft. 2 ins.

SPEEDOMETER TEST

At 30 mph indicated 33.5 mph		11.7% error
At 45 mph indicated 49 mph		10.2% error
At 60 mph indicated 64 mph		6.3% error

GENERAL SPECIFICATIONS

ENGINE

Type	pushrod ohv 90° V-8
Bore and stroke	3¹³⁄₁₆ x 3⅝ ins.
Stroke/Bore Ratio	0.95:1
Cubic Inch Displacement	331
Maximum Bhp	160 @ 3800 rpm
Bhp/Cu. In.	.483
Maximum Torque	312 ft.-lbs. @ 1800 rpm
Compression Ratio	7.5:1

DRIVE SYSTEM

Hydra-Matic four-speed transmission.

Ratios:	First—3.819	Second—2.634
	Third—1.450	Fourth—Direct
		Reverse—4.304

No clutch pedal. 12 quarts oil capacity.
Rear Axle: Semi-floating, Hotchkiss drive, hypoid bevel gears, ratio 3.36:1

DIMENSIONS

Wheelbase	126 ins.
Overall Length	215.5 ins.
Overall Height	60¹⁵⁄₁₆ ins.
Overall Width	80⅛ ins.
Tread	Front 59 ins., rear 63 ins.
Turns, Lock to Lock	4.5
Weight (test car)	4420 lbs.
Weight/Bhp Ratio	27.6:1
Weight/Road Hp Ratio	48.0:1
Weight Distribution (Front to Rear)	52.8/47.2

Sober black and elegant harmony of line make the Cadillac an exemplar of quality in the American style of product.

DATA FOR THE DRIVER

PRICE (at factory), with saloon body, $3,096.83 = £1,106 at $2.80 = £1. Not available in Great Britain.

ENGINE: 46.5 h.p. (R.A.C. rating), eight cylinders, overhead valves 96.84 × 92.07 mm, 5,420 c.c. Brake Horse-power: 160 at 3,800 r.p.m. Compression Ratio: 6.7 to 1. Max. Torque: 312 lb ft at 1,800 r.p.m. 24.4 m.p.h. per 1,000 r.p.m. on top gear.

WEIGHT 38 cwt 0 qr 22 lb (4,278 lb). Front wheels 52 per cent; rear wheels 48 per cent. LB per C.C.: 0.79. B.H.P. per TON: 83.7.

TYRE SIZE: 8.20 × 15in on bolt-on steel disc wheels.

TANK CAPACITY: 16.7 English gallons. Approximate fuel consumption range, 14-16 m.p.g. (20.2-17.7 litres per 100 km).

TURNING CIRCLE: 45ft (L and R). Steering wheel movement from lock to lock: 5 turns. LIGHTING SET: 6-volt.

MAIN DIMENSIONS: Wheelbase, 10ft 6in. Track, 4ft 11in (front) 5ft 3in (rear). Overall length, 17ft 11½in; width, 6ft 8½in; height, 5ft 2⅛in. Minimum Ground Clearance: 7⅛in.

ACCELERATION

Overall gear ratios	From steady m.p.h. of				
	10-30 sec	20-40 sec	30-50 sec	40-60 sec	50-70 sec
3.36 to 1	6.2	6.6	7.0	9.3	13.9
4.87 to 1	4.1*	5.6*	—	—	—
8.84 to 1	—	—	—	—	—
12.84 to 1	—	—	—	—	—

From rest through gears to :—

	sec.		sec.
30 m.p.h.	4.8*5.0	60 m.p.h.	17.1
50 m.p.h.	11.8	70 m.p.h.	25.2
		80 m.p.h.	37.7

SPEEDS ON GEARS :

(By Electric Speedometer)	M.p.h. (at change point)	K.p.h. (at change point)
1st	17	27
2nd	30	48
3rd	59	95
Top	90	145

* Using Low; remainder on High.

Speedometer correction by Electric Speedometer :—

Car Speedometer		Electric Speedometer m.p.h.
10	=	9.0
20	=	18.5
30	=	27.0
40	=	38.0
50	=	47.0
60	=	54.0
70	=	63.0
80	=	71.0
90	=	81.0

WEATHER : Dry, no wind. Air temperature 70 deg F.

Acceleration figures are the means of several runs in opposite directions.

Described in "The Autocar" of April 6, 1951.

No. 1447 : CADILLAC
SERIES 62 SALOON

THE Cadillac division of General Motors introduced four new series of cars for 1951, providing a range of eight models. These include a convertible, a long wheelbase limousine, three two-door fixed head coupés and three four-door saloons; it is in this last category that the Series 62 model is placed. As it occupies a position in the expensive car class, it was interesting to test this car shortly (in Belgium, with the co-operation of General Motors Continental, Antwerp), after having had experience of other less expensive models produced by the same parent company.

Once inside the car it did not take very many minutes to realize that, in the Cadillac, General Motors have produced a car that has really "got something."

The 160 b.h.p. developed by the 5½-litre V eight overhead valve engine is transmited by means of an improved version of the well-known Hydramatic transmission, which automatically provides four forward gear ratios. The result is a car with an outstanding performance, and more especially when its size and weight are considered. A maximum speed of a genuine 90 m.p.h., plus the ability to accelerate from 10 to 30 m.p.h. in 4.1 sec is something that is not possible on some so-called sports cars, and, indeed, one run of just under a hundred miles was covered at an average speed of just over 52 m.p.h. without apparently hurrying, and at a fuel consumption of 14-16 m.p.g.

The improvements made to the Hydramatic drive enable the change from forward to reverse, or vice versa, to be made while the engine is still revving fast, and, apart from preventing accidental damage should the lever be moved by mistake, it is also claimed that this modification enables the car to perform more easily the American manœuvre known as "rocking." For all normal driving the hand control lever is placed in the D position and in this range the car will climb all main road hills quickly and with complete absence of fuss. Even after being baulked on a hill of around 1 in 10 it is not necessary to change down to the Low ratio, but if this is done an extremely brisk getaway will result. The change from one gear to another is particularly smooth, and unless one is looking out for a change point it is hard to detect.

In spite of the fact that there are five turns of the steering wheel from lock to lock, the car handles extremely well at speed, and possesses a certain "quality" feel. On the straight there is a feeling that it will steer itself, yet it obeys the slightest wish of the driver. So much is this so, in fact, that in a very short space of time one thinks of the car as almost a small one, as far as manœuvring is concerned. On corners there is a minimum of roll, and the car has a "solid" feel, although a certain amount of tyre squeal occurs on some

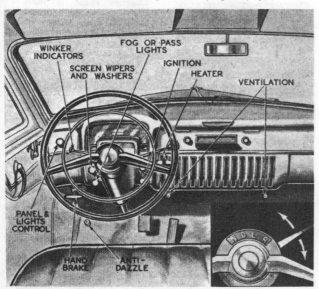

WINKER INDICATORS
FOG OR PASS LIGHTS
SCREEN WIPERS AND WASHERS
IGNITION
HEATER
VENTILATION
PANEL & LIGHTS CONTROL
HAND BRAKE
ANTI-DAZZLE
N D L R

Although large, the Cadillac retains a well-proportioned layout. Width makes the car seem lower than most of its compatriots. Bumpers, both front and rear, are exceptionally massive. The radio aerial is automatically extended by pressing a control inside the car.

More than most American cars, the Cadillac has retained the "pursuit plane" suggestion at the rear. A false duct entry at the front of the rear wing is part of the same conception. The final effect suggests the luxury and high speed that the Cadillac possesses in good measure.

ROAD TEST . . . . continued

types of road surface; but, of course, the suspension is by no means hard. The slight degree of understeer that is apparent does not seem to be affected very much by the small amount of roll produced by normal cornering, and the quick self-centring action of the wheels also helps to produce a general feeling of manœuvrability.

The suspension is by coil springs and wishbones at the front, and long leaf springs at the rear, a combination that produces a very even ride with an absence of pitch and kick up at the rear end. Over all types of surface, including "colonial" sections and Belgian pavé, the car kept a very even keel, with the minimum amount of movement transmitted to the passengers. The noise level from inside the car is very low, and even over the bad surfaces there is only a slight amount of rumble.

With under 18 lb weight per sq in of brake lining area, the Cadillac can be stopped quite easily from normal speeds, with only a light pedal pressure. However, under the conditions imposed during performance testing, a considerable amount of fade was experienced; although the brakes quickly regained their normal working properties on being allowed to cool, the efficiency did not seem quite as high as before. The hand-operated parking brake, situated on the extreme left of the car, is fitted with a warning light which comes on when the brake is applied.

The driving seat is extremely comfortable and gives good support, but by comparison with other G.M. products that have been tried it appears to be noticeably higher, and consequently a much better view and sense of control are obtained. The steering wheel and pedals are very well positioned, and reduce fatigue to a minimum when the car is driven for long periods. The design of the steering

wheel, with two sloping spokes, enables the driver to have an extremely good view of the instruments, which are grouped with the small controls above the enclosed steering column.

Below the large speedometer, and to the left of the column, are two controls; the upper one is a combined windscreen spray and control for the suction-operated wiper motor, and the lower converts the front flashing indicator lamps into pass lights, provided that the head lamps or side lamps are switched on. Below an electric cigarette lighter, to the right of the steering column, is a multi-position ignition switch which operates auxiliaries only, if turned to the left, and the ignition when turned to the right. A further right turn automatically starts the engine, provided that the control lever is in the neutral position. Warning lights are used to indicate dynamo charge and oil pressure, while two small gauges show water temperature and petrol level. Instrument lighting can be varied by means of a rheostat built into the main light switch.

Two small interior lamps are mounted in the facia just above the radio panel. These are automatically switched on when either of the front doors is opened, and may also be controlled from inside the car by means of a small switch built into the left-hand lamp. The glove locker is also illuminated automatically when the lid is opened, and can be locked by means of the ignition key.

The relatively high driving position partially offsets the disadvantage of a fairly high bonnet line, but it is not possible to see the right-hand front wing from the driving seat in a left-hand drive car. However, the general outward vision is extremely good, and there is the minimum of

Considerable bonnet space is well filled by the V-eight engine. The battery is accessible and an oil bath cleaner serves the downdraught carburettor. One of the impeller housings of the air-conditioning system can be seen to the right of the big air cleaner.

Luggage space is more than ample. The lid of the locker is automatically retained in the open position. As shown in the inset, the left-hand stop-light installation opens to reveal the fuel filler cap.

interference from the windscreen pillars. The large wrap-round rear window, in conjunction with a well-placed mirror, ensures good rear visibility. At night the mirror can be dipped by pressing a small catch, to prevent dazzle from following traffic.

On an expensive car one expects certain refinements as regards upholstery and interior trim generally, and in this respect the Cadillac comes up to expectations. It is neatly trimmed in grey cloth piped with leather. A fold-down arm rest is provided in the rear seat only, and this could with advantage be wider. A combined cigarette lighter and ash tray is built into the back of the front seat.

Interior air temperature control, although somewhat complicated, is very comprehensive, and the use of a thermostat reduces the control mechanism to a minimum of two levers, to operate the fans and water supply, plus two controls to operate the forward-facing air intake ducts. Apart from the scuttle mounted heater unit, there is another blower under the front seat, which conveys air to the rear passengers' feet, while a third extractor fan is fitted in the luggage compartment, with a communicating duct behind the rear seats. Adequate de-misting ducts are formed in the interior of the screen casing strip. The quarter lights

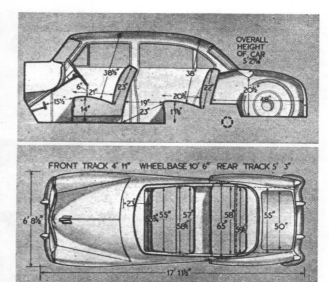

Measurements in these scale body diagrams are taken with the driving seat in the central position of fore and aft adjustment and with the seat cushions uncompressed.

in the front doors can be opened by means of winding handles which hold them against the outside air pressure when in the fully open position, when they act as very effective air scoops.

Even when housing the spare wheel and tools, the luggage locker retains very generous proportions, and is of a most convenient shape to accommodate a large number of suitcases. The lid, hinged at the top, is spring loaded, so that it will remain in the open position for loading.

The head lights, although having the appearance of being of small diameter, prove to be very powerful, and to give the good range essential for night driving at high speed. The note of the horns is also powerful, yet pleasant, and in keeping with the character of the car. Starting from cold was at all times instantaneous.

Judged by any standards of performance, comfort or manœuvrability, this car would fulfil the needs of a most critical driver, but perhaps one is impressed most of all by its extreme silence as regards both engine noise and wind noise. It is a most pleasing car to drive.

The windscreen, it will be seen, has a high degree of curvature. The upholstery, as this view of the front seat cushions shows, is luxurious.

The interior is capacious, and finished in soft pale grey cloth. Arm-rests are fitted to all four doors. Small handles provide a positive, simple opening for the front ventilation panels. The draughtproof ash tray, with roll-top cover, is interesting, as also is the conveniently placed seat adjusting control.

THROUGH THE YEARS the name Cadillac has been synonymous with the word Class. Despite the fact that more than a million cars have been built since the founding of the Cadillac Automobile Company in 1902, the prestige of becoming a "man of distinction" in the circle of your society still goes with the purchase of a Cadillac.

Although it may be questioned how long Cadillac can hold their leadership on the basis of class alone, MOTOR TREND Research's road test of the 1952 Cadillac "62" four-door sedan indicates that the prestige factor should enable them to stay out front for a long time to come. A deluge of questions about the styling and luxury of driving and owning a Cadillac greeted us wherever we stopped on our three-day, 1000-mile-long test through cities, over mountains, and through backcountry. Not once were we asked about performance. And yet the 1952 Cadillac *has* performance, performance to match its class: bounding acceleration, phenomenal top speed, and handling ability greatly improved over last year's product.

Power Steering—A Boon to Driving Ease

After driving the '52 Cad (picked up from the Cadillac Motor Car Division of Los Angeles) around the block once, we were amazed at the difference between it and our '51 test car. At that time we complained of having to tug heavily at the wheel in order to get around corners; what they've done this year is to devise a unit that frees you of this effort. As

Road Testing the 50

Our tests reveal that the '52 Cadillac not only has luxury, but performance to match

An MT Research Report
by Walt Woron

long as the car-buying majority insists on a soft ride (creating the need for large tires, along with soft springs, etc.), power steering (although not standard equipment) provides the antidote.

Cad power steering—a combination of conventional steering gear and hydraulic booster—is fairly simple in operation. Here's the way it works: Whenever the engine is running, a pump creates hydraulic pressure that is used, through the actuation of suitable valves, to assist the driver's steering effort. You begin to turn the wheel to move away from the curb, and as soon as you exert a pressure of more than three pounds the booster goes into operation, and your effort goes down to practically nothing. As you straighten out and drive down the street, the valve closes and steering becomes normal. Out on a straight highway, you're driving with conventional steering. But as you enter a turn which makes you exert an appreciable effort on the wheel, the hydraulic assist again comes into operation. Coming out of a turn, the hydraulic pres-

sure is automatically relieved and the steering wheel returns to normal.

The most important feature of this system, MOTOR TREND Research feels, is that it does not make the driver *completely* dependent on power assist. It still provides most of the "feel" of a conventional system. In the case of hydraulic failure during high-speed cornering, the change in effort would be hardly noticeable; on a slow, city turn, you would feel a definite change.

Unlike a car with conventional steering, at least unlike our '51 test Cad, the '52 Cad did not get whipped from one side to another, either on tar strips, on railroad tracks or going over chuck holes. "Wheel fight" is virtually eliminated. All the hard work involved in parking is no longer there; instead of loads as high as 50 pounds, maximum is eight pounds.

Disadvantages? (1) Until you get used to it you have the tendency to over-control, because you don't realize how easy it is to turn a corner. Without being accused of crying "Wolf" we would like to point (*Continued on page twenty-two*)

20

1902—First car built by Cadillac

1912—First with electric starting, lighting and ignition system

1915—First with the V-type, water-cooled, eight-cylinder engine

Speedometer dominates easy-to-read instrument panel, good safety feature

Six stop watches and an electric speedometer are used for acceleration runs

Fred Bodley and Bob Hoeppner, technical men, and Walt Woron, editor, talk it out at stop near Indio, Calif. Temperature hovered around 110 F. in shade

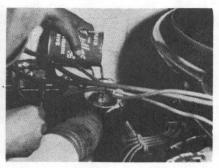

Filling Hydra-Matic unit in Cad requires a funnel and considerable ingenuity; however, filling is not usually necessary between the regular changes

ANNIVERSARY CADILLAC

1923—First to build the inherently balanced 90° V-type engine

1933—First to provide cars with the no-draft ventilation feature

1949—Cadillac builds its one-millionth car since company's founding

Luxury items on Cadillac include automatic radio selector (above, left), cigarette lighter in back of front seat for rear-seat passengers (right), defroster for rear windows, and radio speaker for the passengers in the rear seat (below)

PHOTOS BY ERIC RICKMAN

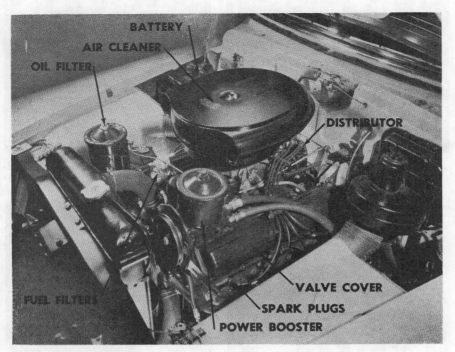

BATTERY
AIR CLEANER
OIL FILTER
DISTRIBUTOR
VALVE COVER
SPARK PLUGS
POWER BOOSTER
FUEL FILTERS

Performance of 190-horsepower engine was outstanding on test. Record run of 115.4 mph top speed was recorded, highest ever obtained on one of our test cars

Cadillac Road Test

out that drivers using this system should become accustomed to its ease of steering effort and the fact that you *can* over-control. Going into a corner, you set the wheel, preparing for a certain amount of effort. When the hydraulic assist takes over, your own unexpended effort turns the wheel an additional amount, causing the car to go through a shorter radius than required (which can cause you to slide or spin). (2) It drains off some of the increased horsepower. (3) The steering gear box is fairly hard to service since it's located under the air vent duct, slightly below the engine left bank, although the pump is right on top.

The steering wheel, quite thick and easy to grip, is set in a good position as far as the seat is concerned. Driver comfort and safety have both been taken into account with the seat being adjustable to the extent that when it is moved forward (either by manual control or the hydraulic-electric system on deluxe versions) it also raises—a definite advantage to shorter persons. The full circle horn ring is recessed below the level of the wheel, and operates at the mere touch of the thumb from anywhere on its circumference.

In general the car handles well, sticks in corners, has little tendency to break loose, doesn't feel mushy, gives a fairly flat ride through corners taken at moderately high speeds. Some road shock is felt in the wheel but not enough to be bothersome. Tire squeal is there, as it will inevitably be with large (8.00 x 15) tires, inflated to their recommended pressures.

One thing that sold us on the way the Cadillac handled was its reaction to crossing a railroad track of the "hump" type, causing any car approaching it over 30 mph to be thrown into an unexpected leap through the air. We crossed it deliberately at twice this speed, becoming airborne for 15 to 18 feet, a good 12 to 18 inches off the ground, returning to earth nose first. You would think it might "pancake" there, but steering wheel jar was at a minimum, there was no swerve, no sway. It just held a straight course, except that after the rear end came down, it made two fairly severe bumps, then quickly settled down.

It Literally Flies—115.4 Top

Starting with a run of about two miles before entering our ¼-mile measured trap, the Cad picked up its speed phenomenally quickly, the needle passing the 110 peg on the speedometer long before the near end of the trap was reached. At the average top speed of 109.6 (the average, incidentally, of four runs, two each in opposite directions) there was only a trifle of "floating" (oscillation of the body on the springs, over a virtually level course). The car held a perfectly straight course on these runs—the fastest we have made

CADILLAC TEST TABLE

PERFORMANCE

CLAYTON CHASSIS DYNAMOMETER TEST

(All tests are made under full load conditions)

RPM	MPH	ROAD HP
1200	29	80
2000	51	80
3000	74 (maximum)	100

Per cent of advertised hp delivered to driving wheels—52.6

ACCELERATION IN SECONDS

(Checked with fifth wheel and electric speedometer)

	LO-D3	D3
Standing start ¼ mile	18.4	18.4
0-30 mph (0-34.5 car speedometer)	4.0	4.1
0-60 mph (0-67 car speedometer)	13.2	13.5
10-60 mph through gears	12.4	12.4
30-60 mph in Third		9.4

TOP SPEED (MPH)

(Clocked speeds over surveyed ¼ mile)

Fastest one-way run	115.4
Average of four runs	109.6

FUEL CONSUMPTION IN MILES PER GALLON

(Checked with fuel flowmeter, fifth wheel and electric speedometer)

	D-3	D-4
Steady 30 mph	14.7	17.0
Steady 45 mph	15.7	17.7
Steady 60 mph	—	15.8
Approximate average in traffic	—	16.3

BRAKE STOPPING DISTANCE

(Checked with electrically actuated detonator)

Stopping distance at:

30 mph	47 ft. 3 in.
45 mph	114 ft. 3 in.
60 mph	204 ft. 5 in.

GENERAL SPECIFICATIONS
ENGINE

Type	Overhead valve V-8
Bore and stroke	3¹³/₁₆ x 3⅝ in.
Stroke/bore ratio	0.95:1
Compression ratio	7.50:1
Displacement	331 cu. in.
Advertised bhp	190 @ 4000 rpm
Piston travel @ max. bhp	2416 ft. per min.
Bhp per cu. in.	0.57
Maximum torque	322 lbs. ft. @ 2400 rpm
Maximum bmep	146.6 psi @ 2400 rpm

DRIVE SYSTEM

Transmission: HydraMatic, Dual Range
Gear Ratios: First, 3.82:1; Second, 2.63:1
Third, 1.45:1; Fourth, 1:1
Rear axle: Semi-Floating, Hypoid Drive
3.36 ratio with 3.07 to 1 optional

DIMENSIONS

Wheelbase	126 in.
Tread	Front—59, Rear—63 in.
Wheelbase/tread ratio	2:1
Overall width	80¹/₁₀ in.
Overall length	215½ in.
Overall height	62¹¹/₁₆ in.
Turning radius	22½ ft.
Turns, lock to lock	5½
Weight (test car)	4510 lbs.
Weight/bhp ratio	23.7:1
Weight/road hp ratio	45:1
Weight distribution (front to rear)	front 54%, rear 46%
Weight per sq. in. brake lining	20.6 lbs.

INTERIOR SAFETY CHECK CHART

QUESTION	YES	NO
1. Blind spot at left windshield post at a minimum?	X	
2. Vision to right rear satisfactory?	X	
3. Positive lock to prevent doors from being opened from inside?		X
4. Does adjustable front seat lock securely in place?	X	
5. Minimum of projections on dashboard face?		X
6. Is emergency brake an emergency brake and is it accessible to both driver and passenger?		X
7. Are cigarette lighter and ash tray both located conveniently for driver?		X
8. Is rear vision mirror positioned so as not to cause blind spot for driver?	X	
TOTAL FOR CADILLAC	75%	

OPERATING COST PER MILE ANALYSIS

1. Cost of gasoline	$166.66
2. Cost of insurance	168.40
3. First year's depreciation	258.00
4. Maintenance:	
a. Two new tires	39.90
b. Brake reline	32.28
c. Major tune-up	8.75
d. Renew front fender	81.52
e. Renew rear bumper	42.29
f. Adjust automatic transmission, change lubricant	16.00
First year cost of operation per mile	8.1c

Cadillac Road Test

(by eight mph) with any American stock car MOTOR TREND Research has tested.

With the new "performance range" Hydra-Matic, the Cadillac can definitely take advantage of its increased power, utilize it with a greater versatility, though at the sacrifice of completely automatic driving. Like other General Motors cars, this transmission provides manual control over two gears (third and fourth) in the driving, "DR," range. For city traffic and mountainous driving you use third, which gives you less lugging, more engine braking, less economy. On the open road you use fourth, which is considerably more economical, giving you two to 2½ mpg more than third gear in 30 to 45 mph speed ranges. Up around 60 mph, of course, you are winding the engine too tightly in third gear for best fuel economy, so it's best to use fourth in the higher speed ranges.

For some reason, or reasons, unexplained at the time of this writing, the '52 Cadillac gave us considerably less fuel economy than our '51 test car. Weights were approximately the same (4420 vs. 4510), rear axle ratios were the same (each 3.36:1), testing conditions were the same. There are, of course, differences between seemingly identical cars. Another explanation could be that the '51 Cads were slightly overboard fuel economy-wise, with the carburetor power jets set too high for best acceleration performance.

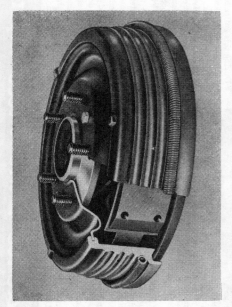

The 12-inch ribbed brake drums in the '52 Cadillac are both stronger and larger, allow for more effective cooling

Unfortunately, the way the Hydra-Matic gear selector is set up, it's sometimes difficult to read what gear you are in. For us it wasn't hard, because in tests such as we make our ears are attuned to the sound of the engine. We can tell by the number of revs it is turning up what

gear it is in. For the person who drives a car automatically, paying little attention to the car once it's rolling, a better selector dial would be desirable. There is only the smallest of tick marks to indicate the difference between third and fourth gears.

Accelerates Like Some Sports Cars

With a power/weight ratio (number of pounds that each horsepower has to push) of one to 23.7, the Cadillac was bound to have much better than average acceleration. As it worked out, running acceleration checks through various gears, using high alone, clocking to certain speeds and to distances, the '52 Cadillac turned in a most creditable performance—best of any stock car tested so far this year. Its "dragging" qualities were comparable to those of some sports cars. As an example, its speed at the end of the ¼-mile trap was 72 mph, a speed attained in 18.4 seconds, much better than average.

Pick-up was somewhat better using the LOW range of Hydra-Matic, then shifting to third gear of DRIVE, which kept the car in second gear for a longer period of time than is possible using DRIVE alone. The shift was made at around 42 mph, whereas in DRIVE the shift is automatically made at around 30 mph.

With a Cadillac you would expect to get a better ride than in any other car on the road—an expectation that is not realized. Although the front and rear seat rides are comfortable and you don't have to brace yourself for ordinary curves (you do for fast, sharp ones), the high spring rates, canted shock absorbers and anti-sway bars still seem insufficient to bring the ride up to Cadillac standards.

Rear end bottoming was not noticeable from the driver's seat, or from any other place within the car, but when we placed the car on a hoist to check the underside, we discovered a point of contact between the left rear leaf spring and the gas tank filler neck. This was probably inadvertent interference, however, and not bottoming.

Plush, Comfortable Interior

It is easy to get into and out of either front or rear seat of the '52 Cadillac. There are 35 and 28 inches, respectively, of space designed to give you plenty of maneuvering room. Once you're seated, you find you have all sorts of legroom. A diagonal drawn from the floorboard to the front of the *front* seat to the seatback measures 44 inches; from the floorboard to the front of the *rear* seat to the seatback measures 38½ inches. Headroom is ample, 34 inches both front and rear. When you're behind the wheel, there's plenty of freedom for your left leg; even if you're the middle passenger in the front seat, the transmission tunnel doesn't cut down your legroom excessively.

The plain instrument panel is free of knobs, incorporates a large glove compartment, but a dull finish would eliminate

some of the glare from the painted top. The instrument cluster (placed behind a glass that picks up too many reflections) has an extremely legible speedometer, fuel and water temperature gauges that are fairly small and located somewhat low for easiest reading. Red lights are used to indicate low oil pressure and low generator charging rates.

Controls are all within easy reach, and though the ratchet-type emergency brake is located on the left side, it's simple to pull to the ON position. When it is on, a red warning light, located above the 50 to 60 mark on the speedometer, flashes off and on. The ignition key is also the starter switch, with a cut-out to prevent the engine from being started when the car is in gear.

No noticeable blind spots are evident from within the Cadillac: the triangular-shaped windshield post is slim and angled properly; the rear quarter panel is down to a bare minimum; the glare-proof, two-

These views show how exhaust is designed into integral part of the rear bumper, another Cadillac refinement

position, rear view mirror has several adjustments to reduce the blind spot normally created to the right front; but a lower hood line, or higher fender (as some of the manufacturers are using) would help distance-judgment in traffic.

All appointments are of usual Cadillac elegance, with the possible exception of the rear quarter windows. These have small pull-and-twist handles that are awkward to operate; it seems that a luxury car like the Cad should have window cranks.

Construction of the body, which has only superficial 1952 styling changes, is about average; here again, its finish did not seem up to the par of what you have grown to expect from Cadillacs. Hood and trunk lid are both easily raised; the well-braced, undercoated hood by an outside

CONTINUED ON PAGE 33

Cadillac taking a fast turn on a rough dirt track. Stability of this car was good.

On this fast jump test, note that this Cadillac's heavy front end barely leaves the ground.

Cadillac makes straight-line panic stop from 50 mph. Brakes on this car were excellent.

Testing the CADILLAC SERIES 62

By JULIAN P. LEGGETT

How wet can it get? Here the Cadillac Series 62 Sedan is being deluged by hoses during 1½ hour test to determine body tightness and seal against moisture.

With fire hose nozzles on this time, pressure is stepped up to 137½ pounds and water streams are aimed at points around windows, doors, hood and luggage compartment where leaks might occur. After 1½ hours of this water penetration test, not over 6 ounces of water got in around window vents and door seam, and none got in trunk—Cadillac has a tight body!

SINCE there are mighty few bathtubs around in which you could dunk a Cadillac, our crew of engineers from Motor Vehicle Research rigged up another way of determining the tightness of the body construction on the new Cadillac they tested for SCIENCE AND MECHANICS. For an hour and a half, they played water from fire hoses against and over the car body, paying particular attention to closed doors and windows, windshield, back window and hood and luggage compartment areas. Over 18,000 gallons of water

were poured on the car from all angles, using fire hoses that delivered 90 pounds pressure with nozzles removed for the first hour, and 137½ pounds pressure with nozzles on for the last 15 minutes.

During this entire test, an observer stationed inside the car with an inspector's magnifying glass checked every point where leakage might conceivably occur,

and, after the tests, a complete inspection for leakage was made of the entire car. Despite this deluge, not more than one glassful of water entered the car, and the only leakage points that showed up under this extreme test were minute amounts through the front window vents and around the center door jamb between the front and rear door. The luggage compartment was absolutely free of any water. And there was no evidence of damage to the car's finish from the hosing under high pressure. This car, the engineers decided, had an

exceptionally tight, well-sealed body.

Road performance of this car kept pace with the quality of the body construction. Its top true speed of 105.75 mph on one radar-timed run places it among America's fastest stock cars. The speedometer hit bottom at 110 and bounced, but the radar and 5th wheel recorded the true speed. At that rate of travel, the 190 hp engine was turning up 4,480 rpm.

For all its 4,175 pounds dry weight, this Cadillac showed itself to be remarkably frisky on acceleration. It stepped from 10 to 50 mph in 7.62 seconds and from 20 to 60 in 9.96 seconds in the two fastest runs. Zero to 60 took longer, 10.89 seconds, but that's still mighty sharp performance. On these acceleration runs, the car carried 360 pounds of passengers.

Braking efficiency tests also produced some top-notch performance, such as the emergency stop from 30 mph, in 27 feet, for an efficiency of 90%. All of the panic stops resulted in efficiencies of 75% or better, with the car coming to a halt straight, with wheels locked, no slewing or side thrust, and a normal weight shift. And, after the initial series of 18 normal and panic stops, an additional series of 14 panic braking stops from speeds ranging from 20 to 60 mph revealed no primary fade and exceptionally fine brakes for this heavyweight vehicle.

Our readers have often asked just what power demands various automatic devices make on an automobile's engine. Since this Cadillac was equipped with both power steering and Hydramatic transmission, MVR's engineers set out to find what power the engine had to. deliver to these automatic units to operate them. With the car at a standstill and engine idling at 600 rmp, the steering wheel was turned, with the booster's aid, ¼ turn. The rpm reading dropped to 585. Turning the wheel all the way to lock position reduced the rpm to 525. On the Hydramatic test, with the engine idling at 520 rpm the gear selector was moved from N (neutral position) to LO (low range) but without setting the car in motion.

The rpm reading promptly dropped to 460. That meant it required that much effort to turn the hydraulic coupling. Turning the steering wheel hard left to lock during this same transmission test further reduced the rpm to 400. The total power loss, 120 rpm, becomes quite apparent— again proving that you can't get something for nothing. For the convenience and comfort of power steering and automatic gear shifting, you give up some engine power. This is true, of course, of all cars so equipped and doesn't apply solely to Cadillacs.

That this car has plenty of power left after the loss to steering and transmission was forcefully demonstrated in two ways. First, MVR's engineers tried a tow, attaching the Cadillac to a tractor-and-loaded-trailer with a total weight of 31 tons or 62,000 pounds. A pull gage in the tow chain showed the Cadillac exerted a 2,700-pound

Another *Science at the Wheel* Report

Science at the Wheel — Cadillac "62" Performance

START OF TESTS: March 11, 1952

MAKE OF CAR: 1952 Cadillac Series 62 4-door sedan

WEATHER CONDITIONS (prevailing at time of recorded road tests): Temperature: 68-73°F. Humidity: 20-58%. Wind velocity: 3-7 mph. Wind direction: W-NW to SE. Barometer: 29.30-30.1

ROAD CONDITIONS (for gas mileage, acceleration and brake efficiency tests): Asphalt-covered crushed rock, clean and dry

MILEAGE AT START OF TESTS: 1,461.3

MILES COVERED IN TESTS: 2,600

GAS USED: Premium (slight ping under load in preliminary run with Regular) **OIL USED:** SAE #10

TEST DATA

GASOLINE MILEAGE (checked with fuel velocity meter, gas volume meter, 5th wheel and Mile-O-Meter vacuum gage. Passenger weight 370 lbs., test equipment weight 97 lbs. Average of two steady runs made in Drive or Hi-Drive range north and south on 2% grade at each speed. Tire pressure 24 lbs. cold, 5th wheel pressure 24 lbs. cold. Speedometer correction not applied to miles-per-gallon readings)

MPH Speedometer	True Speed	Miles Per Gallon	RPM
20	20.5	21	890
30	30.5	20.75	1250
40	40.5	18.75	1680
50	48.85	18.5	2010
60	57.85	17	2380
70	68.25	15.25	2700
80	75.85	12.5	3010
90	86.25	13	3420

FUEL ECONOMY ACCELERATION TEST (both tests made in Hi Drive range): Full throttle from 0-50 mph speedometer, then holding 50 for 1 mile (1 min. 16 4/5 sec.), consumed .075 gal. at an approx. rate of 13.33 mpg. Slow acceleration from 0-50 mph speedometer, then holding 50 for 1 mile (1 min. 25 1/5 sec.), consumed .06 gal. at an approx. rate of 16.66 mpg.

ACCELERATION (checked with dampened pendulum meter and timed electrically. Times subject to speedometer correction. Carried weight 370 lbs. front. Figures are average of two successive runs at speeds specified):

MPH Speedometer	Gear Range	Average Time (Seconds)	MPH Speedometer	Gear Range	Average Time (Seconds)
0–20	LO only	2.15	0–60	LO and shift at 30 mph	10.89
0–30	LO only	3.71			
0–40	LO only	5.29	10–50	Hi Drive	7.62
0–50	LO and shift at 30 mph	7.85	20–60	Hi Drive	9.96

ACCELERATION FACTOR (roughly speaking, a measure of potential pickup performance. Full throttle in gears indicated):

MPH Speedometer	Accelerometer Reading	Pull in Lbs. per ton	MPH per second	Feet per sec. per sec.
20 (LO)	34%	630	7.48	11.66
20 (Drive 1)	34%	630	7.48	11.66
30 (LO)	32%	606	7.04	10.58
30 (Drive 1)	32%	606	7.04	10.58
40 (Drive 1)	27%	530	5.94	9.18
50 (Drive 1)	21%	411	4.6	6.8
60 (Drive 1)	13%	259	2.9	4.2
60 (Hi Drive)	13%	259	2.9	4.2
70 (Hi Drive)	12%	239	2.65	3.95

TOP SPEED AND SPEEDOMETER CORRECTION (average of north and south runs in miles per hour with passenger weight of 360 lbs. and indicated peak rpm of 4480 on each run. Tire pressure 24 lbs. cold, 5th wheel pressure 21 lbs. cold, wind 17 mph with gusts to 24, wind direction W-NW. Speedometer bottomed at 110 mph and bounced):

MPH Speedometer	5th Wheel Check	Radar Timer Check	MPH Speedometer	5th Wheel Check	Radar Timer Check
110 Top Speed	104.5	105.2	50	48.85	48.85
90	86.25	86.25	40	40.5	.....
80	75.85	75.85	30	30.5	.....
70	68.25	68.25	20	20.5	.....
60	57.85	57.85			

ODOMETER CORRECTION (checked with Veedor Root counter and calibrated new "6th wheel," with error checkout of 1/2" in 5,000 ft. Hairline magnifier used. Indicated speed during tests 9 mph): Car's odometer—5,450 feet; true distance by 6th wheel—5,280; error 170 ft. Two-mile checkout, error 347 ft. short of indicated distance. 10-mile checkout, error 1,604 feet short of indicated distance

HILL CLIMBING (checked with pendulum performance meter. All tests at full throttle with 360 lbs. passenger weight, 51 lbs. instrument weight):

MPH Speedometer	Gear Range	Grade in %	MPH Speedometer	Gear Range	Grade in %
20	LO	34	50	Drive (1)	21
30	LO	32	20	Hi Drive	23
40	LO	27	30	Hi Drive	25
20	Drive (1)	34	40	Hi Drive	22
30	Drive (1)	32	50	Hi Drive	17
40	Drive (1)	27	60	Hi Drive	13

BRAKE EFFICIENCY (checked with decelerometer and Sioux pressure cylinder. Tire pressure 24 lbs. cold. Weight in car, 360 lbs. passengers, 87 lbs. instruments. Time between normal stops 4½ mins. average, between panic stops 3 mins. average. Temperature 72°F, barometer 30.1, humidity 58%. Pavement dry. Normal stops all straight, no slewing; panic stops straight with all wheels locked, weight shift normal):

NORMAL STOPS

Speedometer MPH From	Pedal Pressure in lbs.	Efficiency in %	Approx. Time in secs.	Stopping Distance in ft.
20	40	86	1.26	25.8
20	36	84	1.37	29.2
30	32	62	2.11	40.8
30	35	54	2.24	54.1
40	34	59	3.1	87.1
50	32	59	3.24	129.7
60	45	78	4.03	191.6

PANIC STOPS

Speedometer MPH From	Pedal Pressure in lbs.	Efficiency in %	Approx. Time in secs.	Stopping Distance in ft.
20	48	75	1.01	15.4
20	41	83	.99	13.4
30	72	83	1.79	33.11
30	54	90	1.64	27.0
40	64	78	2.24	73.1
50	56	84	2.73	113.1
60	68	80	3.93	142.6

REAR WHEEL HORSEPOWER (checked on dynamometer. Temperature in laboratory 70°F, under hood 90°F, barometer 30.05, air-fuel ratio 13.6-1, rear tire pressure 24 lbs. cold):

At an indicated 2,000 rpm, with 2½-3" vacuum and gear selector at Hi Drive, developed horsepower at rear wheels was 79.653

CAR FRICTION or HOLD-BACK (tractive resistance in lbs. per ton, checked on dynamometer):

Miles Per Hour (speedometer)	10	20	30	40	50	60	70
Declutched	29	31	32	36	55	73	94
Drive (clutched, ignition off)	68	71	73	75	98	120	149

SPECIFICATIONS

ENGINE: 8 cylinder V-type, hydraulic overhead valves. Bore 3.8125, stroke 3.625, maximum brake horsepower rated 190 at 4,000 rpm; compression ratio 7.5 to 1; maximum torque 322 at 2400 rpm; piston displacement 331 cu. in.; fuel specified, premium or high test.

TRANSMISSION: Hydramatic automatic—LO and split drive ranges; rear axle ratio 3.36 to 1.

STEERING: power booster type (power required to start operation); turning circle 45 ft.; lock to lock 5¾ turns sprung; 5 unsprung.

EXTERIOR: wheelbase 126"; overall length 215.5"; overall width 80.1"; overall height 62.68"; weight 4175 dry (before fueling for road), road clearance 7.3", gas tank capacity 20 gals.

INTERIOR: head room, front seat, 35.81"; rear seat, 35.56"; leg room, front seat, 43.94"; rear seat, 42.13"; hip room, front seat, 63.56"; rear seat, 64.25"; shoulder room, front, 58.1"; rear seat, 56.50".

VISIBILITY: windshield area (1 piece) 963 sq. in. approx.; rear window (3 piece), 793 sq. in. approx. Driver's eye to road over left front fender (5' 8" driver, seat in extreme rear) 21' 3.75"; driver's eye to road over hood center 36' 7.5"; driver's eye to road over right front fender 29' 5".

EQUIPMENT: Battery 6-volt, 17-plate, 115 amps, located under hood. Tires 8.00x15", recommended pressure 24 lbs. cold. Luggage capacity 14 cu. ft. with spare tire in place. 10-gallon pumping time 1 min. 37.40 sec. with 2 gallons in tank at start; no surge or spillage. Filler tube neck in rear tail lamp housing (if gas overflowed it would run down fender to exhaust pipe which might produce fire hazard). Powerful backup lights. Springing, front independent coil, rear semi-elliptic leaf.

MOTOR VEHICLE RESEARCH herewith certifies that these are the true and accurate findings in tests conducted on the automobile named under the conditions specified.

A. J. White,
Director,
Motor Vehicle Research

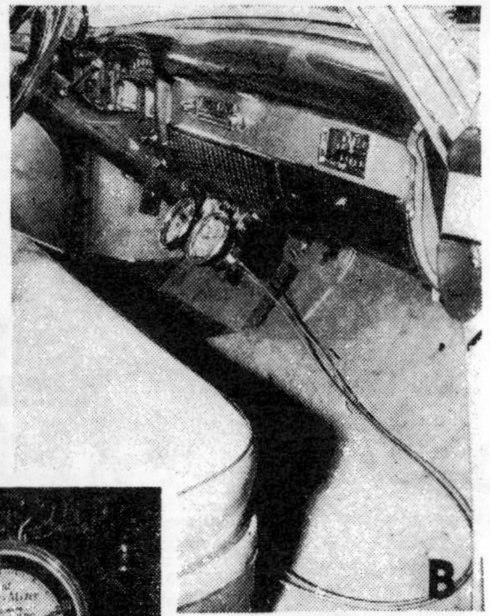

(A) Fifth wheel (right) double-checks car speed and sixth wheel (left) is an entirely new innovation that records actual traveled distance as a check on the car's odometer. Cables from these wheels run to meters shown in photo B inset. (B) Interior showing meters and glove compartment low on dash.

Drivers' Observations

ROADABILITY: This car came equipped with power steering and steering wheel response was excellent, yet retained considerable "road feel" because of effort required in General Motors' system before power mechanism takes over. Front end seems quite heavy—almost logy—at low speeds on rough roads, but this disappears on good roads or as rate of travel increases, evidently a result of intentional design to prevent loss of steering stability when air stream tends to lift front end at upper speed range. Cornering (ability to take curves) very good and side thrust minimum though tires howl in cornering at high speed. Some wander noticeable in 7 mph crosswind.

RIDING COMFORT: Weight and design result in excellent ride on pavement; MVR test on railroad crossties abandoned due to low clearance (7.3"); this car obviously intended for boulevard and open highway, not for rough country roads. Exceptional comfort in rear seat with no extreme side thrust on curves and almost complete absence of noise.

HARMONIC BALANCE POINT (best cruising speed as determined by "feel" of car to driver): 73 mph.

INSTRUMENTS AND CONTROLS: Dials easy to read, although by day the dash picks up pronounced reflection and glare when sun is directly ahead; by night, white letters show up sharply on black background; speedometer figures are easily discernible at a glance. Gear selector quadrant becomes difficult to read while wheel is being turned because horn assembly hides quadrant; light for quadrant is controlled by rheostat on headlamp switch. Word "Brake" lights up on panel in red if hand brake is on; ignition key causes bull's eye to light up on panel if battery is not charging, while another lights if oil pressure drops too low. No ammeter or oil pressure gage on panel. All doors lock from outside without using key (don't leave it inside!). Green direction signals are large and operate with distinct click. Accelerator pedal seems too close to brake for fast foot action and brake pedal could be larger. Windshield wiper, heater and ventilator controls are well-positioned, easy to work. Front seat moves backward or forward automatically at touch of button. Radio antenna has positive vacuum operation. Automatic control raises all four windows in 7.11 seconds, lowers them in 6.05 seconds and works well.

SPECIAL COMMENTS: Service men will find this car easy to work on, fenders are low and mechanic has little bending to do in reaching engine parts. Tests of Hydramatic transmission from standstill to 30 mph indicate low slippage factor, decreasing as speed increases. Hood has no dash release but opens by working primary and secondary catches though the latter was difficult to work on the car tested. With hood open, card for owner's name is visible on frame, giving permanent record. Rear trunk lid required considerable force in closing and trunk compartment matting didn't seem up to Cadillac standards. Twin exhaust pipes extend to extreme outer edge of rear bumper and give appearance of being integral with body. Car received equipped with relatively large fog lights but not undercoated. Car has sufficient power and torque to start wheels in all gear ranges. Place shift lever in Reverse when parking to prevent pushing or rolling. One of flexible hoses between air scoops and car's interior was found disconnected and poorly installed. Air cleaner atop 4-barrel carburetor is one of largest in use and should do a good job of keeping dirt out of the engine. Arm rests are too close to door latches, limiting useful area. Parking brake is one of best tested, giving 33-34% braking efficiency. Glove compartment is set too low on dash, making it difficult to inspect or use, and material in compartment spills easily on opening. Interior is well-finished.

pull to get the load moving on a paved highway. Then the gage was removed and the car took this load in LO range up to 41 *mph* for a distance of 5½ miles on a 1% upgrade, moving along smoothly with little effort. The exceptional potency of this 190 *hp* V-8 power plant was also demonstrated in the regular hill-climbing tests. With 360 pounds of passenger weight, the car took a 34% grade in LO at 20 *mph*, a 27% hill in Drive (1) at 40 *mph* and a 13% hill in Hi Drive at 60 *mph*. That's good climbability!

The Hydramatic transmission has a new performance range in the 1952 version. Suppose we call it Drive (1). On hilly, winding roads, this 3-gear ratio range allows a steady, powerful pull in third, as well as a reserve acceleration surge when needed. It's also handy for downgrade driving for the 3-gear range automatically holds third gear, allowing a coasting speed on the average descent of approximately 25 *mph* without applying the

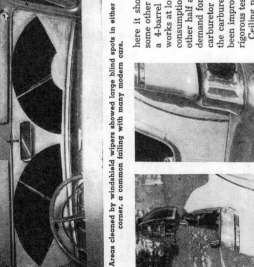

Cadillac

For a Lifetime ... if You Prefer!

brakes. Tests showed, incidentally, that the drag or engine braking effect of this transmission when down-shifted while traveling at speeds rangin', from 20 through 50 *mph*, ranged from 15 to 20% efficiency, with a peak deceleration rate at the higher speeds of about 6.44 ft/sec./sec. On the other side of the gear selector quadrant, the Hi Drive gives not only the normal three gears, but also a gear above third, somewhat like overdrive. This 4-gear arrangement provides the full range for city or open highway driving up to the car's highest speeds. As for axles, you can take your choice of two rear-axle ratios available.

Left above, note blower (1) in luggage compartment that serves as a defroster for rear window. Also note positioning of jack parts which are held well out of the way (rear tire has been temporarily removed).

The 3.36-to-1 ratio will give you the most sparkling acceleration; the 3.07-to-1 axle ratio will give you the greatest overall economy. While the manufacturer recommends premium fuel for this high compression engine (the compression ratio is 7.5-to-1) MVR's engineer's tried out regular gasoline and only got a slight ping when the engine was under load. Right here it should be mentioned that Cadillac, like some other General Motors cars, is equipped with a 4-barrel carburetor. Half of the carburetor works at lower speeds, therefore tends to cut fuel consumption below the rate required when the other half also goes into action upon the driver's demand for more power. Intake capacity of this carburetor is almost doubled in comparison with the carburetor used previously, yet economy has been improved, MVR's experts determined in the rigorous tests.

Ceiling price on the Cadillac as established by the Office of Price Stabilization is $3,636.48 for the Series 62, including Hydramatic transmission. This figure is at the Detroit factory and includes federal excise taxes, factory handling charges and dealer delivery-and-handling charges. It does not include transportation charges, state and local taxes, or optional equipment such as the power steering ($198.43).

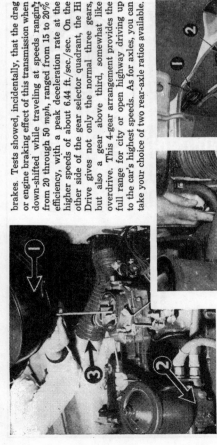

In the photograph above, note the huge air cleaner (1) which should keep this Cadillac 190 hp power plant clean. The power steering unit (2) worked well under test. But the connection of the air intake duct at (3) was quite loose on this car. Inset, screwdriver points to hose found lying on exhaust manifold when car was delivered—hose would have burned through in time after continuous running.

Areas cleaned by windshield wipers showed large blind spots in either corner, a common failing with many modern cars.

Left, gas tank filler is located inside this rear lamp housing and exhaust pipes (right) are built into each rear bumper.

Here is a frank appraisal of why Cadillac gets the 1952 Motor Trend Engineering Achievement Award. How does your car rate?

By Walt Woron

CADILLAC—CAR OF THE YEAR

"CADILLAC—CAR OF THE YEAR!" That's what it says, and MOTOR TREND Research is ready to back up that statement—ready to back it up with facts and figures. For although many cars come close to the '52 Cadillac, *no* other American production stock car can lay claim to the honor of being *the* car of 1952. *Why* is Cadillac the car of 1952? Sure, it has style, prestige, and creates a pride of ownership surpassed by only the princeliest of products, but this isn't what we are talking about. We claim that Cadillac is the car of the year on the basis of performance. handling, safety, economy. How do we determine that? Draw up a chair and we'll go into a detailed explanation.

First of all, most of. the figures used in determining the 1952 MOTOR TREND Engineering Achievement Award were gathered during the road tests of the 20 listed cars. These tests were conducted for publication in MOTOR TREND during 1952. Other figures were added later, but *all* of them, with the one exception of the evaluation on handling, are based on cold, hard, engineering test data.

The staff of MOTOR TREND Research does not claim to be engineers. Practical engineers, yes; theoretical, no. With critical eyes, the guidance of our readers, the use of engineering instruments, and the help of engineering specialists, we are able to come up with figures in which we have the utmost confidence. With these figures in chart form, we are then able to give you an *overall* rating of the 20 cars tested.

We have used a system that places less emphasis on power to determine the 1952 Award winner. The method used in 1951 may have favored more powerful cars. This year's method does not: In first place is a heavy car, in second a light car, third a medium car, fourth a light car, fifth a medium car.

This year's categories are four basic ones that go into a car's engineering qualities: Performance, Handling, Safety, and Economy and Maintenance. The first includes those factors that determine the *overall* efficiency of the engine, by itself, in relation to the transmission, and in relation to the entire car. Handling includes roadability: how the car reacts to movements of the steering wheel under many assorted conditions. Safety includes interior safety as well as brake efficiency. Economy and Maintenance are indicated by fuel consumption, cost of operation, and how much it costs to repair and maintain.

Each of the main categories was assigned a value of 25 per cent, with a possible total cf 100. Since Performance has eight sub-items, Handling only one, Safety three, and Economy and Maintenance four, factors were needed that would result in a total of only 25 per cent for each category. After all the figures were determined, the cars were given positions from first to twentieth in each column. Twenty points were given for first place, 19 for second, 18 for third, etc. The total points each car received under all sub-items in each category were then added. A theoretical total of 160 points was therefore possible for a car that placed first in each of the eight columns under performance. To reduce this to 25 per cent (the total value assigned to each category) the conversion factor of .156, or $^{25}/_{160}$, was used. Each car's total for the eight columns under performance was multiplied by this figure. The same method, but with different reduction factors, was then used for each of the other categories (.417 for Safety, .312 for Economy and Maintenance; no factor was necessary for Handling, which has no sub-items).

How Did Cadillac Rate?

In automobiles, like anything else, a compromise is the rule, rather than the exception. It's therefore not at all surprising that the Cadillac 62 won the 1952 MOTOR TREND Engineering Achievement Award. Cadillac has built a better automobile, on a comparative basis, than the 19 other cars rated. It's a compromise automobile. one that's good in all factors. This enabled it to total enough points to

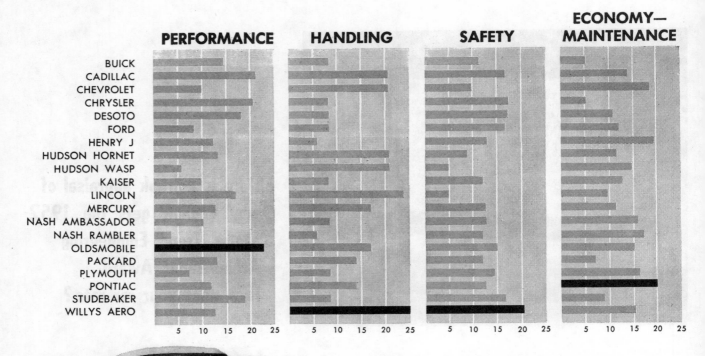

PERFORMANCE HANDLING SAFETY ECONOMY—MAINTENANCE

BUICK
CADILLAC
CHEVROLET
CHRYSLER
DESOTO
FORD
HENRY J
HUDSON HORNET
HUDSON WASP
KAISER
LINCOLN
MERCURY
NASH AMBASSADOR
NASH RAMBLER
OLDSMOBILE
PACKARD
PLYMOUTH
PONTIAC
STUDEBAKER
WILLYS AERO

CADILLAC—CAR OF THE YEAR

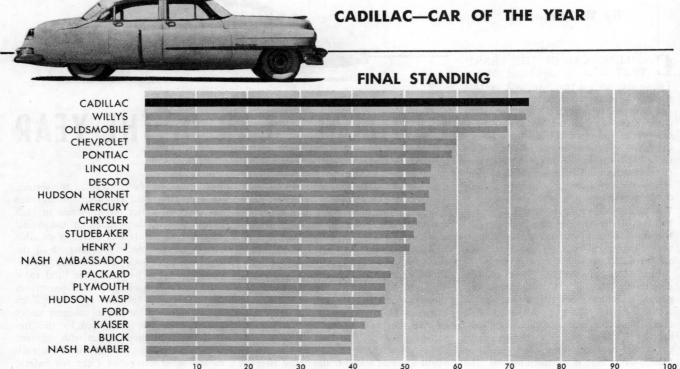

FINAL STANDING

CADILLAC
WILLYS
OLDSMOBILE
CHEVROLET
PONTIAC
LINCOLN
DESOTO
HUDSON HORNET
MERCURY
CHRYSLER
STUDEBAKER
HENRY J
NASH AMBASSADOR
PACKARD
PLYMOUTH
HUDSON WASP
FORD
KAISER
BUICK
NASH RAMBLER

outdistance any other car that was tested.

In Performance, the Cadillac came in second because of its good acceleration, high top speed, low number of pounds car weight for each ft.-lb. of torque and high maximum bmep. These latter factors, plus the relative number of pounds each horsepower has to push, result in the acceleration qualities evident at low, medium, and high speeds.

In Handling, the Cadillac 62 with power steering has been placed in a tie for third

by the MT Research staff. The steering wheel is well-positioned, overall handling characteristics are good, the car sticks in corners, has little tendency to break loose, does not feel mushy, and maintains a steady course with little wind wander.

In Safety, the Cadillac 62 had the least number of pounds loading on each square inch of brake lining (making it tops in this sub-item), and was sixth in the sub-item, interior safety.

The Cadillac is fairly economical to

run and has a high trade-in value (tie for third in cost per mile), is efficient (fourth) in the strictly engineering analysis of fuel economy (ton mpg), and is the most economical in its price class when it comes to repairs, parts, and labor.

So much for the winning car and how it won. A study of the chart will show *why* Cadillac wound up in each position as it did. Now, let's take a closer look at the four main categories and the various sub-items under each of them.

PERFORMANCE DATA CHART

Line No.	Car Make and Model	PERFORMANCE								Handling	SAFETY			ECONOMY & MAINTENANCE				Line No.
		Average 1/4 Mile Acceleration in Seconds	Average High Speed Acceleration in Seconds	Average Top Speed	Per cent of BHP at Wheels	Pounds Per RHP	Pounds Per Lb.-Ft. of Maximum Torque	RHP Per Cu. In.	Maximum BMEP in PSI	(By Position)	Average Braking Distance in Feet	Weight Per Sq. In. of Brake Lining	Interior Safety Check in Per cent	Average Fuel Consumption in MPG	Average Fuel Consumption in Ton MPG	Cost Per Mile	Maintenance and Repair Costs	
1	Buick Roadmaster…	20.2	15.9	100.1	50.0	53.2	16.2	.265	131.8	11T	135'3"	20.7	86	13.9	31.5	13.3	175.07	1
2	Cadillac 62……	18.4	10.9	109.6	52.6	45.1	14.0	.302	146.6	3T	122'0"	18.7	86	16.7	37.7	6.7	183.00	2
3	Chevrolet-Standard..	20.8	19.8	80.9	67.4	52.7	18.5	.286	122.5	3T	121'3"	20.6	43	19.1	31.1	5.3	98.65	3
4	Chrysler Saratoga V-8	19.5	11.3	106.0	54.0	44.4	13.9	.294	142.0	11T	115'3"	21.5	100	15.0	32.5	11.9	192.77	4
5	De Soto V-8……	20.4	13.8	98.1	55.0	46.5	16.3	.317	136.5	11T	125'2"	20.3	100	17.3	35.4	11.3	177.76	5
6	Ford V-8……	21.4	22.0	86.7	58.2	55.1	18.0	.268	123.5	11T	94'0"	20.4	72	17.0	30.0	7.0	139.71	6
7	Henry J-Corsair 6…	20.8	19.5	83.9	63.1	50.0	18.9	.313	124.6	19T	128'0"	19.1	72	23.3	30.1	5.4	113.17	7
8	Hudson Hornet…..	20.2	13.9	99.2	50.7	53.9	15.4	.238	125.8	3T	119'5"	25.0	86	17.3	34.3	11.4	146.03	8
9	Hudson Wasp…….	20.9	18.0	97.8	47.5	62.9	19.0	.231	115.0	3T	130'6"	23.9	72	18.9	36.0	10.5	146.03	9
10	Kaiser…………	19.7	19.2	90.8	50.4	60.8	18.5	.256	126.7	11T	129'6"	20.0	72	17.8	31.2	11.4	120.18	10
11	Lincoln…………	21.6	13.1	98.3	59.2	48.7	16.3	.299	134.9	2	132'7"	23.5	72	17.4	40.4	14.9	250.79	11
12	Mercury… …….	20.1	19.3	91.7	57.6	51.0	17.4	.282	124.5	7T	119'8"	23.1	86	18.3	33.6	8.0	194.79	12
13	Nash Ambassador…	20.6	15.2	95.2	50.0	62.8	17.1	.238	131.4	11T	121'0"	22.1	86	22.2	41.8	11.9	146.21	13
14	Nash Rambler……	22.5	19.6	81.3	51.2	63.0	19.2	.243	120.6	19T	116'10"	27.6	86	22.6	30.0	7.3	119.25	14
15	Oldsmobile Super 88.	19.0	12.2	104.3	60.0	42.7	14.5	.316	140.5	7T	121'8"	21.5	100	18.9	38.7	8.7	148.48	15
16	Packard 300……	20.7	15.9	96.3	57.3	50.9	16.2	.263	124.5	9T	129'6"	21.0	86	15.2	33.3	11.7	186.52	16
17	Plymouth…………	22.9	22.8	85.6	61.9	55.8	19.1	.275	121.2	11T	106'6"	21.1	72	19.6	32.7	7.6	135.02	17
18	Pontiac 8………	21.4	13.9	92.9	57.2	54.2	16.7	.261	127.5	9T	111'3"	22.1	72	19.7	37.3	6.7	126.84	18
19	Stude. Comm. V-8..	20.5	13.7	87.6	74.1	37.0	17.3	.382	127.5	11T	113'4"	20.1	72	16.2	26.7	8.4	143.13	19
20	Willys Aero. ……	20.8	17.2	81.5	60.0	50.2	20.1	.335	126.4	1	113'10"	20.4	100	21.5	29.2	7.5	121.56	20

Performance

The first column under Performance is *Average Acceleration over 1/4-mile* in seconds of elapsed time. This indicates the effectiveness of the power/weight ratio, which provides the car with the pickup required for traffic driving. If the car is too heavy, or if it is underpowered, it will naturally have slow acceleration. MT Research tries all possible combinations of shifting before finally recording the figures, so we are certain to wind up with the best obtainable times (for the particular car and test conditions).

Average High Speed Acceleration is the average of acceleration from 10-60 and 30-60 mph. These tests are conducted by cruising at the indicated low speeds, then stomping the throttle (letting the car down-shift if that is the operation of the transmission) and accelerating until the upper speed is reached. Acceleration at these speeds is important when you have to slow down behind another car on a grade, then wish to pass and need the added push.

Average Top Speed speaks for itself. The figures (derived from two-way runs, two each in opposite directions) give an indication of possible cruising speeds.

Per Cent of Brake Horsepower delivered to the rear wheels is the ratio of bhp *advertised* (by the manufacturer) to road hp (the latter determined with a Clayton chassis dynamometer). Road hp is the bhp *minus* losses through the transmission, driveshaft, rear axle, and rear wheels. A percentage of 50-60 is about average; some cars may be on the low side if *advertised* bhp is higher than *actual* bhp.

Pounds per Road Horsepower is another factor in the performance of the vehicle, and not the engine. The engine will deliver a certain bhp at each rpm, finally tapering off after it reaches maximum bhp. Required road hp for the vehicle to maintain level road speed is somewhere below these values. Where the two curves cross on a graph is the theoretical top speed. The difference between the two factors at any given speed is available for a change of speed, dependent on the weight of the car and the torque. This, then, explains the reason for the next column,

Pounds per lb.-ft. of Maximum Torque. While high torque (for which we depend on the manufacturer's figure) is a highly desired engine characteristic, we tie it in with performance potential by equalizing it with the weight of the car. One car may have considerably more torque than another, but the ratio of torque to the weight it has to push may be higher, resulting in less available acceleration. Torque is also important because although two cars may have the same maximum bhp, one may have more torque throughout the entire rpm range, which will be reflected in more available acceleration.

Road Horsepower per Cubic Inch is a rating that involves engineering "finesse" in the development of power rather than brute strength through size. Since we measure power at the rear wheels, this figure also includes the mechanical efficiency of the drive train.

Maximum Bmep (brake mean effective pressure) is another way of expressing engine torque per cubic inch at the maximum torque speed range. This figure, along with maximum brake horsepower per cubic inch, is a comparative measure of how efficiently an engine develops power per unit of displacement over a fairly wide operating speed.

Top car in the Performance category is the Oldsmobile Super 88, equipped with the Super (dual-range) Hydra-Matic transmission. Its overall engine efficiency (top maximum bmep, high torque per lb., high road hp per cu. in.), its engine-to-rear axle and engine-to-car relationship (tie for fifth in per cent of brake hp delivered to rear wheels, third in pounds per road hp), results in outstanding acceleration and top speed.

Handling

Handling is one category that is based on selective personal opinion; however, it is a consensus of the MT Research staff, all members of which drive all the cars, using unbiased judgement in looking at handling characteristics. These opinions are based on the roadability of the car, rather than the ease of handling.

We take into account the car's versatility at all speed ranges, keeping in mind what the car owner will be doing with his car in traffic, on dirt roads, on smooth asphalt highways stretching beyond the horizon, and on roads that curve over and around mountains. Also, what the car will do when it hits a soft shoulder, how it acts on streetcar tracks, how it reacts to ruts in the road, how mushy the front end is in a tight corner, how much the body leans, how easy it is to correct after going through a corner, how much corrective action it needs to hold it in a straight line, and how much it is affected by crosswinds.

Best car for all-around handling qualities, according to the opinion of MT Research, is the new Aero Willys. The steering wheel is positioned properly to give the driver excellent control, the car maneuvers gracefully in traffic, takes very little corrective action on a straightaway, is barely bothered by powerful crosswinds, does not break loose on sharp turns (except on dirt, where it goes into a safe, controlled slide), does not get whipped aside on streetcar tracks or by shoulders, and has an overall cornering ability on a par with many sports cars (despite the fact that the steering ratio is slow by comparison).

Safety

Safety, as we see it, based on items other than personal opinion, should include braking, how safe the interior of the car is, and how good the vision is. Other items are also important, such as handling ability and acceleration at high speed, but these two factors show up elsewhere in our evaluation.

Average Braking Distance is the overall average of stopping distances required at speeds of 30, 45, and 60 mph. These are obtained for all cars on the same road surface, checked with an electric speedometer, an electrically-actuated brake detonator, and a steel tape. Tires are as provided as standard equipment.

Weight Per Square Inch of Brake Lining is the weight of the car in pounds, divided by the number of square inches of brake lining for all four wheels. This indicates the energy that each square inch of lining has to dissipate during a stop, and possibly indicates the durability of the lining (more square inches means less heat per unit of surface for a given energy absorption).

Interior Safety Check includes items that affect the safety of driver and passengers alike: blind spots in vision, positive locks to prevent rear doors from coming open while driving, a secure locking device on the front seat track, projections on the dashboard, convenient location of lighter and ashtray for the driver.

The ratio of noes to yeses determines this percentage, with the safest cars getting the highest score.

The Aero Willys also rates tops in this category, on the basis of its No. 1 position in weight per sq. in. of brake lining. Actual stopping distance is not outstanding (13th overall) but during our test of this car the brakes were subjected to a destructive beating. Fade did not occur, possibly due to weight loading and the fact that the drums have deep cooling fins. In interior safety, the Willys ties for sixth.

Economy and Maintenance

Average Mpg is the overall average of fuel consumption readings taken at steady, level road speeds of 30, 45, and 60 mph, and during a drive through a 13-mile course laid out through traffic. Type of fuel used (regular or premium) depends on the manufacturer's recommendation.

Average Ton Mpg is an engineering figure based on how much weight a certain car can haul at what fuel consumption. It is obtained by multiplying the weight of the car in tons by the actual fuel consumption.

Its usefulness is in comparing the overall thermal efficiency of the vehicle in converting fuel energy into useful work, and to what extent the transmission and gearing take advantage of the engine's inherent fuel economy.

Cost Per Mile is determined on the basis of four items: cost of fuel operation for one year, cost of insurance coverage, first year's depreciation, and that maintenance which, on an average, may be required on any car (not necessarily every car). To determine fuel cost, it is assumed that the car will travel the national average of 10,000 miles. This figure is divided by the overall mpg average obtained on our road test, multiplied by the cost per gallon of fuel used (regular or premium) as recommended by the manufacturer. Insurance cost is for the following coverage: comprehensive, $50 deductible, public liability of $10,000-$20,000, and $5,000 property damage. Maintenance includes: a wheel alignment, a brake reline, two major tune-ups, an adjustment and change of lubricant of the automatic transmission (if the car is so equipped).

Maintenance and Repair do not necessarily mean that all the items are necessary for a full year's maintenance, but indicate the *relative* cost of maintaining and repairing one car, as compared to another. Cost of parts and labor are taken from *Motor's Flat Rate Manual,* and include: distributor, battery, fuel pump, fan belt, a valve grind, one front fender, one tire, and one bumper.

The most economical car to operate, on the above basis, is the Pontiac Eight, with Dual Range Hydra-Matic. Although it does not excel in any one of the four sub-items under Economy and Mainte-

nance, it falls into the upper range in all four. In fuel economy it is fifth in both miles per gallon and ton mpg, in cost per mile of operation it ties for third, and in maintenance and repairs it is sixth.

A Few Final Words

Well, there you have it. If you can't figure out why your car did not wind up in first place in overall standings, or why it didn't take first in performance (or one of the other categories), take another look at the basic numerical chart. Rate your own car, compare it to the others, see why it finished where it did. You may not agree with our method of selecting the winner, but it's hard to deny the proof of figures obtained during the critical tests we conduct.

On the basis of such searching analysis, conducted over the period of a year in which we road tested 20 different makes, all four-door sedans (except where no such model is manufactured), all equipped with that model's most popular transmission, we are proud to present the Cadillac Motor Car Company with the 1952 MOTOR TREND Engineering Achievement Award.

—*Walt Woron*

Sectioned *Cadillac*

Above: Rear quarter window is too long to roll down into the sectioned body. Here it is slid out of position and subsequently stored in trunk.

Below: Wide appearance of 1952 Cadillac is shown in this head-on view. Section was removed from lower edge of hood eliminating the usual "V".

Seldom Customized, The Cadillac Makes A Good Car For Transformation

By Spencer Murray
Photos by Ralph Poole

"UNUSUAL" is the word for this car. At first glance it appears to be just what it is, a 1952 Cadillac Coupe deVille. A closer look proves, however, that something is missing from, or added to, it.

When Ed Wilder of Los Angeles decided to alter his 1952 Cadillac convertible, he made up his mind that it should be altered radically but still retain the stock Cadillac appearance. Chopping the top, channeling the body, altering the grill, or making any similar changes would detract from the Cadillac quality. The only remaining solution was sectioning.

Many of our readers have written to us asking why Fords seem to be about the only cars that people section. Here is the answer.

Wanting nothing but top quality body work, Ed took his Cadillac to Jay Everett, also of Los Angeles. He told Jay that he didn't want to detract from the stock Cadillac appearance so they put their heads together and finally came up with a workable solution. They decided to section the car *above* the fender line. This necessitated rebuilding the hood and drastically altering the deck lid but, undaunted, Jay set to work.

Two parallel lines, four inches apart, were scribed on the car just below the belt molding (the chrome strip that encircles the car just be-

Drawing attention wherever it is driven, Coupe de Ville looks stock at first glance.

neath the windows). Carefully following the lines, Jay made the two cuts and the upper part of the body was allowed to drop four inches.

Realigning the top to the bottom was a little more work than Jay had originally planned on. The major body sections such as the cowl, the quarter panels, the doors, and inner body panels went together comparatively easily, but the hood and deck lid presented major problems.

The deck lid was removed from the car and a mark was made about four inches in from the outer edge, all the way around. Cutting on this line, the outer lip of the deck lid and the metal immediately surrounding it was separated from the remaining inner portion. The outer section was discarded and a new, wider section of metal was welded to the inner part. By first reworking the deck lid to fit the new body contours, then shaping up the new outer edge and rounding the lower corners, the lid was completed.

The hood also presented its problems. A four inch section was removed from the vertical sides of the hood and from the leading bottom edge. Like the deck lid, a new outer edge had to be built so that the hood would line up with the fenders. At this point it was noticed that, although the sectioning job gave the car a new, wider, appearance, it was still not as wide appearing as Ed wanted it.

The front fenders were each moved out from the body three quarters of an inch. This made it necessary to add still another outer edge to the hood to conform with this increase in width. The remaining portions of the car also had to be widened; the doors, the quarter panels, the rear fenders, the bumpers and the grill.

When the fenders were replaced on the body, it was found that the top edges of the fenders were actually higher than the belt molding, so a panel had to be fitted to the body to conform with this. If the body had not been widened this would have been, probably, an almost insurmountable problem, but the width increase of three quarters of an inch on each side gave Jay some room to work. The result may be seen in the accompanying photographs. This area, above the front edges of the rear fenders, is actually concave, so much so, in fact, that a drain hole had to be made to let the water run off that would otherwise accumulate from rain or from washing the car. Next, the seams between the body and the fenders were filled in.

Always full of ideas, Ed decided now that he wanted a Coupe deVille instead of a convertible. An order was placed at a Cadillac agency and soon a deVille top, complete with windows and hardware, arrived.

The top was installed with no little difficulty, but it was discovered that the deVille quarter windows would not roll down in the conventional manner. It seems that the windows were longer than the body was thick so an alternate method was worked out. The quarter windows are now completely removable from the car. By rolling down the door windows, the quarter windows are slid out of position and stored in the trunk.

With the exterior of the car pretty well along by now, work was directed

Instrument grouping has been slanted in at the top to reduce glare. Hardware is brass plated.

to the interior. The cowl had been sectioned below the level of the instrument panel, so the panel had dropped with the upper part of the body. The results were somewhat astounding; the lower edge of the panel came so close to the floor that the driver was unable to get his feet under it. It was eventually found, however, that a 1950 Cadillac instrument panel was not so deep as the later one, so the earlier one was fitted to the car.

The seats also had to be rebuilt to fit the body and still retain plenty of head room. The seat cushions were dropped closer to the floor and the seat backs were, also, cut down. The result is perfectly proportioned seats, just a little lower in all respects than stock seats.

The only exterior trim that was removed was the trunk hardware and the Cadillac signs on each front fender. The hood "V" was eliminated in the sectioning process.

All metal work being completed, the car was given an outstanding black lacquer job. This is an unusual color to paint so radically customized an automobile and many shops frown on customers who want their cars this color because it has a marked tendency to show up any rough metal work.

The final touch was to lower the entire car three inches in the rear and two and a half inches in front. The result is a beautifully proportioned automobile that is, very unusual.

The cost for a job like this, if anyone has a Coupe deVille that they want sectioned, will run close to $3,000.

Cadillac Road Test

CONTINUED FROM PAGE 23

latch, and the trunk lid by a key and over-center springs that eliminate the effort of lifting.

A Long Line of V-8s

It's inevitable that the Cadillac V-8 for 1952 would have more horsepower, greater efficiency, and easier accessibility for servicing—it has behind it 37 years of engine building, starting with the pioneering of the water-cooled V-8 of 1914—an engine smaller (314 cubic inches) than today's, developing only 60 hp. The present Cad engine, basically the same as the overhead job introduced in 1949, has 30 additional horsepower—developed at a rate higher by 200 rpm than previously—gained through a four-barrel carburetor and a general opening up of the intake and exhaust systems. The carburetor uses two barrels for part-throttle driving, calling on the other two for maximum power requirement conditions. The intake mani-

Coupe De Ville—$3978 FOB Detroit

Limousine—$5300 FOB Detroit

Four-Door Sedan—$3648 FOB Detroit

fold has been enlarged, as have the exhaust valves and exhaust ports. The exhaust system uses independent exhaust pipes (not headers) for each bank of the engine, one large and one small muffler for each pipe, ending through the outer ends of the rear bumper (giving added road clearance over steep driveways and dips, which often cause flattening of the tail pipes). The smaller mufflers, known as resonators, are for removing noise frequencies which cannot be removed by the regular mufflers. Cadillac is striving for a completely silent exhaust system.

Placement of the various components of

the engine were made apparently with an eye to ease of service; the oil filler neck and both fuel filters are out in the open; the distributor is in a good location; all spark plugs (except no. 1 and 4 on the right bank) are simple to remove; valve covers are easily detached; the only thing in the way of servicing the distributor is the removal of the large carburetor air cleaner.

Better Brakes This Year

The only changes, but welcomed, to the '52 chassis (or running gear) are the larger

Convertible—$4128 FOB Detroit

front (12-inch) ribbed brake drums that are both stronger and allow more effective cooling. With the increased horsepower, providing more acceleration and top speed, better brakes are called for. At no time during the normal performance of our test (except at the tail end of our full-on brake stops) did the Cad brakes fade. Recovery was very rapid. Compared to last year's test car, brake stopping distances remained about the same at 30 mph, increased at 45 and were greatly reduced (by 22 feet) at 60 mph (see Test Table).

Another Stride Forward

With the introduction of its Golden Anniversary Cadillac, the Cadillac Motor Car Company has taken another stride forward in producing pioneering innovations: the multi-cylinder engine; the first to equip cars with electric starting, lights and ignition; the first to build a water-cooled V-8 engine. Even though the 1952 Cadillac doesn't have the distinction of introducing another new automotively world-shaking development, the combination of power steering, 190 horsepower engine, luxuriousness of interior and fantastically low depreciation make it a car to be desired.

CADILLAC ACCESSORIES	
Wheel Disks	$ 28.40
Windshield Washer	11.36
Oil Filter	11.34
Fog Lamps	36.91
License Frames	4.28
Outside Mirror	6.24
Vanity Mirror	1.85
E-Z-Eye Glass	45.52
Heater and Blower	113.66
Radio Push Button & R. Speaker	112.47
Radio Sig. Seeking & R. Speaker	129.22
Power Steering	198.43
Autronic Eye Beam Control	53.36
White Sidewall Tires 62 and 60	33.76
Automatic Window Regulators	138.64
Trim Rings	10.69

**luxury, performance, even economy—
the cadillac has them—but above all, it is
the car with prestige**

An MT Research Report
By Walt Woron and Pete Molson

Photos by Jack Campbell

BOX SCORE:

	POORER THAN AVERAGE	AVERAGE	BETTER THAN AVERAGE
ACCELERATION			
Standing ¼ mile			
30-60 mph			
BODY WORK			
BRAKES			
Stopping distance avg.			
@ 30, 45, 60 mph			
EASE OF HANDLING			
FUEL ECONOMY			
Averages @ 30,			
45, 60 mph			
INTERIOR			
RIDE			
ROADABILITY			
TOP SPEED			

This box score is based on the average of all '52 cars tested except for the ratings on Interior and Ride, which refer to the average of other cars in the same price class (see February '53 MT).

IN A LITTLE OVER A FIFTH of a minute, a '53 Cadillac will hit 60 mph from a standing start. In not too much longer, it will top 115. Much more impressive to us at MOTOR TREND, however, is the fact that the fuel economy of the '53 Cad is *30 per cent* better than that of the '52 Cad. For this Cadillac should take a bow. They are increasing engine efficiency in a place where it hits you and us—the pocketbook. Let's hope we see similar increases with other '53 models.

America's Glamour Queen

Cadillac is the car that most Americans —if their purses were unlimited—would choose above all others. It has so entrenched itself on the domestic scene that it has become to many people a symbol rather than a tangible automobile with direct competitors, at least pricewise, among four other well-known and highly respected U.S. cars. The most important factor in Cadillac's desirability is very probably the elusive one of prestige.

People Like Its Looks

In appearance, General Motors' top-drawer offering has grown a little less distinctive since it became virtually undisputed King of the Mountain in 1941. The ever-larger decorative Vs, the chrome wheel discs of 1947, and the fins of 1949 were quickly taken over by other makes, though GM wisely held back whenever possible before using them on its lesser cars. On the other hand, Buick—not only on the Roadmaster but also on the medium-priced Super—has used the same body shell as the Cadillac for many years. The current body was introduced simultaneously on the two cars three years ago and has continued without visible change except for a heightened trunk lid.

CADILLAC-

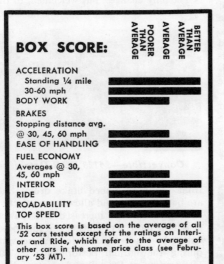

Here sit the country's most envied drivers. Power steering put wheel grips out of their usual position with easy half turn

Cigarette lighter is located conveniently for rear seat passengers. Rope cord has concealed mountings in padded recess

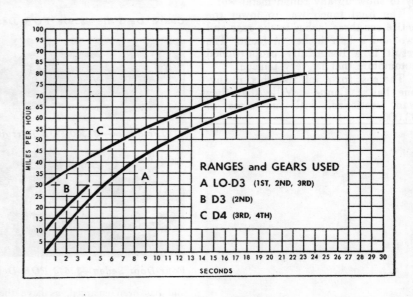

RANGES and GEARS USED
A LO-D3 (1ST, 2ND, 3RD)
B D3 (2ND)
C D4 (3RD, 4TH)

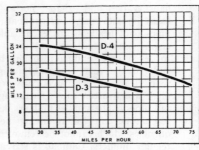

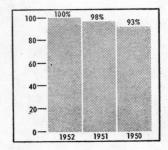

ACCELERATION, FUEL CONSUMPTION & DEPRECIATION CHARTS

This is not to say that it is not satisfactory; in many respects it is extremely so. Not the least of these would seem to be appearance, if the popularity of both makes is an indication. Few Americans will wholeheartedly support something whose looks they don't like. Cadillac represents the heights of the solid GM school of design, whose main stock-in-trade consists of considerable length, width, and weight, even on the Chevrolet. Its second time-proved tactic lies in making all of these dimensions appear greater than they actually are.

Whether the appealing work of the Italian designers will eventually influence all American automobiles remains to be seen. It offers the advantage of better vision and of lower cost through the elimination of chrome. But it is a good bet that General Motors, at least, will not make radical changes in the looks of its standard products for some time to come.

Other Makers Please Copy?

For 1953, the Cadillac grille is even more massive than before. Two raised and

AMERICA'S FAVORITE LUXURY CAR

enlarged bumper guards dominate it. Other cars may shortly adopt two new styling touches: extended chrome "eyelids" on the headlights, and the extremely handsome, optional chrome wheel discs with concave centers. Except for these changes and the squared-off rear deck, the casual observer will find the new car practically indistinguishable from 1950 and later models. From the standpoint of continuing owner satisfaction with a luxury car, this policy is wisdom itself.

From Inside

Let's take a look at the surroundings in which the typical owner of a '53 Cadillac controls his car. We say "controls," for driving, in one sense, is no longer necessary here. In minor respects, such as keep-

ing aware of exact engine oil pressure, it is not even possible. Being typical, our owner has a Series 62 four-door sedan, the model used for testing by MT Research.

Doors, both front and rear, are wide. Getting in and out through them is easy. Their interior panels, like the rest of the interior, are finished in conservative good taste. Armrests are now an integral part of the panel; as a result they are much longer, and more comfortable for a variety of human statures. They incorporate a door pull, whose shape and metal finish make it resemble an ashtray. Fabrics and trim used on the doors, as elsewhere in the car, are excellent, on a par with other 1953 luxury cars.

The seats follow GM practice in being deep, comfortable, and of medium height.

The MT Research car was equipped with optional power seat adjustment and window lifts (the combination costs an additional $138). Travel of the seat is the same as with the standard hand control: It rises as it moves forward; the seat back, rather sharply canted to the rear, does not change its angle.

Instruments, grouped directly in front of the driver, are surmounted by a large and legible speedometer. Fuel and temperature gauges use a white needle on a chrome ground and are not easy to read. Warning lights are provided for low oil pressure, battery discharge, and parking brake position. Replacement of the conventional oil pressure gauge and ammeter with light signals is hard to justify on an expensive car. Lights are an excellent adjunct to dials, but their information is too limited to make them a satisfactory substitute. The Hydra-Matic transmission range indicator has moved to the panel, where it can be scanned with the other instruments. As the staff observed last year, the two DRIVE range "notches" are too close together on the dial.

In many respects the Cadillac's beautifully finished dash does not reflect the best in present-day arrangement. The heater and ventilation controls, though solid and pleasant to operate, are unlighted. Two vent knobs, evidently not considered a part of the panel's design, are awkwardly located under the radio speaker. Twin map lights are a good feature.

Cadillac's wheels are always a center of interest, and for good reason. These unusual concave discs are optional extras.

Cadillac's powerhouse lies in this seemingly crowded compartment, but access for service is not bad. Note 12-volt battery

CADILLAC

The test Cadillac took fast corners, like this one, without discomfort for passengers

New Safety Ratings

This month MOTOR TREND is making a number of changes in its Safety Check, and it is interesting to see how Cadillac stands on the new points, and what improvement has been made over last year. The Cadillac mirror, unlike others, is adjustable up and down, and may be called the industry's safest in terms of effectively eliminating the blind spot. It is free of sharp edges. Again this year, the dash panel glares irritatingly at the driver. At the left side of the dash, where the driver's knees can slide forward quickly in a crash stop of even medium intensity, the hand brake and sharp ignition key protrude at too low a point for safety.

Location of the glove compartment has now joined that of the lighter and ashtray as a safety item. With front seats increasing in width, right-hand compartments have moved farther and farther away from the driver. The "reasonable man" of legal terminology cannot be expected to

stop his car whenever he needs his sunglasses, and reaching across a front seat as wide as the Cadillac's is not at all safe while driving.

On the passenger's side, the dash is commendably free of dangerous projections with the exception of the radio knobs; however, even one projection is a potential hazard. If you order a Cadillac without a radio, the right side of its dash will be as safe as that of any American stock car. It does not deserve a completely clean bill of health in this regard, for—in common with all other U.S. cars—it

lacks a crash pad with high shock-absorbing ability. (Those on the Kaiser and Chrysler, though a step *toward* safety, have little function in a serious crash, but offer protection—especially to children—in ordinary quick stops.)

Safety for rear seat passengers is also a part of the new check list. The back of the front seat should be padded but solid; this the Cadillac's is, but its ashtray and cigarette lighter project from the seat back. Its rear doors cannot be opened, from inside or out, when the pushbutton

---

1953 CADILLAC TEST TABLE

PERFORMANCE
ACCELERATION IN SECONDS
(Checked with fifth wheel and electric speedometer)

Standing start ¼ mile	18.4
0-30 mph (0-32, car speedometer reading)	4.0
0-60 mph (0-63, car speedometer reading)	12.8
30-40 mph (DRIVE range)	2.9
40-50 mph (DRIVE range)	3.2
50-60 mph (DRIVE range)	3.3
60-70 mph (DRIVE range)	3.8

TOP SPEED (MPH)
(Clocked speeds over surveyed ¼ mile)

Fastest one-way run	116.9
Slowest one-way run	113.9
Average of four runs	115.4

FUEL CONSUMPTION IN MILES PER GALLON
(Checked with fuel flowmeter, fifth wheel, and electric speedometer)

	D-3	D-4
Steady 30 mph	18.2	24.2
Steady 45 mph	15.6	22.1
Steady 60 mph	13.4	18.6
Steady 75 mph	—	14.5

BRAKE STOPPING DISTANCE
(Checked with electrically actuated detonator)

Stopping distance at:

30 mph	44.9
45 mph	113.9
60 mph	195.9

GENERAL SPECIFICATIONS
ENGINE

Type	Overhead valve V-8
Bore and stroke	$3\frac{13}{16}$ x $3\frac{5}{8}$
Stroke/bore ratio	0.95:1
Compression ratio	8.25:1
Displacement	331 cu. in.
Advertised bhp	210 at 4150 rpm
Piston travel @ max. bhp	2507 ft. per min.
Bhp per cu. in.	.63
Maximum torque	330 lbs.-ft. at 2700 rpm
Maximum bmep	150.14 psi

DRIVE SYSTEM

Transmission: Dual Range Hydra-Matic
Ratios: Reverse 4.30, 1st 3.82, 2nd 2.63, 3rd 1.45, 4th 1:1
Rear Axle: Semi-floating hypoid drive
Ratio: 3.07:1 on series 60 & 62; 3.77:1 on series 75

DIMENSIONS

Wheelbase	126 in.
Tread	Front—59 in., rear—63 in.
Wheelbase/tread ratio	2:1

Overall width	80⅛
Overall length	215¹³⁄₁₆
Overall height	62¹¹⁄₁₆
Turning diameter	45 ft.
Turns lock to lock	5
Weight (test car)	4660
Weight/bhp ratio	22.1
Weight distribution	Front—53.2%, rear—46.8%
Weight per sq. in. brake lining	18.0

PRICES
(All prices are factory delivered prices and include retail price at main factory, provisions for federal taxes, and delivery and handling charges.)

Series 62:

Club Coupe	$3571.33
Four-door Sedan	3666.26
Coupe de Ville	3994.57
Convertible Coupe	4143.72
El Dorado Convertible	7750.00

Series 60:

Fleetwood Sedan	4304.88

Series 75:

Eight-passenger Sedan	5407.54
Eight-passenger Imperial Sedan	5620.93

ACCESSORIES

Power steering	$176.98
Tinted glass	45.52
Radio (Signal seeking, pre-selector)	131.92
Radio (Signal seeking, pre-selector, remote control)	214.45
Autronic Eye	53.36
Heater	119.00
Wire wheels (chrome)	325.00
White wall tires (5)	47.77
Air conditioning	619.55

SAFETY CHECK

	YES	NO
DRIVER SAFETY:		
1. Blind spot at left windshield post at a minimum?	X	
2. Blind spot at rear vision mirror at a minimum?	X	
3. Vision to right rear satisfactory?	X	
4. Windshield free from objectionable reflections at night?	X	
5. Dash free from annoying reflections?		X
6. Left side of dash free of low projections?		X
7. Cigarette lighter, ash tray, and glove compartment convenient for driver?		X
DRIVER AND PASSENGER:		
8. Front seat apparently locked securely at all adjustment points?	X	
9. Metal strip eliminated between front quarter window and main door window?		X
FRONT PASSENGER:		
10. Mirror free of sharp corners?	X	
11. Right side of dash free of projections?		X
12. Adequate shock-absorbing crash pad?		X
REAR SEAT PASSENGERS		
13. Back of front seat free of sharp edges and projections?		X
14. Rear interior door handles inoperative when locked?	X	
15. Adequate partition to keep trunk contents out of passenger compartment on impact?		X

(MOTOR TREND constantly improves its test procedures. Because of this, we are dropping percentage ratings on the Safety Check Chart to avoid seemingly inaccurate comparisons between cars from month to month.)

OPERATING COST PER MILE ANALYSIS
(In this portion of the test table, MOTOR TREND includes those items that can be figured with reasonable accuracy on a comparative basis. The costs given here are not intended as an absolute guide to the cost of operating a particular make of car, or a particular car within that make. Depreciation is not included.)

1. Cost of gasoline	$149.85
2. Cost of insurance	146.60
3. Maintenance	
a. Wheel alignment	6.00
b. ½ brake reline	13.50
c. Major tune-up (one)	16.50
d. Automatic transmission (adjust, change lubricant)	16.00
First year of operation per mile	3.5¢

MAINTENANCE AND REPAIR COST ANALYSIS
(These are prices for parts and labor required in various repairs and replacements. Your car may require all of them in a short time, or it may require none. However, a comparison of prices for these sample operations in various makes is often of pertinent interest to prospective owners.)

Part	Cost	Labor
1. Distributor	$19.03	$ 2.10
2. Battery	25.80	1.75
3. Fuel pump	17.50	1.75
4. Fan belt	3.34	1.05
5. Valve grind	9.72	33.25
6. One front fender	60.17	12.25
7. Two tires	61.72	
8. One bumper	53.49	1.40
TOTALS	$250.77	$53.55

CADILLAC—America's Favorite Luxury Car

locks are down, which should prevent children from inadvertently opening them.

MOTOR TREND will continue to include in its analyses all items that it considers of relative importance and that could easily be incorporated into all cars, regardless of whether only one car—or, as in the case of an adequate crash pad, none—is satisfactorily equipped.

A Test Drive

Guiding the Cadillac is an almost effortless undertaking when it is equipped with power steering. The wheel position is a high one, in typical GM fashion, and the ratio is high too (25.47:1), requiring five turns from lock to lock. Last year, MOTOR TREND mentioned that the hydraulic booster might cut in too suddenly, causing the driver to overshoot his mark. On further familiarity with the various systems, such a possibility seems unlikely. At any rate, we were utterly at ease in the Cadillac. We did note a small amount of play in the wheel. Many makers claim that their variety of power steering gives a true feel of the road, but seldom has the testing staff noted so little loss of "road sense" as on this car. There is little sensation that the system is a hydraulically assisted one. Rather, it suggests exceptionally easy conventional steering.

Non-slip plastic grips on the wheel are located at the "8:20" position. One driver of average height found that the armrest struck his elbow at this position. In any event, many drivers prefer a "10:20" or even "10:10" position, and grips above the crossbar as well as below it would give them more freedom.

Unlike last year's test car, this one was whipped aside (though not at all badly) by soft shoulders on the highway. Streetcar tracks gave it some trouble, and so did ruts. Very little steering vibration was noted. At high speeds on straight roads, the car held its direction well, requiring no correction.

Parking, which requires so little physical exertion, would be simpler if the fenders were visible. Because of the high hood, the right front one is hidden, and even the right rear tail fin, which could be a useful guide, cannot be seen from the driver's seat. Aside from this, vision is excellent in all directions. Directly ahead of him, the driver has a view of the road close to the car.

Hydra-Matic transmission is standard. Smoothness has increased to the point where this more efficient drive can now be compared (at least, as it operates on the Cadillac) with the torque converters. Unless one is watching for the shift points, they frequently pass unnoticed.

Brake lining area is up from 241.5 to 258.5 square inches; stopping distances showed a slight improvement. Pedal pressure, though not unduly high, is noticeably greater than on the Chevrolet, for example. Cadillac is the only car in its field on which power brakes are not available. Left-foot operation of the brake pedal is rather difficult, the pedal being close to the throttle and a little small.

Riding comfort is fine. Some vibration is transmitted to the body on washboard roads. Sidesway does not disturb the passengers. After a very bad dip taken fast, we noticed some "walking" (the wheels left the road for brief intervals). Aside from this, there were no complaints.

More Performance, More Fuel Economy

Acceleration and top speed, of course, are remarkable, topping the 1952 figures by varying margins. Highest top speed recorded was 116.9 mph, about 1.5 mph faster than last year, but the average of four runs was 115.4 or nearly six mph faster.

Credit for the increase is divided. Horsepower is up 10 per cent. Last year's optional rear axle ratio of 3.07 (3.36 was then standard) is now regular equipment, and there is a new 12-volt electric system.

In the engine itself, a new combustion chamber has increased the compression ratio to 8.25:1. Flame travel is shortened and turbulence is increased. Longer aluminum alloy pistons are slipper type, permitting them to nest between crankshaft counterweights. Valves now open wider. The 1952 dual exhaust system continues in use.

Already an economical car to drive, this large V-8 shows increased gasoline mileage in nearly every department. Most startling were comparisons with the '52 model in fourth gear (D-4 range). These yielded increases of 7.2 and 4.4 mpg at 30 and 45 mph, respectively. Engine changes (see above) are responsible. Improvement here, too, must be credited to the higher rear axle ratio and, in lesser degree, to the 12-volt system. Mobilgas Special fuel was used, the car, of course, requiring premium gasoline.

Some Trifles—Pro and Con

In small items of finish and detail, a mixed impression is presented. A rain seal at the forward outside edge of the doors prevents unexpected showers when leaving the car in the wet. Metal pads on lower surfaces throughout the car will effectively halt much evidence of wear. Door jambs, though they compare favorably with those of most other cars, are not finished with the care one expects to find. Variations in the fit of door panels are clearly visible. The new wheel discs fit the valve stems too closely for convenient tire checks.

For neatness under the hood, the fiber blanket is trimly bound in plastic, making it easy to keep clean. Considering the large number of standard and optional engine accessories that have to share the compartment, accessibility is good except for the power steering gearbox, which is under the left-hand exhaust manifold and the heater duct, as it was last year.

Accessories

As far as publicity goes, GM's leading accessory this year is unquestionably its air conditioner. This is, of course, made by Frigidaire, and on the Cadillac it costs a little over $600. Operation is simple for the driver. For particularly hot climates, cool air flows from continuous ducts above the doors; for temperate zones, it comes from the parcel shelf behind the rear seat and above the evaporator itself. The evaporator and blowers take up surprisingly little space in the trunk. Separate controls are provided for the two sides of the car, so that the sunny side can be cooled more than the other. Since the air-conditioner operates with the windows closed, freedom from wind noise, with its consequent lessening of fatigue, is a pleasant feature. Wind noise is of average intensity in the Cadillac with windows open.

The "Autronic Eye" on our test car appeared identical with the one on the Pontiac. (MOTOR TREND is planning an accessory trial for the photo-electric unit.)

Undercoating and an oil filter still are extra on this car, costing, respectively, $45 and $11. The MT Research staff feels that both these items should be standard equipment on this luxury car.

Summary

The Cadillac could be better, like any other car we ever heard of. It has few truly unusual features; compared to the American classics of yesterday, it isn't even very big. But it will give you comfort and luxury with its thickly padded seats, high-grade materials from floor to ceiling, and room for everyone. You can sell it for a high percentage of what you paid for it.

It is very easy to handle, economical to run and a top-notch performer. No doubt this combination, along with reputation, will sell many '53 Cadillacs.

—*Walt Woron and Pete Molson*

"This little gem comes complete with radio."

Cadillac's El Camino

THIS is a two-passenger hardtop coupe, bearing a Spanish name which means "the highway," and features what its designers term "aircraft styling and "supersonic" tail fins on the rear fenders. The car has a 115-inch wheelbase and the Cadillac V-8 engine is similar to the 1954 production type which has a power output of 230. Overall length of the body is 200.6 inches, while height is 51.5 inches. Highly streamlined, the silver-grey El Camino has a brushed aluminum roof top coated with clear lacquer, tinted glass panoramic windshield, twin tail lights with side slots for a warning effect, and a keel below the tail lamps for extra protection when backing. The tail lights are mounted in cylinders of bumper material. Below the trunk is a spare tire compartment with a concealed, hinged door. Horizontal flutes sweep along the sides to provide both fresh air intake, by means of a compressor, and a hot air exhaust from the engine compartment. Four hooded headlights have been incorporated into the front end—an outer pair for normal city driving and an inner pair for long range, pencil-beam use. The latter set are put out of action automatically by an Autronic eye when in traffic. Below the headlights are a gull-type front bumper, sharp and slim, with two "bombs" projecting forward. On the hood is a recessed V crest, flush with the surface. Inside, the car has a cluster of instruments around the steering wheel. Between the two leather-covered seats is a tunnel housing the Hydra-Matic gearshift selector lever. This lever is of the "aircraft stick" type with a locking button on top that is pressed when the lever is to be moved into reverse position. Behind the gear lever is a radio and vanity compartment. Heater and air conditioning controls are forward of the gear lever.

Camino

Espada

Park Avenue

Cadillac's Park Avenue

WHAT Cadillac stylists have in mind in the four-door sedan field is pointed up in the Park Avenue model. Constructed of fiberglass, design is more restrained than the sport models—yet it is undeniably futuristic. Exterior is dark blue trimmed with bright chrome and topped with a hand-brushed aluminum roof.

Cadillac's La Espada

A FIBERGLASS experimental convertible finished in Apollo gold and trimmed with chrome and aluminum is the La Espada. High luster black leather and brushed aluminum is the interior theme. Wheelbase is 115 inches, with overall length running to 200.6. Engine, of course, is the 1954 Cadillac V-8 of 230 hp.

Cadillac 62 SEDAN

by **ROBERT JOHNSON**

THE CADILLAC Motor Car Division of General Motors has retooled for 1954. The new Eldorado special convertible plus 7 body styles comprising the 62, 60, and 75 series—has been extensively re-engineered. And in doing so, primary consideration was given to increased comfort, safety, and ease of handling.

We road tested the Series 62 Sedan. The test car had many extras, including air conditioning, power brakes, and Autronic Eye. This Cadillac had close to 3000 miles on it, for which we were grateful—putting a *brand new* automobile through its paces is not only rough on the engine but results in unjust performance figures.

The sedan was driven extensively both in town and on the highway, taken up and down Los Angeles' famous Fargo Street hill (32 percent grade) and tested on rough and winding mountain roads for maneuverability.

Let's take these locations one at a time, discuss the Cadillac's performance and handling characteristics under the varying conditions offered:

IN TOWN

Hydra-Matic Dual Range is standard. Stop-and-go driving is fun when you *don't* have to select the gears; the Hydra-Matic in the test car was surprisingly quiet and smooth, with a barely noticeable momentum surge characteristic of automatic transmissions. An acceleration graph from zero to 40 mph shows this clearly, with gear "peaks" hardly breaking an

otherwise clean curve. It is impressive on paper—and in the car.

The GM panoramic windshield offers greater visibility, lends an up-to-date, functional look to the '54 models. However, the windshield in the test car had a certain amount of distortion in its curved outer corners, which was distracting.

Power steering is standard equipment. Approximately 3 lbs. of manual pressure on the wheel is the extent of required driver effort; the rest of the job is done for you. This mechanism has been re-engineered too, is now a simpler, more compact unit with a better steering ratio, offering better road "feel" and ease of handling.

Despite the 3 inch longer wheelbase on the '54, the test car parks easily; the power steering is a blessing here, of course, as is the fact that all four fenders are visible from the driver's seat.

ON THE HIGHWAY

Cadillac is proud of their comfortable, quiet, vibrationless ride. They have a right to be. Generous use of insulating materials, including fiberglass mat, in body panels, top, hood, and deck, make the interior virtually soundproof. Engine noise, even at high speeds, is little more than a whisper; a 35 percent stiffer frame for '54 helps to eliminate chassis and body torsion, a major source of eventual annoying rattles.

While the seats in the test car were not as soft as they could be, a ride in the Cadillac on the highway *is* soft, and without an unnerving undulation often associated with soft springing. The ratio of length of the leaf springs fore and aft of the rear axle on all '54 Cadillacs has been changed, minimizing axle "wind-up" and propeller shaft shake.

ON FARGO STREET HILL

This steep pitch is a breath-taker in any automobile! Under no other circumstances are you more aware of the need for extra power and good brakes. It was necessary to shift into low in the sedan but in this gear the Cadillac went up the grade like going home. Bear in mind that the 230 hp V8

engine was handicapped by approximately 400 lbs. of optional equipment.

Coming down the hill, we deliberately tromped on the brakes; the extra-light rear end (in this attitude) showed no tendency to move over, and the brakes were as effective here as on the flat. Cadillac has, incidentally, a design change in the '54 brake lining; a new lining material increases brake life and a groove cut through the center of the primary lining *(see "car Brakes Rate a Break!," page 30)* makes for more even heat distribution, elimination of hot areas. Cadillac's power brakes (optional equipment) are noteworthy, compared to other types, due to their smooth action. A vicious characteristic with some is their *over*-light touch, requiring too soft, delicately applied pressure to avoid jarring stops. The Cadillac power brake is smooth, has the solid feel of a standard brake—without giving the driver's leg muscles a workout.

ON MOUNTAIN ROADS

A lower center of gravity (the engine has been dropped 2 inches), plus improved suspension, gives the Cadillac better all-around roadability. The compromise between a truly comfortable ride and great handling qualities is always a difficult one, but without sacrificing the comfort associated with Cadillac, their engineers have done much to improve roadability. We drove the sedan hard and fast around corners—the body *does* heel over, but not abruptly or severely; the car tracks well—an under-steer tendency is not alarming.

RESALE VALUE

The primary purpose behind automobile purchase is transportation suitable for the individual need; however, the smart buyer considers later resale value. Without a doubt Cadillac resale value is excellent, particularly with the 1948 and later models (since introduction of the tail light "fins"). This fact is an indirect compliment to the Cadillac Motor Car Division; Cadillac prestige is a symbol of fine styling and engineering. •

The PARADE of NEW CARS

YOUR 1955 CADILLAC should be of even higher quality than those of the past because even though more cars will be built, the time required to build each car will be greater. This, of course, means the addition of another work-shift over on Clark St. The standard models have actually been restyled rather extensively, even though it is not too noticeable in pictures or on the road. Side chrome has been changed so that it now forms a true character line (accentuates a line actually formed in the sheet metal), and the Florentine-curve rear window treatment of last year's coupes has been extended to include sedans. Grilles have a wider mesh, and the parking lights have been squared off and moved outward. Trunk ledges are all graced by a series of vertical chrome strips which purportedly create the illusion of lowering Cadillac's prominent bustle back.

BIGGEST STYLE CHANGE is in the Eldorado, this year a $6000-plus convertible that has a rear end straight from the La Espada and El Camino show cars. It looks good enough to make us wonder why it is not available throughout the line, but perhaps they are saving this for 1956. The Eldorado is powered by a 270-horsepower, 331-cubic-inch V8 that mounts twin, four-barreled carburetors and has a 9 to 1 compression ratio. This engine is available as an option on other models, which normally have a single-carburetor, 250-horsepower version. The Eldorado's revolutionary and attractive aluminum-spoke wheels are also an option throughout the line. Standard equipment on all models includes power steering, windshield washer, and a smoothed-out, dual-range Hydra-Matic.

CADILLAC'S ENGINEERING PHILOSOPHY is premised on the statistic that over 90 per cent of their customers want the utmost luxury in a car that is the least possible work to drive. Agility is a secondary consideration, a fact which makes it the more amazing that Cadillac was our top performing road test car in 1954. Chief Engineer Fred Arnold has his problems because he would like "to do the most things for the most people." For example, shocks on the current model could be tightened up and "export" springs used for better cornering, but the "boulevard" ride would suffer. He would like to give you both, and does wherever a compromise is not necessary.

CADILLAC'S STYLING PHILOSOPHY is premised on what the public wants, not what they ought to want. Time and again, the so-called experts (ourselves included) hand out the concours ribbons to competition; in fact, others seem to have won everything lately but sales leadership in the high-price bracket. While sales leadership doesn't put one above criticism, it helps. It also causes people, especially those who don't own Cadillacs, to gripe about little things.

VANCLEEFF AND ARPELS' JEWELRY, as well as Harry Winston's, has become familiar to millions of common folk through the medium of Cadillac advertising. Honey-rich copy drives home one theme: you haven't arrived until you've bought your first Cadillac. While a few sensitive souls have undoubtedly been driven to Lincolns and Packards in defense against this clever sophism, it works beautifully on most people. Surprisingly enough, the default of others gave Cadillac its current hold on the prestige market. Back in the late Thirties, both Lincoln and Packard put their chips on middle-priced cars. They sold a lot of them, but in the process lost much of their prestige; the road back has been slow and painful.

A LITTLE KNOWN FACT is that General Motors nearly dropped Cadillac back in 1933 when the division was losing millions on its ponderous V-12s and 16s. Non-philanthropic GM gave it one last chance when the late and great Nicholas Dreystadt was moved up from service to production and then to general manager. He soon boiled the line down from four engines on eight different wheelbases to a standardized, modern V8 that actually excelled the multicylinder jobs in power and smoothness. A peculiar paradox during this hectic period was the LaSalle. Theoretically, it

Cadillac again shows two convertibles, the workaday version (above) and the Eldorado, with its new wheels and rear end

Note how deftly Cadillac stylists have refrained from outdating earlier models, but have given freshness to the '55

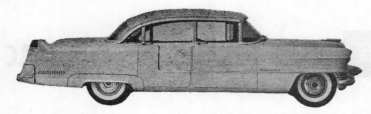

The Fleetwood Sixty Special has its usual long tail, but a new narrow center post, first sign of the four-door hardtop car

should have backfired on Cadillac the way the Zephyr did on Lincoln. However, this didn't happen because for some reason, the public never associated La-Salle with Cadillac, and secondly, La-Salle by 1940 was basically a Cadillac with a different nameplate. It became the Series 61 in 1941, and sold faster than Dreystadt could make them. Cadillac went into the war years with a top quality, relatively low-priced ($1345) car that still commands a premium on the used car market. This car is given credit for their enviable position today.

FRED ARNOLD'S CHIEF WORRY is the old saw that complacency is the downfall of the leader. He tries to keep one jump ahead of competition and this applies particularly to certain other GM divisions whose initials begin with "O" and "B." Cadillac saves a lot of money by sharing a body with Buick and in the process, gives you better value. Even more could be saved if the relatively low-production Cadillac (this year's goal is 150,000) used an engine or frame in common with another GM division. Right now, horsepower-leader Cadillac (270 in the Eldorado) is hard at work on a brand-new V8 which might be ready for production in 1956.

A PERFECT CADILLAC IS RARE, and so is a lemon. Regardless of how high the delivered price, truly fine workmanship is a problem on any assembly line. Twenty-five years ago, one craftsman (*Continued on page* 78)

Chrome on the attractive coupe de ville's sides is also done with restraint. The horizontal bar accentuates an indentation in the metal itself this year

Most popular car in the line will be the Series 62 sedan, this year with the Florentine curve rear roof line that GM pioneered on its '54 hardtops

With everyone else going rear-end happy, Cadillac shows surprising restraint in this back view of the new Sixty Special

Here is the 270-hp Eldorado engine, a souped-up version of that on the lesser Cadillacs. But you can have it on them, too

Better than the Best!

Cadillac say their new Eldorado will make people forget about the Rolls-Royce. Larry Foley points out that's a tall order.

PROTOTYPE of Cadillac Eldorado Brougham was shown at 1955 Motorama. Blonde does not go with the car.

TWO leading United States carmakers have at last got round to considering the needs of their most-neglected customer — the multi-millionaire.

They believe it is high time he got a car worthy of his bankroll—an American equivalent of the Rolls-Royce.

So does he.

For years now this poor fellow has been the saddest thing on the highways. No one could tell how rich he was merely by looking at his car—which puts him at a disadvantage in the U.S., where you size a man up by the car he drives.

Now, the only obvious car for the extra-rich man here (known as the "Big Rich") is a Cadillac (or, possibly, a Lincoln or Packard).

Imported high-priced super-sports jobs don't rate among the Big Rich generally—only among their young sporting offspring as playthings.

No Longer Exclusive

To the driver of an Essex or an Overland the latest-model Cadillac may seem the last word in swank. But the truth is that the Cadillac has become so common on the U.S. highways that the man at the wheel is no longer necessarily a man of distinction (i.e., wealth).

Many quite ordinary people drive Cadillacs. They may be poor, but they want to look rich. So—a Cadillac. No one else need know that they are taking three years to pay it off. The postwar Cadillac cult has made the multi-millionaire just another pebble on the beach. The manufacturers have simply ignored him. All they have done is gone on making bigger, better and dearer Cadillacs. The Big Rich have been reduced to buying strings of Cadillacs, which is not really satisfactory because they can only drive one at a time.

I know of one family in New Jersey, where the eggs come from, which owned seven Cadillacs—one for each member. Their way of showing their contempt for the commonplace Cadillac as a symbol of wealth was to use Cadillacs as farm-waggons, for transporting pig-food, poultry feed and crates of eggs.

About the only solace left the Cadillac man to whom money is no object is to be first with the new year's model. He who gets his delivered first by the town dealer is obviously top dog in local society.

But this is a short-lived triumph, lasting from late October to December, by which time anybody who is anybody should be burling around in the new model. Anybody who drives last year's model is a nobody. Down in Miami, where the sun goes in winter, it's not enough to own any old Cadillac. The girls sneer: "Yeah? What model? If it's last year's, you're out, son. If it's not air-conditioned (or not a convertible), son, you're still out."

Relief in Sight

Well, that's all going to be changed. By the end of this year there will be a new class of car-owner. Two new cars, intended specifically for the Big Rich, are on the way:

● The Lincoln Continental Mark II, being made by the Ford people.
● The Eldorado Brougham, by Cadillac (General Motors).

Of the two firms, the more vociferous so far have been Cadillac. By comparison, Ford have been restrained. Ford are promoting the coming Continental with quiet, dignified advertisements which contrast sharply with the Power! Zoom! Glamor! school of modern motor ads: it favors a poetic picture of a four-pointed star against a star-filled sky, captioned "Rebirth of a proud tradition . . . the Continental Mark II," with blurb recalling that the old Lincoln Continental, created in 1940 and scrapped in 1948, was "considered one of the most distinctive and most admired cars in America."

But, says the blurb, the new Continental, "a daring and dramatically modern car," will "embody elegance and dignity" and "will surpass even the beloved Lincoln Continental . . . for we are determined to make he new Continental as fine a motor car as the world has ever known."

Ford will present this snazzy new job "with deep pride."

Move Over, R.R.

Cadillac have been much more characteristically American in their advance promotion of the Eldorado Brougham.

The Cadillac people announced, simply, that they were going into competition with Rolls-Royce of England.

'Their new luxury car, they said, "will make people forget about the Rolls-Royce."

Rolls-Royce of England, who might perhaps have been amused by such presumption, appeared not to hear. Judging by the description of the Eldorado Brougham, R.R. have nothing to fear from the proposed transatlantic competition. With its racy, low-slung lines (overall height only 4ft. 6in.), four headlights, "quad" exhaust pipes, "projectile-shaped" rear bumpers and massive, flashy chrome-plating, the Eldorado Brougham is hardly likely to appeal to the gentry for whom Rolls-Royce of England have always catered—apparently to their mutual satisfaction, since R.R. have been going strong for 51 years and still need no more resounding form of advertising than their traditional plain, modest little insertions in such journals as The Times: "The best car in the world".

Nobody has ever gainsaid this claim—so you will either admire or smile at Cadillac for their brash prediction that their Eldorado Brougham will depose the Rolls.

The true test of a car's value in the eyes of the world is the legends which form around it. On that score Cadillac lags far behind Rolls. It is not true, for instance, that a Rolls-Royce engine is sealed at the factory and is never accessible except to a qualified Rolls mechanic dressed in morning clothes and cravat and presenting credentials signed by the Archbishop of Canterbury. Nor is it true that the buyer of a Rolls signs a life contract never to sell it except back to an authorised dealer, and is liable to prosecution if he sells it to a mere person whom the Rolls people would consider unworthy.

But a product that gathers such folklore about it must have something. It remains to be seen whether Cadillac, with their new superduper car, can match that something. I doubt it. For one thing, the Eldorado Brougham won't even have a decent price-tag.

The best they will be able to do, it seems, will be something around 10,000 dollars. Why, that won't even beat their American rivals, Ford, who are expected to charge around 12,000 dollars for the Continental Mark II.

With such low prices, both will be far behind the Rolls, which costs 14,000 dollars—before the real work is put into it, like upholstery to match the linings of milady's furs, or hot and cold running water, or jewelled vanity-cases (3000 dollars alone), or gold-plated dashboards with diamond-studded clocks by Cartier, or twin folding-mirrors by Mappin and Webb of London, or concealed bars, or silver-plated bonnets, or costly fur lap-robes, or petit-point upholstery (all featured variously in the Rolls-Royces of well-known contemporary Britons, Indian rajahs, and Americans).

One comfort for the prospective buyers of these two new models: their mass-production will not threaten the exclusiveness of their cars. Production of both will be limited—to 1000 a year for the Eldorado Brougham, and to about eight a day for the Continental.

As for the Continental, it will be hand-made, to order. Chances are no two Continentals will be exactly alike. Buyers will get a wide choice of fabric, trim, color and gadgets. They may even be invited to watch the final assembly of their car.

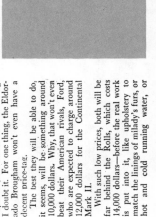

Both are being produced in great secrecy, and neither maker has yet come out with pictures and details. However, it is assumed that the Continental will retain some of the lines of the old Lincoln Continental; and the Eldorado when unveiled is expected to be even less surprising, because its prototype was featured, and got wide publicity, as a "dream car" at this year's Motorama, the annual road-show of General Motors.

The dream car was in fact called the "Eldorado Brougham," but the production model will be a modified version of the Motorama exhibit.

One of the modifications will be the slinky blonde in a white evening gown who appeared to be part of the Motorama model. Discreet inquiries at Cadillac headquarters indicated that the blonde will not go with the production model.

That's too bad. I thought the blonde was one feature on which the Cadillac boys really had poor old Rolls-Royce licked.

· · ·

Fifth wheel is checked prior to gasoline mileage tests. Cad is surprisingly economical, can travel all day on single fill.

ROAD TEST

Cadillac

FLEETWOOD 60 SPECIAL

This car has the reputation . . . does it have the stuff to back it up? Here's a good look at all its features

Photos by Dean Moon

Cellular grille was derived from Park Avenue experimental shown in GM's '54 Motorama. Bullets are fixed to frame.

Cadillac probably is fastest volume production car on the road, with accelerating ability exceeded only by its top speed. When taken over 60 miles of hilly dirt road, as shown here, passenger and trunk compartments remained free of dust.

CADILLAC is regarded by millions of Americans as the ultimate in automobiles. Much of this reputation seems to be derived from the fact that ownership of a Cadillac has a certain amount of social significance. So it is interesting to determine if such extraordinary opinions are supported by the quality of construction, performance and design.

For road testing purposes, a Fleetwood Series 60 Special four-door sedan, with 76 miles on the odometer, was obtained. No customary break-in period was required, however, since Cadillac advises its owners that new models may be driven without limitations on maximum speed.

During an eight-day test, the Cadillac was driven over 1400 miles of California and Nevada, which provided a wide variety of city and open road conditions. Runs for top speed were made in the Mojave desert, while balance of the performance figures were secured near sea level.

The car does not have a clear monopoly on any important feature. Each separate item can be found on one rival make of car or another. But it is the *only* car that combines the maximum number of desirable features in a single package. In brief, Cadillac has just about the best of everything that is available on a modern car, plus a few items that come as extras.

The performance picture can be read at a glance in the accompanying tabulation. It reveals that Cadillac is the fastest volume production car on the road, at an actual 116 mph under the clocks. This high speed run was made with a strong sidewind, yet the driver found the car held to the road with perfect control.

This enormous performance potential has been achieved in Cadillac without sacrificing economy. Over-the-road fuel consumption figures are genuinely remarkable, considering the horsepower output, car weight and loading of powered accessories.

Refinements in Cadillac's engine compartment for 1955, which contribute to the overall performance increase, include boosting the compression ratio from 8.5 to 9-to-1. Valve rocker arms have been redesigned for better breathing on both intake and exhaust. The crankshaft has been strengthened, connecting rod bearings are now narrower, and the water pump is a new unit which gives 20 per cent better circulation at lower speeds, for more even engine operating temperatures. Horsepower is rated at 250 at 4400 rpm, against 230 in 1954, while torque is 345 ft.-lbs. at 2800 rpm, in contrast to 332 on last year's car.

Servicing ease on engine and accessories rates high on Cadillac. The fuel pump is above and in front of the block, with the sediment bowl visible and conveniently located. The generator also is favorably positioned. Spark plugs are above the exhaust manifold. All units involving liquids—oil filter, windshield washer, radiator cap, dip stick, power steering tank, and brake master cylinder—are handy to a wrench from the same side of the car. The voltage regulator has been removed from heat of the engine compartment for simpler adjustments and is immediately behind the grille. These are but a few examples how careful design has provided for efficient mechanical care.

On the roadability side, the reactions of various drivers of the test car were almost identical: the car has a "solid" feel. Road and engine noises are virtually absent, the result of good quality control and ample quantities of insulation in the body and under the hood (where the glass fiber is vinyl covered!). Handling, despite the Cadillac's size, was easy (power steering is standard equipment) and parking seemed to be no more of a problem than with any average car. All four fenders are visible from the driver's seat. The steering wheel itself has superior feel, with gripping areas cleverly designed for firm control. Riding in the Cadillac is exceedingly comfortable, even over long distances, without being excessively soft.

It was noted during the highway travel that drivers would sometimes run the car up to 50 and 60 mph with the selector lever in third gear of the dual-range transmission. While this is further evidence

(Continued on page 78)

MOTOR LIFE ROAD TEST

CAR TESTED: CADILLAC FLEETWOOD 60 SPECIAL

TEST CONDITIONS

Altitude	210	feet
Temperature	53	degrees
Wind	4	mph
Gasoline	MOBILGAS PREMIUM	

ACCELERATION AND TOP SPEED

MPH	Seconds
0-30	3.6
0-45	7.5
0-60	11.2
30-50	5.3
40-60	5.9
Standing ¼ mile	19 seconds
Fastest one-way run	116 mph
Top speed avg. 4 runs	114.1 mph

BRAKING DISTANCE

MPH	Stopping distance
30	40.2 feet
45	88.7 feet
60	159 feet

FUEL CONSUMPTION

MPH	Average
30	21.7 mpg
45	20.5 mpg
60	16.5 mpg

SPEEDOMETER CORRECTIONS

Car speedometer	Actual speeds
20	19
30	27.5
40	37
50	46.5
60	55
70	64
80	72
90	80.5
100	—

REMARKS: ALL SPEEDS ACTUAL. PAVEMENT - DRY ASPHALT.

Although Cadillac is a big, heavy car, its brakes brought it to a quick stop in a straight line. Distinguishing feature of Fleetwood style is Florentine curve on rear window styling, which is shared with Series 62 coupe and Coupe de Ville '55 models.

Attention to detail can be found everywhere. For example, rubber molding catches water runoff when door is open.

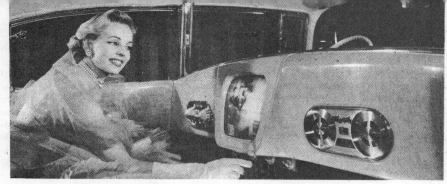

The 1955 Cadillac Series 60 Special Sedan offers such luxury features as 14-inch TV set, telephone, tape recorders, Korina gold wood paneling and mouton carpet.

Cadillac Specials

CADILLAC, never surpassed in the "show car" field, has come up with another one—the Eldorado St. Moritz, a little number that features a white pearlescent body with a smartly-styled interior finish of white ermine trimmed in pearlescent white English grain leather and floor carpeting of white mouton fur. Sounds cozy, in St. Moritz or Miami.

On a more practical plane, Cadillac also has introduced the Eldorado Brougham with an overall height of 54.4 inches and without a center door pillar. Fenders and characteristic tail lines are complimented by a tinted brushed aluminum roof. Dual headlight assemblies, Cadillac says, provide the most efficient road lighting yet devised. The outer lamps are flat beam city lights and inner lamps are highly penetrating highway lights. Both sets are controlled by an Autronic Eye mounted at top of windshield.

Using new methods of construction, Cadillac has reduced all outside dimensions without sacrificing passenger comfort. All seats are individual and are tailored to fit the body. Wheelbase is 124 inches, overall length is 209.6 inches and width is 77.5 inches. A highly iridescent exterior color—Chameleon Green—has been developed expressly for the Brougham and the interior is trimmed in matching paint, leather and imported French silk.

A third model, the Westchester, is a specially styled Series 60 Special sedan featuring television, a tape recorder and a telephone in the rear seat. This job also employs a novel interior treatment—Korina gold wood paneling, upholstery of black cloth interwoven with gold thread and a black mouton fur carpet. ☆

Cadillac's 270-horsepower Eldorado, the "St. Moritz," offers the latest word in luxurious upholstery—white ermine fur and white English grain leather.

THE ELDORADO BROUGHAM—

A NEW CADILLAC FOR 1956

The class of super-luxury cars, neglected since the 1930's, is on the way back, and this one is sure to be a style-setter in advanced features

TWIN HEADLIGHTS at the front end of each fender have five-inch lenses. Outer lamps are flat-beam city lights; inner lamps are for highway use. An Autronic Eye will switch from one to the other as conditions on the road require.

INTERIOR includes padded instrument panel with recessed controls. Driver's seat pivots outward for easy entry and exit, while center of both front and rear seats contains storage compartment. Note absence of small ventilator windows, considered unnecessary in car having air conditioner and heater as integral unit.

QUAD EXHAUST is what Cadillac is calling the system that has dual pipes issuing from rear fenders on each side of the car. This could be said to balance dual-dual headlights in front, but benefits in engine efficiency are unknown.

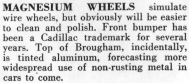

MAGNESIUM WHEELS simulate wire wheels, but obviously will be easier to clean and polish. Front bumper has been a Cadillac trademark for several years. Top of Brougham, incidentally, is tinted aluminum, forecasting more widespread use of non-rusting metal in cars to come.

REAR DOORS open into the wind (above), a characteristic of four-door hardtops. But Cadillac engineers say they have developed an adequate safety device to forestall mishaps. Note triangular section that forms upper rear of door. Only chromed strip on side of body (right) is vertical trim, another Cadillac trademark in recent years, which may point the way to more restraint in exterior treatments for the future. Significant item: the Brougham's wheelbase is 124 inches, five less than the current Cadillac 62 series. Are scaled-down cars coming from other U.S. auto manufacturers?

The Cadillac's contours are smooth and graceful. Twin exhausts protrude through the rear fender trim. The bulges behind the rear window are part of the air-conditioning intakes.

CADDIE COUPE

THIS month we've let our head go and put what we think is a lush combination on our cover. The car is a late 1954 model Cadillac Coupe de Ville; the girl is Sydney model Eve Newton; the background, for those of you who don't live in N.S.W., is the Sydney Harbour Bridge.

The Cadillac, which is identical with the latest 1955 model except for a slight power increase in the engine, belongs to an American business man who lives in Sydney. He is Mr. J. T. Rethers. He told us a few things about the car.

Everything is power assisted. There is power steering; there are power brakes; the windows and front seat are power lifted and ad-justed. The Cadillac also has Hydramatic transmission.

The car is not as bulky as one would expect—it's around the size of the present Ford Customline.

It is a two-door saloon, and would seat five people very comfortably and six reasonably.

Important features are a real air-conditioning system (which dehumidifies and cools the interior air) and complete appointments for all passengers.

There are individual ashtrays and cigar lighters all around; the rear passengers can control the volume of their radio speaker or turn it out; the radio tunes automatically to the next station when a button is pressed.

Mr. Rethers bought the Cadillac in the U.S.A. and drove it for some time there before bringing it to Australia. He reports that its normal-cruising petrol consumption is 18 m.p.g.

The Cadillac's vital statistics are: ENGINE: V-8 ohv, comp. ratio 9 to 1, capacity 5,430 c.c., 250 S.A.E. bhp at 4,600 rpm, 345 lb/ft. torque at 2,800 rpm. TRANSMISSION: Hydramatic automatic. OVERALL DIMENSIONS: Wheelbase, 10' 9"; length,, 18' 5.3"; width, 6' 8" height, 4' 11.7"; clearance, 6.17".

The Cadillac Coupe de Ville has been converted to right-hand drive to meet local traffic requirements. The upholstery is two-tone dark green and light green leather and cloth.

the 1956 cadillac

HIGHLIGHTS: top of 305 hp, new sedan de ville and Eldorado Seville body styles, redesigned Hydra-Matic, aluminum grilles

IN KEEPING with its policy of gradual refinement and evolutionary development, rather than sweeping overnight changes, Cadillac for 1956 is offering a line of cars that have a lot of new features but aren't so different that you can recognize them as Cadillacs at first glance.

There are styling changes and innovations. Engines are bigger, more powerful. Two entirely new body styles have been introduced. The Hydra-Matic transmission has been completely redesigned. Many detail improvements have been made.

Big news in the engine compartment is a displacement increase from 331 to 365 cubic inches, brought about by a boost in the bore from 3.81 to 4 inches. Stroke is still 3.625 inches. This, plus higher compression and improved breathing, has raised horsepower from 250 to 285 horsepower on regular Cadillacs and from 270 to 305 on Eldorado models. Torque is up from 345 to 400 foot pounds on all models.

To go with the bigger engine, Cadillac has the redesigned Hydra-Matic, of which GM is very proud. (It reportedly cost some $35 million to develop and ready for production.) It features a controlled fluid coupling and sprag clutch arrangement, with a new fluid cooling system and oil-submerged gear units.

Big advantages of the new transmission, standard on all Caddies, of course, are smoother, quieter operation, improved acceleration and easier maintenance.

Styling is characteristically Cadillac. Grilles are slightly different, with a finer "egg-crate" cellular texture. A new idea is the anodized aluminum grille with a gold finish available as an option. Hoods have been lowered and front fenders widened.

Rear fenders now have fairings flowing rearward to new oval exhaust outlets at the outer ends of the restyled rear bumpers. New fluted chrome wheel discs are standard on all models except the Eldorado which retains the aluminum spoke design.

The interior features a new and seemingly more functional instrument panel arrangement. The speedometer, something those who have to run performance checks on cars notice particularly, is very readable. The glove compartment has been moved to the center for greater convenience.

Performance, particularly in low and middle speed ranges, has been improved due to the new engine-transmission combination. Zero to 60 times of just over 10 seconds are claimed for the new models.

The two new body styles are the Eldorado Seville, a two-door hardtop introduced as a companion to the Eldorado Biarritz convertible, and the sedan de ville, a four-door hardtop. The Seville has styling features similar to the Biarritz. The roof panel, however is covered with a padded material resembling leather (Cadillac call the material "vicodec").

One detail feature that impressed in a pre-introduction peek at the cars was a side view mirror that is controlled from inside the car—like a spot light.

New power seats which permit the angle of the seat back to be adjusted in addition to the fore and aft and up and down movement is a comfort improvement also.

Brake pedals are much bigger, permitting right or left foot operation, and are supported by two arms instead of the single arm formerly used.

Incidentally, although an Eldorado Brougham was displayed at the press preview of the new Cadillac line, word is that it will be some months before this $8500 model will be in production. Tooling has been released for its production on a limited basis, however, so it definitely will appear later this model year.

Cadillac is backing its optimistic outlook for 1956 by expanding facilities to enable it to build 15,000 more cars than during the '55 model year. (That would boost production to 156,000—and there will probably still be a waiting list.) This move is not much of a gamble, since Cadillac sales manager, Jim Roche, claims to have orders already on hand for the first seven months' production. •

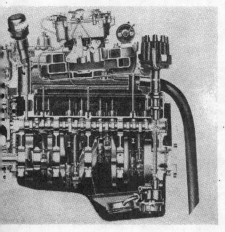

Sedan de Ville (four-door hardtop) is one of two new body types; other is Eldorado Seville, similar to Eldorado Biarritz convertible but with padded top. Rear end changes include inset plates and integral exhaust ports that are oval insteal of round.

Cadillac has 285 hp (Eldorados are 305) from engine with bigger bore that gives 365 cubic inches. Block is new, with more rugged crankshaft on larger journals, redesigned heads that have larger ports, increased intake and exhaust manifolding.

A BARRIS BONANZA

with glittering silver
and gold to whet the desire
of the most exuberant advocate
of "gracious living"

photos by George Barris

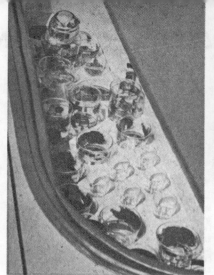

by Bill Babbitt

BOASTING a television set, radio-telephone, tape recorder, and cocktail bar among its many other expressions of all-out individualism, this Cadillac Le Mans by Barris cuts a wide swath anywhere.

Its basic chassis is the experimental Cadillac Le Mans, which was shown over the country in the GM Motorama exhibits of 1953. This modification (by Barris Kustom Autos, 11054 Atlantic Blvd., Lynwood, Calif.) was submitted to Harry Karl, the shoe store executive, before construction began.

The body is mostly Fiberglas with the exception of the lower fender panels, which are formed of body steel and then blue-white chrome plated. Trim between the lower chromed parts of the fenders and the Fiberglas part of the body is ½-inch steel bar, plated with 24-karat gold. To stop rattles before they start, a strip of ⅛-inch rubber separates the gold-plated trim and the body panels. Hubcaps are done in a combination of gold and chrome; the 30 individually inserted "spokes" and the protruding center are gold, with the remainder in chrome.

Paint is 30 coats of "platinum dust" sprayed over a polychromatic base sealer.

The rear window and top are trimmed with chrome-plated steel. The whole top assembly including the rear window can be removed, or the window may be left in place and the top removed (photo at right below).

The engine is the 300-horsepower Cadillac with dual 4-throat carburetors set up by the factory for the original Le Mans model. All engine accessories, valve covers, etc., are chrome plated, of course.

A dynamotor, installed by Ernie's TV (8133 Compton Blvd., Paramount, Calif.) converts power from the 12-volt system to the proper voltage for the television, tape recorder and radio-telephone. The TV, wired thru the ignition switch, can be played only when the engine is not running.

C. & C. Bar Specialists (6826 Crenshaw Blvd., Los Angeles) styled the bar in Formica, inlaid wood, and gold leaf. It hides under a red leather panel, which matches the upholstery.

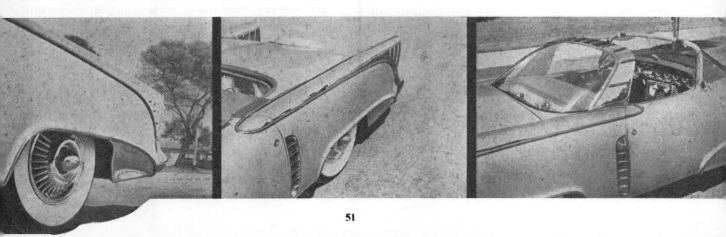

YOUR CHECK LIST

☑ ☑ ☑ ☑ ☑ means top rating

PERFORMANCE ☑ ☑ ☑ ☑ ☑

New Hydra-Matic with second fluid coupling for gear change is exceptionally smooth under all conditions. Teamed with a 285-hp engine, it delivers outstanding performance.

STYLING ☑ ☑ ☑ ☑ ☐

Typical Cadillac; long, low and massive. Graceful sweeping curves of wraparound windshield, roofline and rear window are its most outstanding style features.

RIDING COMFORT ☑ ☑ ☑ ☑ ☑

The combination of long (129″) wheelbase, 5000-lb weight, excellent suspension design plus lavish cushioning makes for most all around comfort. Some well-damped body shake sometimes crops up on rough roads.

INTERIOR DESIGN ☑ ☑ ☑ ☑ ☑

Everything that could be wished for with the possible exception of extra headroom. Vision all around is superb, and deep, firmly-padded adjustable front seat most comfortable.

ROADABILITY ☑ ☑ ☑ ☑ ☑

Excellent, particularly at high speeds when the car gives an unusually secure feeling even in sharp curves.

EASE OF CONTROL ☑ ☑ ☑ ☑ ☑

Somewhat less than perfect because power steering "off-and-on" effect requires close attention and an unusual amount of tiresome small corrections. Power brakes and transmission are extremely satisfactory.

ECONOMY ☑ ☑ ☑ ☐ ☐

Was disappointingly less than Cadillacs of previous years which used phenomenally little gas for their weight and performance. Car tested gave less than 15 mpg, which is average for the luxury class but poor for Cadillac.

SERVICEABILITY ☑ ☑ ☑ ☑ ☐

Engine accessibility is neither better nor worse than any medium or high-priced car where the engine compartment is filled with power-assist units. Multitude of power-operated gadgets may need expensive repairs later in car's life.

DURABILITY ☑ ☑ ☑ ☑ ☑

Gets top rating on the basis of record of past Cadillacs with similar engineering features and high-quality manufacture.

WORKMANSHIP ☑ ☑ ☑ ☑ ☑

At a uniformly high level throughout the car. Interior fittings and upholstery are particularly outstanding.

VALUE PER DOLLAR ☑ ☑ ☑ ☑ ☑

Exceptionally low rate of depreciation plus traditional mechanical longevity make Cadillac the "buy" in the high-priced field. An excellent transportation investment for those who can afford it.

SPECIFICATIONS

Model:	Sedan DeVille
Wheelbase:	129″
Length:	221.9″
Engine Displacement:	365 cu. in.
Bore and Stroke:	4.0″ by 3.625″
Compression Ratio:	9.75:1
Brane Horsepower:	285 @ 4600 rpm
Torque:	400 ft. lbs.
Electrical System:	12 Volt
Factory Delivered Price with standard equipment:	$4569

ALTHOUGH A sizeable amount of money has been spent on the 1956 Cadillac for essentially minor styling changes the car still looks typically Cadillac, with the sweeping rear fender line topped by its much-copied fin. Cadillac still retains its rather high, squared-off hood line, the twin "bombs" on the front bumper and the vertical "leading edge" on its rear fender.

Thus Cadillac protects the investment of last year's buyers by continuing its gradual style change rather than making sweeping changes that would make all preceding models obsolete from a styling viewpoint.

The most important change in the current model is the redesigned Hydra-Matic transmission which matches the overall smoothness of Cadillac's ride and performance. Gone forever are the power "surges" long-associated with the automatic transmission's upshifts and downshifts. Acceleration from a stand-still is one long, smooth increase in speed. Even moving the selector lever from "D-3" range to "D-4" at near full throttle merely increases the rate of acceleration with syrupy smoothness.

The famed Cadillac ride, which has long separated this car from the rest of the large cars, is better than ever. The suspension and insulation have virtually eliminated sound or feel of rough pavement. There is some evidence of well-absorbed body shake on the four-door hardtop "Sedan de Ville," a model added to the line this year. However, this is not noticeable on the conventional four-door sedan.

Cadillac's body designers have not made the mistake of

ANALYSIS:

1956 cadillac

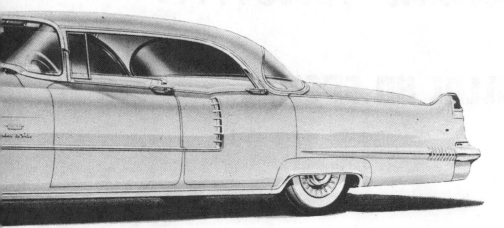

SEDAN DE VILLE

putting overly-soft padding into the deeply upholstered seats.

More than ever the car is supremely comfortable on long trips at high speeds. Money has been well spent on sound-deadening insulation and noiseproofing of the traditionally quiet V8 and its large-bore dual exhaust system. Cruising at 85 in the Cadillac is less tiresome than riding in smaller cars at 55.

Roadability is better than ever, with no roll and very little tire squeal evident even in sharp turns at considerable speed. The car has rocklike stability on undulating, high-crowned blacktop roads that often prove the undoing of softly suspended cars.

There is still room for some improvement in handling on the open highway. The "off-and-on" action of power steering can be annoying at road speeds. Starting a turn, the driver exerts a certain amount of force on the wheel, then the power assist "takes over." Until the driver gets used to it, the action seems too abrupt. This makes the wheel turn just a bit more than necessary and the driver must compensate with an increased pull in the opposite direction. Thus steering becomes a continuous series of minute "adjustments" when traversing the gentle curves of a superhighway.

Parking or handling the car in congested traffic is effortless despite its size and weight. The excellent rear vision and prominent rear fender fins (tail lights are visible from the driver's seat), make backing the car nearly foolproof. The power brake (standard on all models) is now operated by a broad pedal suspended from the firewall by two rods, one on either side of the steering column. This change makes left-foot brake operation a natural.

The instrument panel is little changed from last year, with its sweeping, hooded speedometer dial directly in front of the driver; other controls and gages are neatly grouped around it. Readability of all instruments, including the Hydra-Matic quadrant, is equally easy day or night.

Interior accessories leave little to be desired; there are two cigar lighters and two ash trays, an optional six-way power-adjusted seat, a powerful fresh-air heating system with ducts leading through the doors into the rear compartment, and of course power windows. When fully equipped (including air conditioning), there are 13 small electric motors scattered about the car, including one to operate the trunk latch.

One highly desirable feature of the air conditioning enables the blowers to draw in fresh air through the scoops located on the rear deck and "de-mist" the rear windows without operation of the cooling system. The air-conditioner blowers and cooling coils are neatly stowed on a shelf at the forward end of the trunk leaving more usable space than most cars without such installations.

Summing up: Cadillac offers a well-nigh unbeatable package of high performance, unequalled riding comfort and handling ease coupled with high prestige value and low depreciation. For anyone who can afford upwards of $4000 the Cadillac is unquestionably the buy. ●

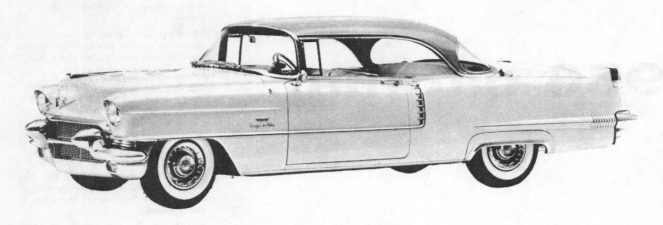

Bill Holland Tests.....

THE CADILLAC 60 SPECIAL

▶ The car furnished by Cadillac Division at Detroit for this driver test turned out to be one of their regular courtesy cars, in use every day and driven by anyone that can get the O.K. from Mr. Gillespie to use a car. I mention this so you'll know it wasn't a special car, or a finely tuned one for this particular occasion. It was a Sixty Special, four-door sedan, with the works on it. By that I mean it had just about all the equipment the factory can supply, such as, power steering and brakes, which are now standard equipment, as is the all new Hydramatic transmission. There was also a six-way power seat, new electrically controlled radio antenna, air conditioner, and many other features I'll mention later. This car delivers as equipped in Detroit for about $6,200 plus taxes.

Ted O'Hearn of the Public Relations Department took me to the garage and checked me out in the car; then I drove around the downtown area of Detroit for awhile to see how it handled in the heavy stop-and-go traffic. I can't say that I was surprised that it drove so beautifully; you just naturally expect a Cadillac to be tops in every way, and this '56 Cadillac is not a disappointment. It's wonderful how easy the power assists make this big 5,000 pound automobile drive.

In only a few blocks I discovered one of Cadillac's firsts. It is no longer neces-sary to put the window down and put your arm out in the cold or rain to adjust the side view mirror. The mirror is fully adjustable from inside the car by a small handle located near the front of the door, just forward of the power-window control switches.

This is the kind of engineering I think all the car manufacturers should turn to, instead of concentrating so much on in-creased horse power. In my book 300 or 350 hp is enough for any amateur to be loose with on the highway. There are so many of these little things to be worked out that would make driving for the aver-age person much more pleasant.

Having been in the automobile air con-ditioning business, I was very interested in the 1956 Cadillac unit. Believe me, this air conditioner is a honey and don't let anyone tell you they have one just as good for less money. The only independent unit that is even comparable to this factory unit, in my opinion, is the A.R.A. unit made in Ft. Worth, Texas.

I couldn't get definite figures regarding the percentage of Cadillacs now being de-livered with air conditioners by the fac-tory, but it is estimated to be at least 20% of production and increasing very rapidly. For solid comfort in the hot sticky sum-mer weather we have in most parts of the country, brother, this is it.

It takes a lot of engine to run this 2½-ton car with all its power equipment. Holland feels that this 365 cu. in. job has nearly reached its capacity, expects to see a new, bigger engine in the near future. Compression ratio is up to 9.75:1.

EASE OF HANDLING, LUXURIOUS FEATURES

IMPRESS MOTORSPORT'S CHIEF TEST DRIVER

Holland points out large running lights on new Cadillac. Style changes this year affect hood, bumpers, new aluminum grille.

Cadillac's system of distributing the cool air through built-in ducts in the roof is the best I've seen. There are four distributor outlets, one over each door. Each distributor outlet has three vents that can be adjusted for both the volume and direction of air desired, or can be shut off entirely. With this system each passenger can regulate the amount of cooling desired.

The compressor is made by Frigidaire and is quite unique, having five cylinders and pistons, but no crankshaft, making it an axial type. The pistons are forced up and down by a wobble plate. It is extremely smooth in operation and uses very little power. In fact I checked the top speed with the air conditioner on, then checked it again with it off and got the same answer both times: 110 mph.

The interior trim of this car is, as expected, both beautiful and serviceable. The dash is new and combines beauty with the utmost in functional arrangement of instruments and driving controls. It isn't necessary to be an engineer to operate the heating system either; there are only two levers to operate: one for heat on the left side of the instrument panel, one for defrosting on the right.

The glove compartment location is center dash, with a drop-down door. If too much junk is collected in this type compartment, not only does the door drop down, but everything in it drops down onto the floor. I have no idea why it was there, but in the compartment was a Decca record #9-29721 by Connie Boswell. I think someone was needling me: the titles were "I Compare You" and "No Other One."

The door latches are the so-called safety type that most of the cars are using now. The safety feature consists of a little piece of thin metal that laps over the "white metal" striker plate. This is a step in the right direction but I question their effectiveness in a fast end-for-end flip. Engineers certainly will come up with something better in the future.

After driving around in the city for awhile, I drove out the Edsel Ford Expressway to the open spaces. The concrete on the expressway is very rough and I noticed considerable body shake between 50 and 60 mph, caused, I think, by the shock absorbers trying to stop the wheel bounce caused by the rough concrete. Cadillac uses two sets of valves in their shock absorbers to control the ride. One set takes care of the small bumps at slow speeds in city driving and gives a nice soft ride. The other set takes over on the big bumps and at higher speeds. One setting is much stiffer than the other; in fact, they are a little stiffer than on the '55 models. Under certain conditions this has a tendency to transfer the jolt through the shock absorbers to the frame and body. However, this also gives a much safer ride when cornering at high speeds. On this subject, I'll note here that there is quite a bit of body lean when cornering fast, but this big sedan is built for the boulevards, not for the race tracks.

The noise level is good except for the noise made by the engine fan. The extra power packed in the engine evidently needed a little more cooling, thus requiring a larger fan. This noise, I think, could and should be lessened.

The engine in this '56 model has so many improvements it could be called a new engine. To begin with they have added 34 cubic inches by boring the block to four inches, making the displacement 365 cubic inches this year. The horsepower is up too, from 250 to 285, and the torque (that's what gives the acceleration) is up from 345 pounds-feet at 2800 rpm to 400 at 2800 rpm.

I have read that the block is entirely new in the '56, but this is not true. It's the same block pattern altered slightly, and the foundry is using a slightly different method of casting. The crankshaft is a little heavier (a pound, to be exact) than the '55. All forged V-8 crankshafts when they are first forged are 180° jobs and look like four-cylinder crankshafts. Then they are heated and twisted until the crankpins are 90° apart instead of 180°.

There are also new cylinder heads, exhaust manifolds, main bearing caps, camshaft, valve springs, valve guides, exhaust valves and pistons. The rods are the same as in last year's models.

The breathing of the engine has been improved by opening up the intake and exhaust manifolds and ports. The intake valves are the same size, but stay open longer due to the new cam. The exhaust valves are a little bigger (1/16-inch), making them 1-9/16 inches. The compression ratio is higher too. It is now 9.75 to

SPECIFICATIONS
1956 CADILLAC SERIES 60 SPECIAL

ENGINE

Type: OHV V-8
Displacement: 365 cu. in.
Bore & stroke: 4" x 3.625"
Compression ratio: 9.75 to 1
Brake horsepower: 285 at 4600 rpm
Torque: 400 ft. lb. at 2800 rpm
Piston travel per car mile: 1334 ft.

BODY & CHASSIS

Wheelbase: 133"
Height: 62"
Length: 225.9"
Width: 80"
Minimum road clearance: 6.1"
Turning circle: 45'
Transmission: Hydramatic
Steering ratio: 19.5 to 1 (power steering standard)
Rear axle ratio: 3.07 to 1 (3.36 to 1 optional)
Tire size: 8.00 x 15

1, and was 9 to 1. The combustion chamber is machined, giving the head a smooth interior surface. It is of the "squish" type, and gets its name because about one-third or more of the piston is covered by the head, when the piston is at top dead center with practically no clearance. This makes the gas that was in that part of the cylinder "squish" into the space left for combustion in a very high state of turbulence, making it possible to use a higher compression ratio, get better fuel consumption and smoother performance.

There are also new spark plugs, a new sealed voltage regulator, a higher torque starting motor, new easily adjusted distributor, an improved fuel pump and improved hydraulic valve lifters which prevent power loss at high engine speeds.

The Hydra-Matic transmission is entirely new, both in principle and mechanical parts. The four-speed design is retained, and a new so-called "controlled coupling" has been added. This hydraulic unit softens the grab that was so noticeable in the old Hydra-Matics, while shifting. The new unit retains the reliability of the old transmission, I'm sure. Don't try to convert one of the old ones; very few of the parts, if any, will be interchangeable.

In smoothness of operation the new transmission is very comparable to any of the other type transmissions on the market. The only fault I could find with it was a slight noise at about 35 mph while it was shifting, but it wasn't enough to be objectionable. A new park position which may be used when the engine is running is included on the transmission quadrant, providing positive lock against car movement when engaged.

Although this is not a high-performance sports-type car, especially with all the power-consuming accessories on it, I put it through the usual acceleration and top speed tests, with the following results. The readings were taken from the uncorrected speedometer.

Using low drive range:
0-30 mph: 3.6 seconds
0-60 mph: 10.7 seconds
Using high drive range:
0-30 mph: 3.7 seconds
0-60 mph: 10.7 seconds
30-60 mph: 7.1 seconds
50-80 mph: 10.3 seconds
Top speed: 110 mph (same with air conditioner on and off)

I call this very satisfactory performance for this big car.

Although the engineers at the factory would say nothing about the future plans of the engine department, I think they are almost to the limit of the present engine. They can bore the block out another 1/8-inch safely, but that's about it. The cam is just beginning to be a little rough at idle now. So don't be surprised to see a completely new and bigger engine in the '57 Cadillac, with the horsepower about 350 to start with and a possible 450 when the competition starts pushing them.

It's even possible we'll see real fuel injection on some models in '57. Who knows?

THE 1957 CADILLAC

Rear of 62 series coupe has relatively simple styling of standard Cadillacs. Bumper is massive, but very straight, with enlarged exhaust outlets. Taillights resemble earlier Eldorados.

Sedan de Ville of 62 series. The 60 Special looks much the same, except aluminum panel on rear fender over wheel well.

STYLING—New body that averages three inches lower, revised fins, all coupes and sedans are now hardtops, new interiors.

PERFORMANCE—Slight boost in engine output likely to shave some time off 1956 figures, but no sensational changes.

ENGINEERING—Biggest news is a unique frame, previously unknown in contemporary U.S. production. Ball-joints added.

BODY TYPES—All series about the same as in '56. Radically new Eldorado Brougham due later with fuel injection setup.

TAKE A LOOK at a '57 Cadillac. Be it a 62, 60 Special or Eldorado model, it has ties with the past. In fact, it's amazing that so many changes could be made in a car and still retain those ties. This doesn't mean the new Cads aren't different; the look you took a second ago told you they are!

The front view has been changed a lot —but is still definitely Cadillac. The hood height has been reduced so there is practically a single flat plane from fender to fender. The grille (it's still anodized aluminum) and bumper arrangement has been changed, but the gull-wing half-bumpers with protruding pods are a link with the past.

No attempt has been made at a dual headlamp setup, but this trend is recognized in the use of two small lamps under the bumperettes—parking and turn signal lights.

The 62 and 60 Special models have rear quarter panels which are a development of Eldorado designs of the past few years. Eldorados have a treatment reminiscent of GM dream cars of similar vintage—and may, to some extent, be previews of the forthcoming Brougham.

Tail lights set into the rear part of the fins have been discarded in all models. In 62 and 60 Special cars they straddle the trailing edge of the rear quarter panels—which extend back of the deck— much like last year's Eldorados. The new Eldorado has three lights, two set in the short bumperettes and one in the quarter panel directly under the fin.

Those are just a few of the detail highlights, of course. The pictures tell more of the story. What you can't tell from the pictures is that standard Caddys have been lowered three inches (59 vs. 62 inches last year). Eldorado models are proportionately lower. Nor can you detect the half-inch increase in wheelbase (from 129 to 129.5 inches).

(Incidentally, both 62 and 60 Special Cadillacs use the new GM "C" body shell, of course. Major difference is that 62 Specials have a 5-inch longer rear deck— plus different interior and exterior trim.)

An interesting example of Cadillac's awareness of trends is that there are no center pillars on *any* 1957 model. All coupes and sedans are so-called hardtops. This will be true throughout the industry before long. •

CADILLAC BODY TYPES

62 SERIES
 Two-door hardtop
 Four-door hardtop
 Convertible

60 SPECIAL SERIES
 Four-door hardtop
 Eldorado Biarritz
  (convertible)
 Eldorado Seville
  (two-door hardtop)

75 SERIES
 Four-door sedan
  (eight-passenger)

Note—All Cadillac standard sedans and coupes are now hardtops.

Eldorados are the hardtop (Seville) above and similar convertible (Biarritz), with a Brougham due later. The exterior styling is especially good, particularly at the rear where the sloping lines recall some masterful roadsters of the 1930's.

CADILLAC ENGINEERING

CADILLAC'S STYLING, though actually changed very much, can still be termed evolutionary. There are certain phases of its engineering, however, which can't be called anything but revolutionary.

The frame is the backbone of a car and it's right there we find the most drastic change in Cadillac for 1957. The conventional ladder-type or X-member designs have been discarded completely.

Instead, Cadillac is using a frame that might be best described as two wishbones superimposed on each other.

Most engineers in their efforts to get lower overall heights for 1957 stuck pretty much with conventional frame designs, only they brought the side rails out closer to the edge of the body. Cadillac engineers have *eliminated* side frame rails!

This means the body, at most points, is secured to outriggers or hangers which extend out from the central frame. An important point that might be overlooked by a layman is that this allows a lot of flexibility for the future. Just by juggling the size of the frame's central section—at the crossover point of the X, or where the two "wishbones" overlap—it can be adjusted to accommodate various body sizes and wheelbases. (This is particularly important to Cadillac, since it builds limousines, ambulances and other special-bodied cars—or is used by custom builders for such purposes.)

This naturally meant that Cadillac engineers had to change their whole approach to frame construction to insure the necessary rigidity. Just as naturally,

that's exactly what they've done. (And many of them will tell you privately that they expect the entire industry to come to a related type of frame design in the future. Especially since there are so many rumors about unit construction being not too far off.)

There are not earth-shaking suspension changes in Cadillac for '57 . . . some that have been made were dictated by the new frame. Rear springs obviously had to be mounted outside the frame, but they are still conventional semi-elliptics. And other than the expected switch to ball joints, there are no basic changes to front suspension.

As far as engines are concerned there are no big changes either. Horsepower has been boosted to 300; largely as a result of higher compression and other detail modifications. Displacement is same as 1956—365 cubic inches. Carburetors are still used, although this is something that could change before the year is over.

To get the extra 15 horse, compression was raised from 9.75 to 10-to-1 and a larger diameter—but still wedge-shaped—combustion chamber incorporated. Intake ports have been modified while intake valves have an eighth of an inch larger and exhaust valves are just that much smaller!

Shoe-and-drum brakes essentially the same as last year are retained and Cadillac is still using 15-inch tires and wheels.

Thus, you can see that the 1957 Cadillac is a blend of the old and new. And it's a better-than-even bet the result is one which will keep Cadillac firmly ensconced in the same comfortable position it's enjoyed these many years. ●

Revolutionary for Cadillac is its new frame which incorporates highly unconventional feature of stressing entirely through central wishbones and abandoning side-rails entirely. The design probably will be extremely adaptable for future changes.

CADILLAC SPECIFICATIONS

Wheelbase: 129.5 inches
Height: 59 inches
Transmission: Hydra-Matic
Horsepower: 300
Cubic Inches: 365
Compression Ratio: 10:1

LONG-AWAITED BROUGHAM FINALLY APPEARS, BUT WITHOUT THE RUMORED INJECTION OR REAR-END AUTOMATIC TRANSMISSION.

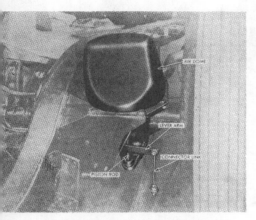

AIR SPRINGS, one on each wheel, hold car level and keep the overall height at 55½ inches regardless of the load of passengers.

BROUGHAM CHASSIS is the same new X-frame layout used on all 1957 Cadillacs, except for the addition of air suspension. The engine utilizes two four-barrel carburetors, is rated at a maximum of 325 hp with a "standard" compression ratio of 10-to-1.

Eldorado Brougham for '57

CADILLAC'S Eldorado Brougham, the first American car to use a true air suspension system, has finally reached production reality.

The super-luxurious four-door hardtop made its debut at the National Automobile Show in New York. Public introductions will be held in key cities throughout the United States after February 1.

Although it contains several industry "firsts," the Brougham does not have several of the features expected. It uses conventional carburetors rather than fuel injection, for example.

(The decision to stick with carburetors was a last-minute one. Cadillac engineers have been working frantically to ready an injection system, but were not fully satisfied with test results. It would not be surprising to see Cadillac make a running changeover to fuel injection later in the year, however.)

Only 55½ inches high at the top of its stainless steel roof, the Brougham has a 126-inch wheelbase and is 216 inches long overall. This makes it a compact car by Cadillac standards. (It has a shorter wheelbase and is narrower, but about the same overall length, as current 62 Series models.)

The 325-hp engine is the same one used by other 1957 Eldorado models. It uses two four-barrel carburetors, displaces 365 cubic inches and has a 10-to-1 compression ratio.

The Brougham's frame is similar to the one used by other 1957 Cadillacs. It has a tubular backbone and is shaped roughly like a big "X."

The air suspension system features air spring units at each wheel. Air is supplied to the spring units thru leveling valves so the car remains level with varying loads and road conditions. This contributes to easy handling and exceptionally smooth riding qualities.

Anti-dive characteristics are built into the ball-joint front end to keep the

CONTINUED ON PAGE 78

CADILLAC

By JAMES WHIPPLE

THE year 1957 was one of the big change for Cadillac. All models got new frames, suspension systems and bodies not to mention bumpers, grilles, hoods, tail-lights and instrument panels.

The engine has been given a conservative boost from 285 to 300 horsepower on the 60 Special, 62 and 75 models. The increase is due to a higher compression ratio of 10.0 to 1 and larger intake and smaller exhaust valves.

The Eldorado coupe and convertible are powered with a 325 bhp engine, basically the "standard" engine with the exception of carburetion by two four throat units instead of the single four barrel unit used on the 300 bhp engine.

One of the first things we noticed behind the wheel of the '57 Cadillac was the improved vision due to a 3½-inch lower hood which is now lower than the fender line. Short-statured drivers will welcome this change particularly in maneuvering their Cadillacs in close quarters.

The new windshield provides noticeably better vision than the one on last year's Cadillac because it is deeper (i.e. continues further into the roof panel), and because it wraps further around at each side.

Driving the new Cadillac both in traffic and out on the highway we were less conscious of the windshield corner pillars cutting into our field of vision. We're glad to report that there was absolutely no distortion in the corners of the new windshield and that the lower corners or "doglegs" of the windshield pillars do not jut into the door opening and interfere with entry and exit.

One of the Cadillac qualities that we've always felt to be particularly outstanding is the seating comfort. The furniture industry could well take some lessons from the men who design and make Cadillac seat cushions. For people who find driving (or even rid-

ing) in a car uncomfortable due to back and leg strain, a Cadillac may well be their salvation.

Quite rightly, Cadillac's designers believe that the seat that gives the best support is more comfortable than a seat that is merely deep and soft. The Cadillac's seat backs give firm extra support at the lower part of the spine which is one part of the driver's anatomy most likely to protest at the end of 300 or 400 miles behind the wheel.

Seat cushions have been designed to give especially firm support under the thighs. This eases the strain on the driver's right leg and makes cornering and driving on high-crowned roads much more comfortable, as the driver and passengers do not flounder helplessly in billowy cushions.

Although the entire Cadillac line has been lowered from two to three inches in overall height, there has been no reduction in headroom either in front or rear compartments of the sedan. Retaining a full 35 inches of headroom

Price range (Factory list price)
$4,212 (Series 62 coupe)
to $6,648 (Eldorado Biarritz convertible and
Eldorado Seville hardtop)

CADILLAC
is the car
for you

if... You want the Number One prestige car on the American market.

if... You appreciate the most comfortable seats available in an American car plus a thoroughly soundproof car.

if... You value really excellent workmanship in all details of upholstery, hardware, trim and finish.

if... You want the best investment, dollar for dollar, in the luxury car field.

CADILLAC SPECIFICATIONS

ENGINE	V-8		
Bore and stroke	4 in. x 3.625 in.		
Displacement	365 cu. in.		
Compression ratio	10.1:1		
Max. brake horsepower	300 @ 4800 rpm		
Max. torque	400 @ 2800 rpm		
DIMENSIONS	**SERIES 62**	**ELDORADO**	**FLEETWOOD**
Wheelbase	129.5 in.	129.5 in.	133 in.
Overall length	215.9 in.	222.1 in.	224.4 in.
Overall width	80 in.	80 in.	80 in.
Overall height	59.1 in.	57.9 in.	59.1 in.
TRANSMISSION	HydraMatic		

Eldorado Biarritz convertible is '57 Cadillac version of open-air elegance. Side trim has been reduced, tail fins have been moved inboard.

New Cadillac chassis features tubular center—X frame. Frame has no side rails, permits lowering of car. Body is secured to "outrigger" brackets.

is mandatory for Cadillac whose customers are not inclined to appreciate crushing their fedoras.

The lowering process was made possible by Cadillac's new "cruciform" frame which has a massive "X" member but no side rails. The body itself is supported by frame outriggers. This new design permits lowering of the floor and doorsills as well as the seats.

Thus the relationships of roof seat and floor dimensions remain the same and the owner of last year's (or the year before's) Cadillac will feel comfortably at home in any one of the '57's. He'll be aware of the difference only by means of the increased forward vision, the changed shape of the rear quarter windows and the new instrument panel.

Evidently encouraged by public demand and the expected rigidity of the new frame, Cadillac has scored as the first U.S. automaker to completely drop the conventional center pillar and door frames of the four door sedan.

With the exception of the seven passenger "75" models, all Cadillacs are hardtops (or convertibles). This means a dividend in vision for passengers except for the outside rear seat passengers whose vision is somewhat blocked by the rear window support pillar which angles down from the roofline in a forward dogleg.

We hope that in future models the designers will find a means of eliminating this annoying pillar which seems to have no purpose other than to stabilize the raised rear door glass when the door is swung open or the car is driven with the window half open.

With all windows closed, the new Cadillac hardtop, we tested a "62" Sedan, showed no tendency to rattle or squeak in or around the doors and window frames on rough, cobblestone roads.

This may be more a tribute to a well-designed body than to the stiffness of the new frame because there is more shake on these same rough roads than in last year's model—in fact, a good deal more shake than is to be expected in a car as massive, well-constructed and expensive as Cadillac.

In our opinion, the only real answer to the problem of body shake and vibration is a complete one-piece body and frame structure of extreme stiffness to counteract the absence of center pillars in the four-door hardtops which are by far the worst offenders.

Although body shake is to be expected on almost every heavyweight four-door hardtop made today, it comes as an unpleasant surprise to find it on a Cadillac which in previous conventional sedan models was an exceptionally solid and well-behaved car.

Cadillac's riding qualities are solid and substantial and have improved as far as better chassis stability has re-duced swaying at high speeds on rough roads.

As far as interference from surface vibrations is concerned, the '57 Cadillac does not seem to have improved as much you would suspect from an entirely new engineering job. In fact, we felt that the overall riding qualities had fallen somewhat below last year's car which was up to standard for the Cadillac price range.

The two major problems that we found in the Cadillac ride were that the minor bumps caused by rough cobblestones, railroad tracks and the like were not completely absorbed and that sharp bumps such as caused by pot holes and abrupt dips were not sufficiently controlled.

In other words, despite the cushioning of large, low-pressure tires and the coil and leaf springs, and the control of large shock absorbers, the jiggle of minor bumps and the choppy rebound from larger ones got through to the passenger compartment.

Roadability has been much improved by the new chassis and ball joint front suspension layout. Brake dip which used to be a major annoyance in big Cadillacs has almost completely disappeared even in panic stop conditions. The car is no longer the slightest bit inclined to "wallow" or dive when pushed into turns of decreasing radius at high speed. Steering action (power assist is standard) is a

Lowered hood of Cadillac is beneath fender line. Split bumper has rubber tips.

Re-arranged dashboard brings instruments and knobs within driver's easy reach.

good compromise for the average driver—not "quick," not too slow.

There's a nice balance between oversteer and understeer so that the car doesn't tend to "come around after you" in a tight bend, nor does it have the sluggish, plowing tendencies of a car with too much understeer.

For those who do a lot of driving in warm climates, Cadillac has relocated the air conditioning in the front compartment. Cooled air is blown at considerable force from three plastic doors at the base of the windshield which are not connected with the regular defrosting system. Removing the evaporator and blower from the trunk has added much needed luggage capacity to a trunk which is actually smaller than last year's model and smaller than that found on several lower-priced cars.

SUMMING UP: Cadillac is, as always, a very solid, well-built automobile with an impressive look about it. Performance is powerful and incredibly smooth, while handling and control is extremely easy and free from problems. Despite its obvious bulk and length, the Cadillac is easy to maneuver and park if the space is long enough. The quality of manufacture and traditionally low rate of depreciation make it an excellent buy for those who are able to afford the initial investment. ●

CADILLAC CHECK LIST ☑☑☑☑☑

5 CHECKS MEANS TOP RATING IN ITS PRICE CLASS

Category	Comments	Rating (out of 5)
PERFORMANCE	Cadillac performance is smooth and powerful but not sensational. Acceleration rate from standstill to 60 mph 11.9 seconds. Response in D-3 range of HydraMatic is smooth and very fast.	4 checks
STYLING	In our opinion the restyling of the '57 Cadillac represents a backward step to an overall shell that's less handsome and dignified than the previous models.	3 checks
RIDING COMFORT	Undeniably a comfortable car with its large, soft tires and deep, firm, well-designed upholstery. Some jiggling of the heavy unsprung axles and wheels transmitted to body. On very rough going there is some body shake and pitching on sharp bumps.	4 checks
ROADABILITY	The '57 Cadillac is very stable and roadable for a heavy sedan, with noticeable improvement over last year's car which was better than average. Behavior in sharp curves is good with no plowing or nosing under.	4 checks
INTERIOR DESIGN	Although Cadillac was lowered from two to three inches this year, excellent interior dimensions are maintained. Doors provide comfortable entry and exit. Seat cushions are exceptionally comfortable on long drives. Vision is considerably improved.	4 checks
EASE OF CONTROL	Power steering on Cadillac requires somewhat more effort than on other large cars but does not over-control when the steering wheel is moved fast when making a right hand turn. Power brakes are smooth-acting and reliable.	4 checks
ECONOMY	HydraMatic Drive fourth gear gives Cadillac an edge in superior gasoline mileage over other heavy luxury cars, but more powerful engine which was new in '56 models doesn't give mileage equal to lighter medium-priced cars as was the case several years ago.	4 checks
SERVICEABILITY	New compact engine compartment with lower hood and a crowd of power accessories makes easy servicing a tough proposition — tougher still with air conditioning piled on top.	3 checks
WORKMANSHIP	The continued high quality of paint, finish and trim found on Cadillacs is one of the big reasons for its continued leadership in the luxury field. Body shake was the only flaw in the car we tested.	5 checks
VALUE PER DOLLAR	Cadillac has next to the lowest depreciation rate of all cars at any price. This fact plus Cadillac's reputation for low incidence of repairs makes the car an excellent investment in luxurious transportation.	5 checks

CADILLAC OVERALL RATING... 4.0 CHECKS

CADILLAC ROAD TEST...

THE 1957 Cadillac is paradoxical in many respects. In the first place, it's a brand-new car with practically nothing left over from 1956 except the engine and transmission.

Yet the Cadillac tradition of evolutionary change has been followed so closely that many people won't recognize the real newness of the car!

The Cadillac used for test purposes was a 62 series four-door hardtop. As is true of most Caddys these days, it had a full complement of accessories.

Among them were power brakes and steering and Hydra-Matic, all standard non-extra cost items, plus power seats and windows, signal seeking radio with rear speaker. In short, everything but air conditioning.

With this type of load aboard, a full tank of gas and the driver, the performance turned in was about what you would expect—good, but not outstanding. That's as it should be, since most Cadillac buyers are more interested in the car's comfort and prestige than blinding acceleration.

Performance figures were just about the same as those of the 1956 test car; even slightly slower at the low end of the range, in fact. This is due to the fact that the engine displacement was unchanged and, although 15 hp was added, there was no increase in peak torque. In addition, rear axle ratio went from 3.36 to 3.07. This shows up in slightly better economy and top speed, but hurts acceleration.

Ride and handling of the '57 Cadillac are noticeably better than last year, however. Riding comfort isn't actually much smoother under straight-ahead, smooth road conditions—Cadillac has long been outstanding here.

Major ride improvement is noticed in turns; the current model feels more stable and sway has been reduced, adding to passenger comfort.

Credit for this can go to the new chassis design and resultant lower center of gravity.

As everyone interested in cars should know by now, Cadillac has ditched the traditional side-member-type frame in favor of a huge X-shaped affair. Outriggers extending from this frame help support the body.

Elimination of side frame rails permits floor height to be lowered and Cadillac claims the X-shaped design has more pound-for-pound rigidity than the "cow-belly" frames with swept-out side rails used by most other makes which were lowered drastically for 1957.

If Cadillac had any important quality problems with its all-new car this year they were licked by the time the test car was produced. All switches, gages and accessories did their job properly and finish details, interior and exterior left nothing to be desired.

Two accessories the car had which were especially appreciated were the six-way power seat and the side view mirror controlled from inside the car.

The first is the only type of power seat which really makes sense. It seems ridiculous to go to the extent of adding power just to move a seat fore and aft a few inches. The six-way seat, which can be adjusted to an almost infinite number of positions, is a different matter.

It is of particular benefit on a trip of any length because the driver can change his seating position—up, down, forward or back—easily and quickly. And it's surprising how slight variations every so often will help reduce fatigue and muscle strain.

The side view mirror is nearly a necessity with a seat of this type since it permits the outside mirror to be adjusted easily to conform to the new driving position. In fact, this type of mirror is a boon in *any* car and, since it can be adjusted without opening the window, is always at the correct angle for providing optimum vision to side and rear.

A driver getting into a new Cadillac for the first time will likely have trouble locating all the instrument switches immediately. Not all are in the conventional position directly in front of the driver.

Light switches are in the corner angle where the left side

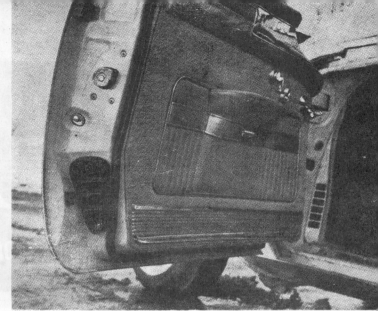

INTERIOR features are very lush and somewhat dazzling to many people. Instruments are grouped in front of the driver and hooded to prevent glare. Radio speaker is mounted below dash in the center.

WARM AIR for rear seat heater is ducted through the doors, as can be seen here. This is making the most of waste space, in the lower portion of the doors, which is most generally left unused.

of the cowl wraps around—directly under the left wraparound section of the windshield.

Windshield wiper and washer controls are even more around at the left side; just a few inches from the separation point between A-post and door, in fact.

These controls are all easy to reach, however; easier than when in the conventional location, actually, once you get used to them.

Cadillac uses flashing generator and oil pressure warning lights, following the current trend. A feature retained from the past which is useful surprisingly often is the trip mileage indicator.

This gadget is helpful not only on long trips, but in checking gas mileage, etc. Salesmen and others paid expenses on a per-mile basis should find it especially valuable!

Speaking of gas mileage, the Cadillac turned in averages just about on a par with other cars in its class. City driving under varied traffic conditions resulted in an 11 mpg average. Highway cruising average was about 16-17 mpg at steady speeds of 50-65 mph. Overall average was just under 14 mpg.

Another point noted about the '57 Cadillac was that its radio was up to the consistently excellent standard of recent years. The test crew hi-fi fan remarked that few test cars have equalled Cadillac in this respect since 1955.

As far as styling is concerned this year, about all you can say is that it's still definitely Cadillac! You would never confuse this new model with any other make, even if you were seeing a '57 Caddy for the first time.

This was demonstrated by the number of people who asked: "Is this the 1956 or 1957 model?"

This surely proves the success of Cadillac's efforts to be evolutionary rather than revolutionary.

How much longer it can hew so closely to this policy is problematical, however. It appears even now that the radically re-styled 1957 Chrysler is taking away a few Cadillac customers. All of the new customers Lincoln was won in the past year and a half can't be former medium-priced buyers moving up a notch, either.

On the other hand, Cadillac's policy is one of the big reasons for the terrific resale value of its cars. This has become one of its most important sales weapons.

When you combine Cadillac's almost unequalled prestige value, the comfort it offers, relatively low depreciation, high quality and very acceptable all-round performance, it isn't hard to figure why the car has been so successful. ●

CADILLAC TEST DATA

Test Car: 1957 Cadillac 62 four-door hardtop
Basic Price: $4780.96
Engine: 365-cubic-inch ohv V-8
Compression Ratio: 10-to-1
Horsepower: 300 @ 4800 rpm
Torque: 400 @ 2800 rpm
Dimensions: Length 221 inches, width 80, height 59, tread 61 front and rear, wheelbase 129.5
Dry Weight: 4600 lbs.
Transmission: Hydra-Matic
Acceleration: 0-30 mph 4 seconds, 0-45 mph 6.9, 0-60 mph 10.9
Gas Mileage: 13.9 average
Speedometer Corrections: Indicated 30, 45 and 60 mph are actual 32, 45 and 58.5

TAILLIGHTS on all Cadillac models have now been moved down (from their former position at the top of the fender fin) to a spot just above the bumper tip exhaust. Bumper is simple, efficient.

OUR TITLE MAY SOUND STRANGE, but all indications point out the truth of the fact. If you take into consideration that the Cad has the lowest depreciation, percentage-wise, of any domestic car; that repairs should be at a minimum; and that the fuel economy we obtained from our test car without using any gimmicks was the best of any large car tested this year, it all makes sense. Then throw in quality workmanship and materials, practically all the comforts of home, a superb ride, prestige . . . and what have you got to lose?

The Cadillac that we drove was a 60 Special Fleetwood. It has the longest wheelbase (133 inches) and is one of the largest passenger cars overall (224 inches) built in the U.S. Only the Cadillac 75 limousine and the Lincoln are longer. The engine is the same as in the series 62 and 75, with 365 cubic inches developing 300 horsepower. Total weight, with a full tank of Mobilgas, is 5140 pounds.

THE RIDING QUALITIES are just about the best found on any present day automobile: super soft with but very little pitch and roll. Recovery after hitting a bad dip is quick and, even on washboard type roads, vibration can hardly be felt. The car does lean quite a bit in sharp turns, but this characteristic is hardly felt by the passengers.

HANDLING IS EASY, though not as good as on some other domestic cars. The great weight makes itself felt when driving through sharp corners, where the car heels over noticeably, and generally has an adverse effect on performance. The power steering gives enough road feel and is very easy, but at higher speeds on rough roads it needs frequent correction. And, if you're unfamiliar with this car, it's wise to keep an eye on the speedometer, since the absolute silence of operation can be deceiving.

PAINT, FINISH AND TRIM are very good, with body panels and chrome strips meeting where they should—in line, which can't be said for all makes. Interior materials and workmanship are excellent, giving the impression of a custom-made car; and, certainly, with the wide variety of fabric and color combinations offered, it can easily be suited to the individual's personal taste. From the leather-padded dash and leather-covered window sills to the rich upholstery, it spells sheer luxury. Every detail has been worked out for the comfort of the owner.

As a matter of fact, Cadillac would seem to be stressing workmanship, quality, and comfort even more than in previous years. Aside from the consistently fine calibre of the overall craftsmanship, a very successful effort to eliminate the small annoyances and to anticipate passenger and driver wants has been made. The extra large glove compartment, for instance, besides being located amidship, has the

Buy a CADILLAC

ROAD TEST OF '57 CAD 60 SPECIAL

release button located far left, within easy reach of the driver. The same is true of the radio, both the volume and tuner knobs being on the left side. All levers, as a matter of fact, have either been recessed or located behind the dish-type steering wheel.

The instruments are well grouped, large, and highly legible. There is no need to squint, squirm, check the road, then squint some more. One glance should do the job. And speaking of glancing, the side view mirror is adjustable from an inside lever.

TIRED OF OPENING THE TRUNK LID? It's now power assisted. Insert the key, turn, and an electric motor will free and partly raise the lid, with the manual effort being reduced to a minimum. It works the same in reverse, both operations being a boon to ladies, children and those who like to play "Open, Sesame." You can also unlock the trunk with a button located

in the glove compartment. A red light reading "trunk" will flash on, signifying a successful disengagement and warning you not to drive with the lid open. It is, incidentally, commodious, to say the least.

FUEL ECONOMY WAS ASTONISHING for a 5100-pound automobile. Our tank average for 332 miles was 14.0 mpg, and at steady speeds of 30 mph we averaged 24.1 mpg and at 60 mph, 16.9 mpg. It proves that good fuel economy *is* attainable from a high compression, modern engine, *provided* it's coupled to the right rear axle ratio. In the case of this particular car, the high-speed axle (3.07 to 1) gave good economy, but lessened its acceleration qualities.

PERFORMANCE IS NOT the highest on the list, but don't hold that against the car. It was not, after all, designed to be a hot rod—anything but!—and its 300 horses can move you from place to place very,

PHOTOS BY WORON

ACCELERATION FIGURES compiled with the aid of the fifth wheel indicated that despite size, weight of car, performance was more than adequate.

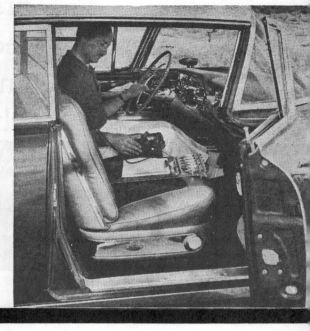

AN MT RESEARCH REPORT
by Otto Zipper

FOR ECONOMY?

REVEALS FANTASTIC FUEL ECONOMY

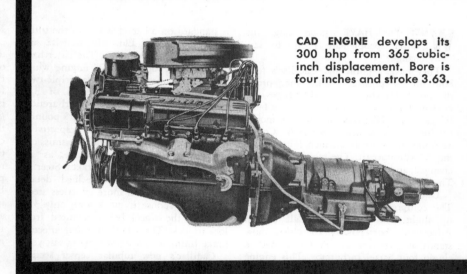

CAD ENGINE develops its 300 bhp from 365 cubic-inch displacement. Bore is four inches and stroke 3.63.

very quickly, indeed. Acceleration through the gears is smoothness itself and top speed is well over a hundred.

CADILLAC'S TWO MAIN DOMESTIC competitors in this price-class range have some fine offerings; and, in certain categories (e.g., performance, handling and, some might say, styling) Cad is short of being tops. But in an overall analysis it would be difficult to say that another make is better.

We do know this: while coming back to Los Angeles from our testing site at El Mirage Dry Lake, we drove through an area called Mint Canyon. Maybe it was that magical, just before dusk, time of day —maybe it was the splendidly buoyant semi-desert air—or maybe it was a combination of those natural phenomena and a fine mechanical achievement that made us think we had never before so much enjoyed an automobile ride.

PERFORMANCE
(300-bhp engine, 3.07 rear axle)

SPEEDOMETER ERROR
Read 31 at true 30, 45 at 45, 52 at 50, 62 at 60, 78 at 75, 84 at 80.

ACCELERATION
From Standing Start
0-45 mph 7.7   0-60 mph 12.4
Quarter-mile 18.6 and 75 mph
Passing Speeds
30-50 mph 5.0   45-60 mph 4.7
50-80 mph 12.1

FUEL CONSUMPTION
Using Mobilgas Special
Steady Speeds
24.1 mpg @ 30   19.7 mpg @ 45
16.9 mpg @ 60   14.0 mpg @ 75
Stop-and-Go Driving
14.0 mpg tank average for 332 miles

(285-bhp engine, 3.54 rear axle)

Read 34 at true 30, 49 at 45,
64 at 60, 78 at 75

From Standing Start
0-45 mph 6.6   0-60 mph 11.4
Quarter-mile 17.8 and 78.5 mph
Passing Speeds
30-50 mph 5.3   40-60 mph 5.0
50-80 mph 11.0

Using Mobilgas Special
Steady Speeds
21.4 mpg @ 30   20.2 mpg @ 45
17.4 mpg @ 60   14.7 mpg @ 75
Stop-and-Go Driving
12.8 mpg tank average for 512 miles

first feel behind the wheel

CADILLAC

by Joe Wherry
Detroit Editor

"WHEN YOU HAVE a good thing," the Cadillac people are prone to say, "why change?"

They have a point and Cadillac's firm hold on the prestige market may prove the point. Of course several changes are evident, but they are definitely in the face-lift category. Take our introduction model for instance, a luxurious Series 62 Coupe de Ville; it's scarcely an inch longer than the '57 counterpart. The wheelbase is unchanged, and the overall width is the same. The height overall, too, is unchanged.

Under the hood there are few changes. The compression ratio has been stepped up, slightly, to 10.25 to 1 on all models. Advertised horsepower, therefore, now stands at 310 bhp at 4800 rpm with a single four-barrel carburetor. This engine is standard on all models except the ultra-luxury jobs—the Eldorado Biarritz and Seville and the Brougham. The latter have the otherwise optional "Q" engine which shares the same block but has triple-two-barrel carburetors with ratings of 335 bhp at 4800. Regardless of carburetion, the torque of each is stated at 405 pounds-feet at 3100 and 3400 rpm respectively.

Dual range Hydra-Matic transmissions are standard on all, of course, as are power steering and power brakes. Steering has been improved, unspecified details having enabled even more effortless steering, and response is quick with only 3⅔ turns of the wheel being required from lock-to-lock. The wheel size and effective brake lining area are the same as last year.

Cadillac's new tubular center section X-type frame, introduced in '57, is little changed except for modification necessary to accommodate air suspension, an option on all models except for the Eldorado Brougham where air is standard. A new four-link-type trailing arm rear suspension is used across the board. Our steel-sprung first feel car was equipped thusly. A trailing arm attaches, on each side, to a crossmember extending far outboard of the wasp-waisted frame forward of the rear wheels. These two arms precisely position the rear axle. Another trailing link, actually two links in one and shaped in outline like an asymmetrical circle, attaches to the differential cage, in the rear, and is hinged to the rear frame crossmember.

Take a new Cadillac, one with coil springs, through a fast series of S-bends and you'll gain new respect for the roadability that can be built into a large and heavy car. Solidly positioning the rear axle in this manner prevents torque and road-induced misalignment of the rear axle. The big car holds firm at speeds at least 50 per cent greater than could formerly be held. On fast corners there is still considerable heeling over, but no longer is this accompanied by as much rear end sway as formerly. Rear end breakaway is less likely, there's more warning, and correction is easier and less violent.

STARTING OUT from scratch, with the Hydra-Matic selector in top DRIVE range, our 310-horsepower Coupe de Ville made the following acceleration times: 0 to 30 mph, 3.9 seconds; to 45, 7.4; to 60, 11.7. The 50-80 time was 11.8 seconds.

A cold rain hampered these acceleration tests; despite this, however, rear wheels did *not* hop; they stayed put under maximum torque, slipped remarkably

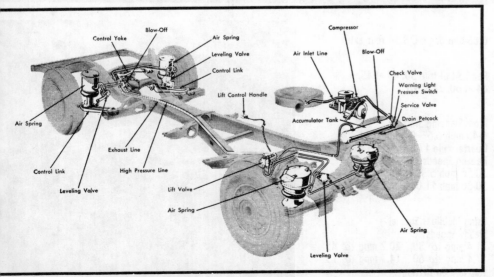

FRAME has only slight modifications to accommodate air suspension system.

little, and evidenced the benefits of the trailing links in the rear with better traction and less squat.

On a high-speed test track this heavy car snuggled down in the curves and, though the road was wet, it was solid and unaffected by a moderate crosswind that blew all day. It gave excellent feel of the road. The optional air suspension would, theoretically at least, give a softer ride. How this could be, or better yet how the air bags could improve ride and driver feel and control proportionately, is difficult to imagine since the new rear suspension now allows a more violent type of driving with increased road adhesion.

But Cadillac buyers are not usually so concerned with handling approaching that expected of sports cars as they are of the quality evidenced and the appointments. There are no less than 55 interior trim and color combinations available on all series below the Brougham; the latter has 44 available interior trims. The power window controls have been extended, in scope, to include the front vent windows. All four-door models now feature rear vent windows as well. Stylish and just as practical is a new molded Fiberglas headliner for the hardtop models. Easy to clean, this headliner has sound-deadening properties as well. The buyer can choose

conventional two-way power seat controls or six-way controls; the latter are now controlled from the driver's armrest. Also optional is power operation for the rear deck lid—a switch in the glove compartment does the trick. Electrical door locks are also optional on any model with power windows.

Passenger comfort in the front seat has been improved by relocation of the radio speaker in the dashboard—it was in the center of the floor. The instrument panel now includes, at the right side, the clock. Vacationers will find that their '58 Cadillac, regardless of model, will hold more luggage than formerly. The trunk has a new floor that is perfectly flat.

OUR TEST CAR was a run-of-the-mill job and so we noted, particularly, that assembly and workmanship generally were excellent. In '57 we experienced drafts, in one hardtop, caused by badly out-of-line doors and weatherstripping. We have been told that Cadillac is tightening up on quality control. Even fine car manufacturers have to watch final assembly; the new models should show improvement to the point where they will undoubtedly be the best assembled high-priced cars made domestically.

Cadillac has not released the percentage

of air-suspended cars they expect to build, but the ratio will probably be the highest in the industry. This system is refined over that introduced on the Brougham last spring but is technically the same. Incorporated in the air suspension system is a lift valve actuated by an under-dash handle which forces the air bags full of air, puts the car at full-jounce position to enable the driver to clear obstructions, high road centers in an emergency, or to back out of steep driveways without damaging bumper guards, etc.

Distinctive styling in the Biarritz and Seville models in the Eldorado series is maintained by rear quarter panel trim, by a different bumper bar, and by vertical strips between the outer bumper sections. The Biarritz features Cape Buffalo leathers with both grained and metallic finishes, or one may optionally choose combinations of leather and metallic-threaded nylon materials.

The 133-inch wheelbase Fleetwood Series 60 Special is distinguished by an extruded aluminum panel across the lower portion of the rear quarter panel—this grooved decoration is matched on the rear deck between the backup lights. Stainless steel gets a new nod from Caddy on the Fleetwood 60 with a rocker sill molding beneath the doors. /MT

BODY STYLING for '58 (below) is not greatly changed from '57 (above) except in front end.

CADILLAC

By JIM WHIPPLE

IN THE FACE of the first serious competition in many years, Cadillac has stepped down off its Rolls Royce-like pedestal and, with the '57 and '58 models, commenced to make really worthwhile improvements in riding qualities, handling and roadability.

Having the uncontested leader of U.S. luxury field for so many years, made Cadillac management feel that it was enough just to come forth with a large, quiet-running, beautifully-made luxury package year after year.

The fact of the matter is that they were right. Until 1957, when the eye-stopping new Imperial and a vastly upgraded Lincoln caught the luxury buyer's eye, Cadillac's conservative, massive good looks and high prestige was enough to give each and every Cad salesman a happy backlog of potential customers, not only for new cars but for well-kept trade-ins too!

In 1958, Cadillac is still the sales leader although the margin of sales supremacy has been cut down. For

those who may be waiting for a new Caddy or making a choice between the big three we've got good news; the engineering progress that did much toward winning Cadillac its crown is under way in earnest once more.

The '58 Cadillac is more than just an elegantly facelifted new edition of a perennial favorite; it is a very noticeably improved automobile. When we got behind the wheel of the Series 62 Sedan DeVille test car, we were once again impressed by the deep, firm comfort of the upholstery which is second to no other U.S. car.

The driving position is as comfortable as ever and vision through the wrap-around windshield is nearly distortion-free. For short-statured drivers, the '58 Cad's 5-inch longer hood is no help as it cuts down view of the road immediately ahead of the car.

Whether the owner's pleasure in a longer, more massive-looking car (wheelbase remains 129 in.) will counteract the annoyance of groping

blindly into narrow driveways or bumping into curbs is for him to judge. Happily, the longer hood and fenders and the longer backslanted tail fins do not impair safe vision on the open highway.

The familiar Cad instrument panel is, as always, an irritating paradox. The instrument dials are wonderfully readable white on black, perfectly placed so that they can be read through the steering wheel, softly lighted yet surrounded by dazzling chrome trim as thick as whipped cream. The glitter from this needless frosting manages to be equally annoying in daylight and after dark and makes you think seriously of spending an hour or so working it over with a small brush and some lusterless enamel.

Cad's power steering is as good as ever. It has just the right balance of gradually increasing boost and true feel of forces reacting between front wheels and road surface. This doesn't mean that Cadillac steering transmits

Series 62 four-door hardtop snows Cadillac's returning
to high, swept-back tailfins and longer hood of '56.
Its 310-hp engine is standard throughout the line.

CADILLAC
is the car
for you

if... You want the top prestige
car in America today.

if... You liked everything about last
year's Cadillac, yet found its
ride and roadability inferior
to its '57 competition: the '58
solves your problems.

if... High quality of finish and
workmanship are important
to you.

if... The lowest rate of depreciation
in the luxury field makes
economic sense to you.

CADILLAC
SPECIFICATIONS

ENGINE	V-8	ELDORADO "Q" V-8	
Bore and stroke	4 in. x 3.625 in.	4 in. x 3.625 in.	
Displacement	365 cu. in.	365 cu. in.	
Compression ratio	10.25:1	10.25:1	
Max. brake horsepower	310 @ 4800 rpm	335 @ 4800 rpm	
Max. torque	405 @ 3100 rpm	405 @ 3400 rpm	
DIMENSIONS	62 SERIES	60 FLEETWOOD	75 FLEETWOOD
Wheelbase	129.5 in.	133 in.	149.7 in.
Overall length	216.8 in.	225.3 in.	237.1 in.
Overall width	80 in.	80 in.	80 in.
Overall height	59.1 in.	59.1 in.	61.6 in.
TRANSMISSION			
Hydra-Matic			

Cadillac's air-suspension system illustrated below is a '58 option.

Eldorado series is available only in convertible, below, and two-door hardtop.

road shock because it is completely free of it.

The steering on Cadillac's competition is good but we give Cad the edge for best "feel" under all conditions.

One of the first things that we noticed out on the road was the greater stability of the car. On a rough high-crowned rolling macadam road the '58 Cad seems to knife through the uneven sections rather than roll over them or sway to one side.

Cadillac engineers attribute the improvement to the new rear suspension set-up in which the car is supported by coil instead of leaf springs and the axle is precisely positioned by three rubber-cushioned links rather than flexibly shackled by leaf springs.

This new set-up raises the car's "roll center" or point of lateral oscilation some 5 inches which cuts down sway very considerably and makes the car feel much closer to the road even though its center of gravity is no lower than on last year's model. This new rear suspension has done a lot to improve ride as well. There is noticeably less pitching (now almost none) than last year and even less vibration from surface roughness is transmitted. Cadillac's ride with standard all-coil spring suspension compares very favorably with Lincoln's similar system and Imperial's torsion-bar, leaf-spring set-up.

It is hard to say which is more comfortable. The three cars are very close. In the final accounting we'd give Lincoln a slight edge because of the shakeproof rigidity of its one piece body and frame.

Cadillac's frame, a tubular-backboned X-shape has been changed slightly in respect to body mounting and the body sills which bridge between the open sides of the X have been beefed up. As a result of these fairly minor changes there is a great reduction in body shake on rough roads. The amount of shake on last year's Cadillac was, in our opinion, barely excusable in a car costing $5000 and up. The '58 Cadillac has as little shake as any car with conventional separate body and frame construction.

Handling has improved on the '58 Cad, and it's an important item to be upgraded on a car of the size power potential of a Cadillac. There's nothing that will make a big car seem elephantine more quickly than sloppy handling qualities. The new, precisely positioned rear suspension is again responsible for the improvement.

You can snake the '58 Cadillac down narrow winding dirt and macadam roads at 50 and 60 mph with ease and security never known before. The car is steered, not aimed as was the

case with many luxury cars of the past which were not only bargelike in dimension but equally clumsy in maneuvering.

Probably few of the sedate and successful middle-aged buyers of '58 Cadillacs will fully appreciate the improvements in ride, handling and roadability over previous Cadillacs, but they may take our word for it that these changes have made trading in the old Cadillac more desirable than perhaps ever before.

Performance of the '58 Cadillac is just about the same as last year. Engine horsepower has been raised from 300 to 310 (325 on the Eldorado models) which has made no measureable difference. However, those accustomed to reading higher figures on smaller, lighter and lower-priced cars (e.g. 345 on Chrysler and Edsel, 400 on the top Mercury engine) shouldn't come with the impression that the '58 Cadillac is a laggard in acceleration. Moving a 4800-lb. sedan from 0 to 60 mph in 11.5 seconds is no mean feat and should raise few legitimate complaints. Much of the responsibility for Cad's brisk performance goes to the excellent four-speed Hydra-Matic transmission. Coupled with a 3.07 to 1 rear-axle ratio, this transmission makes the best use of the Cadillac engine's

Fleetwood Sixty Special four-door hardtop has an advertised delivered price of $6,232.

Eldorado Brougham is basically unchanged from '57, rates as most expensive car built in U.S.—$13,074.

Dashboard arrangement holds big, bold speedometer, transmission indicator.

405 lbs. ft. of torque which is developed at 3100 rpm. Only hot rodders, and Cadillac doesn't angle for their business, would be discontent with performance. Hydra-Matic's top ratio corresponds to an overdrive ratio and makes Cad one of the quietest cars on the road at high (80 mph) cruising speeds.

Summing up: Cadillac is, as usual, an extremely well-built and well-finished car with a roomy and comfortable interior and traditionally rich General Motors styling. This year's models offer top notch riding comfort and roadability to match quiet, powerful performance. ●

CAR LIFE'S overall rating for the '57 Cadillac was 4.0 checks. The following car in Cadillac's price range has already been tested by CAR LIFE. The issue in which it appeared may be obtained by sending 35¢ to CAR LIFE, 41 East 42 Street, New York 17, N. Y.: Lincoln, January, 1958.

CADILLAC CHECK LIST

5 CHECKS MEAN TOP RATING IN ITS PRICE CLASS

PERFORMANCE	Cadillac's smooth running, exceptionally quiet engine gives entirely satisfactory performance in all speed ranges, although acceleration is not as fast as its competition.	✔✔ ✔✔ ☐
STYLING	Cadillac styling for '58 with its lower grille, longer hood and more sweeping fins manages to look both up-to-date and conservative at the same time. Only fault is non-functional spattering of chrome trim.	✔✔ ✔✔ ☐
RIDING COMFORT	Much improved over last year's models which were good. Pitching, swaying and annoying body shake have been almost eliminated in coil-spring suspended cars.	✔✔ ✔✔ ☐
ROADABILITY	The '58 Cadillac shows perhaps its greatest improvement in roadability which is now on par with Lincoln and close to the sensationally roadable Imperial. For the first time in years it's fun to drive a Caddy on bad roads as well as good.	✔✔ ✔✔ ☐
INTERIOR DESIGN	Cadillac maintains its excellent interior dimensions. Seats are 65 inches wide have 35 inches of headroom in both front and rear compartments of sedans. Upholstery is firm (as it should be) and seating positions are good.	✔✔ ✔✔ ☐
EASE OF CONTROL	New suspension system has improved control and makes steering very accurate and precise. Power steering is good, giving enough assistance yet maintaining adequate road feel.	✔✔ ✔✔
ECONOMY	Although the buyer of a $5000 automobile is not primarily interested in the ultimate in gasoline economy, the Cadillac's efficient four-speed Hydra-Matic gives best mileage in its field.	✔✔ ✔✔ ☐
SERVICEABILITY	The big V-8 engine is crowded enough in its tight low compartment make force removal of many components a necessity for servicing of others. With air suspension compressor, air conditioning, power steering and power brakes, conditions are pretty rough.	✔✔ ✔☐ ☐
WORKMANSHIP	Cadillac's continued high standards of finish and assembly leave little to be desired and cannot be topped this side of the Atlantic.	✔✔ ✔✔ ✔
VALUE PER DOLLAR	Improved roadability, ride and handling coupled with Cadillac's remarkable low rate of depreciation and generally high quality make it once again the best $5000 worth of car on the market.	✔✔ ✔✔ ✔

CADILLAC OVERALL RATING... 4.1 CHECKS

QUALITY, prestige and comfort are three big reasons for Cadillac's continued success in the luxury car field. That's been true for some years, and it's true again in 1958.

Originally, however, the make established itself on the basis of continued engineering advances and progress. There have been concrete reminders of this in the past two years.

Cadillac introduced the X-type tubular center frame for 1957 and pioneered air suspension on its Eldorado Brougham.

The 62 series hardtop sedan tested was equipped with this type of suspension (standard only for Broughams, but optional for all other 1958 Cadillacs) and it showed up in the form of more comfort than ever!

Cadillac riding qualities have always been considered excellent, so the advantages of air suspension might seem only like frosting on the cake. That isn't completely accurate.

While it's true that Caddys of recent years have offered a ride that was extremely soft and smooth under most conditions, it's equally true that compromises made to obtain this softness have resulted in some adverse effects under less normal conditions.

They had a tendency to bound slightly on adverse surfaces and were not exceptionally well controlled over really bad bumps. In short, boulevard ride was outstanding, but there were a number of situations in which Cadillacs didn't react so favorably.

The air-suspended 1958 test car was quite different. Degree of ride improvement on smooth roads was difficult to measure, true. On rough surfaces or over bumps, however, this car was noticeably better than previous Cadillacs tested.

Admittedly there probably are few Caddy owners who drive their cars through the boondocks, but our road system is far from being so perfect that there is no advantage in having an automobile which furnishes a stable, controlled ride over both smooth and beat-up highways.

Even more important in many respects is that 1958 Cadillacs have far better handling qualities than those of several years back. Improvements in this area were noted when 1957 models were checked and it was encouraging to note that even more progress had been made for 1958.

A major reason for both the better ride over rough surfaces and improved handling is the new four-link suspension arrangement.

Introduced on Broughams (and new Chevrolets are using a similar setup), this design has resulted in Cadillacs having a roll center almost six inches higher than in 1957. This makes for increased stability and better cornering characteristics; body heeling and side sway is reduced markedly as compared to Cadillacs of the middle and early 1950's.

CADILLAC ROAD TEST

CADILLAC STYLING has retained its basic look for a number of years. As father of the fin it must continue the tradition. The jewel-like grille was hailed immediately by car customizers and can be seen today incorporated into a number of their productions.

BEAUTIFULLY finished interior revealed no flaws in the paint, trim or fitting. The quality throughout appeared extremely high.

Again, it's obvious that Cadillacs aren't built, or billed, as sporty-type automobiles and their buyers normally don't plan to drive them with abandon. The effortless way in which these cars cruise at high road speeds makes the extra margin of controllability in 1958 models a praiseworthy step forward, however.

This improvement, incidentally, holds true for both air-suspended Cadillacs and those with standard steel springs. (Caddys with steel springs now use coils at all four wheels; in previous years coils were used at front and semi-elliptics at the rear.) The basic suspension is the same, only difference being that air bags are substituted for the normal coil springs; the design permits easy interchangeability between the two suspension media during production.

Another virtue of air suspension as compared to steel springs, well-known by this time, is that car height remains constant regardless of amount of positioning of load. Another benefit is that a lift control handle near the steering column permits the driver of an air-suspended Cadillac to raise his car an additional five inches.

This height control is handy when tires have to be changed, when driving up steep ramps or driveways and when additional road clearance is needed for a short period.

One factor in which Cadillac has fallen behind somewhat recently is performance. One of the first makes to adopt the modern short-stroke, overhead valve V-8, Cadillac was deservedly known as

one of the "hot ones" up until a couple of years ago. This isn't the case anymore.

When the first 331-cubic-inch Caddy V-8's were introduced they were regarded as big engine. Displacement went up to 365 cubic inches in 1956 and has stayed there. Meanwhile, many newer engines have appeared and now a number of lower priced cars than Cadillac have larger, more powerful engines. Even the so-called low priced Big Three now sport powerplants of only slightly small size, either as standard equipment or extra-cost options.

The result is that Cadillacs have dropped from their former status as hot performers to the strictly mediocre class —which disturbs its makers not at all.

"We aren't building cars for drag racing," as one engineer put it last fall. "We feel our cars offer all the performance their drivers need—and can use with safety."

The point is well taken. Acceleration from a standstill is far from blinding in today's terms, but it's plenty adequate for any type of day-to-day driving. Mid-range punch is good, offering ample surge for highway passing. Top speed is well above the maximum most drivers ever use.

The current Cadillac V-8 is a much-modified version of the original 331-cubic-incher. Compression is up to 10.25-to-1 (compared to 10-to-1 in 1957) due to a redesigned combustion chamber shape, which utilizes a depression in the piston head, incidentally. Valve sizes were increased this year and a different cam

grind is now used. This has resulted in a modest 10 hp increase from last year, plus a slight torque boost (405 vs. 400 lb.-ft.).

(All Eldorados have essentially the same engine as this one, but it uses three two-barrel carburetors and is rated at 335 hp at 4800 rpm.)

Despite Cadillac's apparent unconcern about the falling prowess, relatively, of its V-8, it would not be surprising to see a new one appear in the not too-distant future.

Quality was mentioned in the beginning as a Cadillac strong point and the test car was proof that there has been no letdown.

This is just about what the test crew has come to expect, however. Cadillac is one of the few makes which, over the years MOTOR LIFE has been testing cars, has been remarkably free of the petty and annoying defects often found during the test period. This has invariably been the case with Cadillacs checked and such a record is rare enough to be worth mentioning!

Add all these things up and you begin to understand why Cadillac has maintained an even sales pace this year in the face of reduced demand. Latest figures available show the make to be less than 2,000 sales under 1957 and that it is firmly perched in the number nine sales spot—well ahead of competitors in its price class, even in front of many cars which sell for considerably less! •

Test Data

Test Car: 1958 Cadillac 62
Body Type: four-door hardtop sedan
Basic Price: $4891
Engine: ohv V-8
Carburetion: single four-barrel
Displacement: 365 cubic inches
Bore & Stroke: 4 x 3.675
Compression Ratio: 10.25-to-1
Horsepower: 310 @ 4800 rpm
Horsepower per Cubic Inch: .85
Torque: 405 lb.-ft. @ 3100
Test Weight: 4874 lbs.
Weight Distribution: 53% of weight on front wheels
Power-Weight Ratio: 15.7 lbs. per hp
Transmission: Hydra-Matic, four-speed planetary incorporating fluid coupling
Rear Axle Ratio: 3.07-to-1
Springs: Air
Steering: 4.5 turns lock-to-lock
Tires: 8.00 x 15 tubeless
Gas Mileage: 11.7 mpg average
Speedometer Error: Indicated 30, 45 and 60 mph are actual 28.5, 43 and 56.8 mph, respectively
Acceleration: 0-30 mph in 4 seconds, 0-45 mph in 6.8 and 0-60 in 11 seconds

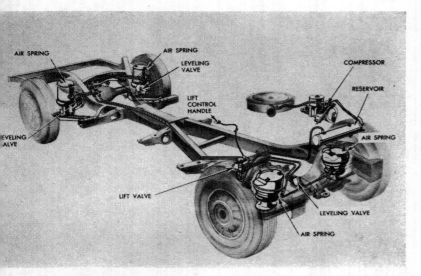

AIR SUSPENSION system was pioneered by Cadillac in its 1957 Eldorado Brougham. Although the Cadillac ride has always been good, the introduction of the air system did away with a few compromises retained for ride which had harmed handling in the past.

AN ENGINEER'S ANALYSIS
By DALE KELLY, SAE
Registered Professional Engineer

1958 CADILLAC TEST DATA

MODEL TESTED: 1958 Cadillac Series 62 four-door hardtop with four-barrel carburetor, dual exhausts, automatic transmission, power brakes, steering, seat and windows, air suspension and air conditioning. Tires: 8.20 by 15. Weight: 5128 pounds with gas tank half full (55½ percent on front, 44½ percent on rear). Rear-axle ratio: 3.36 to 1. Wheelbase: 129.5 inches. Mileage on car at time of test: 4350 miles. Barometer: 28.98 inches. Temperature: 80 degrees F. Payload: 200 lb.

ACCELERATION TIME FROM STANDING START (in seconds)

Ignition timed for:	0 to 20	0 to 40	0 to 60	0 to 80	¼ mile
Regular gasoline	3.4	7.3	13.3	21.9	19.9
Premium gasoline	3.2	6.6	12.4	21.2	19.4
Super-premium gasoline			No improvement		

(Gasoline used had the following octane ratings by Research method: Regular 90; Premium 97; Super-premium 105.)

FUEL ECONOMY (miles per gallon)

Ignition timed for:	Steady 30 m.p.h.	Steady 50 m.p.h.	Steady 70 m.p.h.	Traffic Route
Regular gasoline	19.1	15.4	13.2	7.7
Premium gasoline	20.2	15.1	12.55	7.8
Super-premium gasoline		Not tested (see Observations below)		

(In traffic test, car makes 10 full stops per mile and is driven fast enough to average 15 miles per hour.)

ESTIMATED AVERAGE ANNUAL GASOLINE BILL: $245 for 10,000 miles

(Based on all cars using premium gasoline)

SPEEDOMETER ERROR (miles per hour)

Speedometer reading	20	30	40	50	60	70	80
True speed	21	31	40	50	60	69	79

ODOMETER ERROR (miles traveled)
Odometer registered 101 miles for an actual distance of 100 miles.

DRIVER'S VISION

Driver could see part of road 20 feet in front of car, full width of road 23 feet in front of car.

GROUND CLEARANCE (unloaded car)

26 feet* 24 feet*

Worst dip that could be crossed...26-ft. radius*
Worst hump that could be crossed 24-ft. radius*
Deepest rut that could be negotiated......7.0 in.
Curb clearance for door opening..........13 in.
* See Observations below

STEERING

Steering-wheel turns for 100-ft. circle.0.80 turn
Curb-to-curb turn-circle diameter..........47 feet
Wall-to-wall turn-circle diameter..........49 feet
Steering-wheel turns, lock-to-lock......3.7 turns
CENTER OF GRAVITY: 19 inches

OBSERVATIONS

Speedometer scale has been straightened out and as a result the five-mile-per-hour intervals in the middle range (where most driving is done) are very small. Excessive chrome impairs visibility of entire panel.

With air suspension at maximum height (a separate control is used to elevate at maximum height) the radius of the worst dip drops to 19 feet, and the worst hump drops to 14 feet. This is excellent clearance. With air suspension at normal height, clearance was fair under rear overhang and relatively poor amidships. Deepest rut clearance is normally determined by the differential housing and cannot be increased by changing air-suspension height. However, with the engine dead and the air bags deflated, the front end dropped so low that a rut deeper than three inches would have stopped the car.

MISCELLANEOUS

TRUNK CAPACITY
13 cartons (one cubic foot each)
WATER RESISTANCE: Fair
Splash-pan test: No leaks. Brakes only slightly affected.
High-pressure test: Leakage at tops of all doors.

Because no acceleration improvement was noted with the spark advanced for super-premium fuel, there is no reason to use this extra-cost gasoline. Therefore, no fuel-consumption test was made with it. During full-throttle acceleration above 60, there were signs of vapor lock on two different commercial gasolines. The time to 80 m.p.h. might have been a little better in cooler weather or with a less volatile gasoline.

In spite of poor gasoline mileage in traffic, the over-all gasoline bill was no more than the average for the Chevrolet, Ford and Plymouth cars tested a few months ago.

Power-brake reserve vacuum was enough for three full applications with the engine dead. When the car was allowed to run out of gas, a little more than a gallon was required to move the pointer.

"Handles well in city traffic. More like a small car."—Louisiana Chevrolet dealer.

"Easy handling. Easy to park, power steering greatly improved."—California property owner.

"Styling. The car draws many glances and comments from people. When stopped for gas, drivers of other cars start asking questions. Neatest and best-looking car on the road."—New York physician.

"Long, smooth profile, beautiful colors."—Illinois housewife.

"No excessive flares."—Michigan foreman.

"Each line and feature reflect expert craftsmanship."—Michigan executive.

But Cadillac Is Not Perfect

Although a high percentage of Cadillac owners make no complaints at all about their cars (44.6 percent), the majority mention a few bad features. First on the complaint list is poor workmanship, followed by poor gasoline economy and body noises. Here are quotations describing these troubles:

"Not meticulous in final inspection. There is always a series of minor adjustments. Nothing serious, just annoying."—California executive.

"My first Cadillac. It should have been a dream car, especially for the price. But, alas and alack, it wasn't put together as well as the car I traded."—Maine salesman.

"Low gas mileage. It averages 9 miles per gallon in city (I got 11 and 12 on previous Cadillacs)."—Ohio chemical research director.

"I would like more gas mileage. I wish I could get two more miles per gallon (I get 14 on long trips)."—Texas salesman.

"No gas mileage. Have had it in the shop one third of the time since December 15th. They can't seem to do anything about it. I get 8 miles per gallon in the city."—Oregon club operator.

"A car costing $7000 should be engineered for quietness. All my Cadillacs (this is the 4th) rattle like a truck."—Texas investor.

"Car is not prechecked for body rattles and squeaks. It must be brought in time and again on the same complaints."—Illinois lawyer.

CADILLAC PIPES HOT AIR INTO REAR SEAT VIA A DUCT INSIDE DOOR AND A CENTER-POST GRILLE

Always the same complaint! Certainly some way can be found to catch production faults on a $7000 car before the customer finds them.

For years Cadillac owners bragged that they got more miles per gallon than small-car owners. The honeymoon seems to be over at last.

Test car had no rattles. In fact, its main virtue was its absolute quietness. It was much quieter, both in engine and road noise, than either of the other two cars. He must use his Cadillacs to round up the cattle.

SUMMARY OF CADILLAC OWNERS' OPINIONS:

OVER-ALL RATING: Excellent 80.9% Average 17.3% Poor 1.8%

Best-liked features	
Riding comfort	46.4%
Handling ease	40.2%
Exterior styling	21.4%
Power, performance	20.5%
Heavy, safe feeling	8.9%
Quiet, smooth running	11.6%
Prestige	5.4%

Most-frequent complaints	
None at all	44.6%
Poor workmanship	14.3%
Poor gas economy	13.4%
Body rattles, squeaks	11.6%
Engine noise, trouble	3.6%
Brake trouble	3.6%
Rear-view mirror location	3.6%
Poor acceleration	3.6%

Had trouble with engine?	
No trouble	89.1%
Some trouble	8.2%
Considerable trouble	2.7%

What was engine trouble?	
Carburetor	2.7%
Valve trouble	1.8%
Oil leaks	1.8%

How is dealer service?	
Excellent	60.7%
Average	30.4%
Poor	8.9%

Would buy from him again?	
Yes, would	75.9%
No, would not	36.6%
Undecided, no answer	8.0%

Have optional air suspension?	
Yes, have it	55.4%
No, do not	16.1%
No answer	76.8%

Is air suspension worth price?	
Yes, it is *(asked of those with it)*	7.1%
No, it is not	3.6%

No answer, undecided	10.7%

What make was traded?	
Cadillac	73.3%
Other GM make	8.0%
Ford Motor make	7.1%
Chrysler Corp. make	1.8%
No trade, no answer	9.8%

What make will buy next time?	
Another Cadillac	75.9%
Other GM make	0.8%
Ford Motor make	6.3%
Chrysler Corp. make	4.5%
Undecided, no answer	12.5%

What other car owned?	
Another Cadillac	8.0%
Other GM make	42.9%
Ford Motor make	14.3%
Chrysler Corp. make	5.4%
Other U.S. car	3.6%
Foreign car	2.7%
No answer	30.4%

Cadillac Owners Rate Riding Comfort First

Fourth on the complaint list is engine noise, although it is mentioned by only 3.6 percent. The same number complain about brake trouble, principally with the parking brake. Other complaints involve mirror location and poor acceleration. Here, in order of frequency of mention, are these additional owners' complaints:

"Excessive roar in exhaust system at high speeds and when taking off."—Iowa dairy farmer.

"Engine too noisy. Suspect it is because r.p.m. is away up. Noise commences at 60 miles per hour. Sounds like a truck going by in 7th gear."—California owner.

"Poorly placed parking-brake release. Could be operated more efficiently by hand knob on dash."—Maine general contractor.

"Brakes require 1000-mile attention. Won't release. Engine must be tuned every 1500 miles."—Tennessee owner.

"My only complaint is that the rear-view mirror is too low. It makes a blind spot which is very hazardous."—Wyoming retired owner.

Suggestions to Industry

Cadillac owners offer some interesting answers when asked to make one suggestion to the entire automobile industry (not just to Cadillac):

"Don't go any lower to satisfy styling at the expense of seating position."—Michigan engineer.

"Make it look like an automobile again."—New Jersey funeral director.

"Don't make the cars any longer or wider."—Pennsylvania bakery owner.

"Cut back on horsepower to increase gas mileage."—Minnesota businessman.

"Make more distinction between different cars."—Texas funeral director.

"Build a quality American car. I saw some foreign makes that seemed better built."—Pennsylvania salesman.

"Get off the emphasis on tails."—New Mexico engineer.

"For higher-price models, stop changing to cheaper styling."—Florida school principal.

"The industry tries to create a car 'out of this world' to beat its competitor, rather than to create the kind of car the average motorist really wants. The extreme fins, the wraparound windshields, increase the cost of the car and are not what the public really wants. The average American businessman would prefer a car on the conservative side."—Kentucky contractor.

More Best-Liked Features

Fourth on the best-liked list is power and performance, followed by that heavy, safe feeling of the big car. After these come roadability, quiet operation, prestige and others described in the following quotations (given in order of frequency of mention):

"Engine seems to respond promptly when power is needed."—Pennsylvania salesman.

"I like the safety factor of a heavy, well constructed car. Also it gives me prestige away from home."—California real-estate investor.

"It has a solid feeling. It's the safest feeling car on the road I have driven."—Oregon contractor.

Most cars have gone to a foot-operated parking brake. Now comes the foot-operated release. It's just another skill to be learned and it's hard to see the advantage.

CADILLAC MOUNTS ITS BATTERY IN FRONT FENDER BEHIND HEADLIGHTS—A VULNERABLE SPOT

When Cadillac owners talk like this, it is time for Detroit to get on with it!

Cadillac (nor the other two for that matter) is no car for the dragstrip. But it gets away quickly and without jerking your head back uncomfortably. You feel the power, but it doesn't kick you in the pants.

It feels so heavy that its inertia is a bit frightening. There seem to be tons in motion. Braking requires an unusual amount of pedal pressure even with power assistance.

"Well balanced. Hugs road on curves."—North Carolina executive.

"I like its absolute quietness on the road."—California retired owner.

"The name 'Cadillac' has the sound and feel of prestige due to good propaganda advertising."—Pennsylvania owner.

"Cadillac prestige."—Texas investment executive (and to prove he's most interested in prestige, he adds a complaint that there is 'not sufficient identification of Cadillac on the side of the car').

"The Cadillac is not as good as the reputation it has. It is better than most cars, but you pay for this in a number of ways. I would say that the best thing about a Cadillac is that it builds up one's ego."—Louisiana sales engineer.

"Dollar for dollar, the least expensive car to own."—Arizona sales engineer.

"I find now that I can trade Cadillac for a Cadillac about as cheap or cheaper than when I drove a new Dodge or new Buicks. My 1955 Cadillac I sold outright for cash within $950 of what I paid new at end of one year."—Michigan real estate dealer.

"Gives a durability that I have been unable to get in any other car."—Wisconsin real estate man.

"Starts good in cold weather."—Idaho farmer.

"The car has a nice view from every seat inside. Instrument panel is excellent with everything at your fingertips. The car is built solid."—Illinois motel manager.

And the Other Complaints

Mentioned by a small percentage of the total, but still by enough to be of interest are the following:

"Too much slippage in Low. Motor races and car barely moves off. Pickup speed too slow. Dangerous in heavy traffic."—Oklahoma owner.

"There is something wrong with the transmission, I think. A heavy noise that we don't like and the garage can't detect the trouble. We have been waiting two months to get it fixed, if and when a factory representative gets here."—Illinois decorator.

"Body slightly too long."—North Carolina surgeon.

"Nice car, but price much too high. Everything but the four wheels, body and steering wheel is extra cost."—Washington, D.C., executive.

"Rear springs are too soft. Car sags in the rear with very little luggage in trunk."—Ohio businessman.

"Poor paint job. Many spots are bare where body panels meet."—New Jersey housewife.

"Front grille is a car-washer's nightmare."—Ohio mechanical engineer.

"Dust fogs in the trunk and back seat when driving on country roads."—Colorado farmer.

"Window cranks are in awkward position. Difficult to use."—New Jersey executive.

"Door opener is hard to reach. Foot parking brake hard to release. I prefer a hand release."—Connecticut physician.

"Hands on the clock and the pointer on the gas gauge have little white dots on them and are very hard to read."—Texas housewife.

"I certainly don't like that 'seven minute warmup' racing period to warm up the engine in cold weather."—Illinois publisher.

That is the story of the 1958 Cadillac as told by the owners themselves—owners from all over the country who know the car best.

Balance is something you can't measure — you have to feel it. Railton ranks Imperial best in this department. You should drive all three and make your own judgment.

There's no sin in buying a car to build up your ego. The error comes when you buy it for this reason, but justify it on other grounds.

He must have latched onto a live one!

CADILLAC'S FRONT DOOR HAS A CLUTTER OF HANDLES, NOT ALL OF WHICH ARE WELL POSITIONED

Added comments: Seats of excellent height and comfortable. Very good speedometer dial. Vent and heat controls simple and convenient. Ash trays handy, lighter location not. Steering not so precise as in the other two cars, seems to have less road sense too. Front end shakes on washboard. Ride too soft on undulating roads. Fuel-gauge needle a masterpiece of uncertainty. A huge dot on end of needle covers almost a quarter of the scale. Heater blower runs all time heat is needed. Extreme display of chrome on dashboard seems out of place in a top-drawer car. Some windshield reflections at night. Vacuum wipers slow down on acceleration, just when most needed. High-beam indicator lamp almost invisible, as are the hands of the clock.

CADILLAC ROAD TEST
(*Continued from page 45*)

of engine quietness, the mileage benefits of top gear are lost. It would not be surprising if GM shortly produced some kind of visual reminder for forgetful motorists in this respect.

Cadillac's heat and ventilating system employs the cowl intake, with warm air conducted through the vented front door panel to the rear seat area. The arrangement is an elaborate one, but is simply controlled and highly functional. Unlike many modern cars, it can be mastered without undue study of the owner's manual furnished by the division.

Today's wrap-around windshields have created an annoying situation caused by wipers which are inadequate for the curved glass. On Cadillac, a cam guides the blades effectively around the curve, wiping cleanly to within two inches of the corner posts. The windshield washer-wiper system is fully automatic—touch of a button puts both into operation and the cutoff takes place a few seconds later without further attention.

Additional evidence of manufacturing care can be found inside the vast trunk, which is upholstered more luxuriously than the passenger compartments of many other automobiles. Cadillac provides its owners with a rubber covered lug wrench, jack is fixed to the floor in a non-rattling position by a spring, while a triangular piece of wood (painted black) is included for blocking the tires while jacking.

Cadillac likes to point out that some of its models cost no more than comparable cars in other makes. This is true, but in order to enjoy many of the features commented upon here, you will have to pay a high price. As of this moment, a fully equipped Cadillac is one of the costliest American cars on the road.

On the other hand, Cadillac depreciates at a slower rate than almost any other car. This, along with good mileage and dependability, gives the expensive vehicle certain qualities of economy. It's a paradoxical situation, but actually an honest argument which Cadillac salesmen have found highly effective. ●

SPECIFICATIONS

TEST CAR: 1955 Cadillac Fleetwood Series 60 Special sedan.
ENGINE: ohv V-8. Bore 3¹³⁄₁₆, stroke 3⅝. Displacement 331 cubic inches. Compression ratio 9 to 1. Bhp 250 at 4600 rpm. Torque 345 ft.-lbs. at 2800 rpm. Crankcase capacity (with filter) 6 quarts. Fuel tank capacity 20 gallons. Cooling system capacity (with heater) 22 quarts. Electrical system 12 volts.
TRANSMISSION: Hydra-Matic standard on all models is dual-range with four forward speeds and fluid coupling. Ratios: 1st 3.82, 2nd 2.63, 3rd 1.45, 4th 1.0, reverse 4.03. Rear axle ratio: standard 3.36, optional 3.07.
OVERALL DIMENSIONS: Wheelbase 129 inches. Tread 60 front, 63 rear. Length 227.3, width 80, height 62.1. Dry weight 4540 lbs. Turning circle 45 feet. Tire size 8.00 x 15 tubeless.
PRICES: Series 60 Special four-door sedan $4728. Radio $214. Power brakes $47. Electric seat adjustment $53.

'55 Cadillac
(*Continued from page* 42)
built some five or six Cadillac engines a day. He took pride and a personal responsibility. A progressive assembly line precludes this type of workman, so recourse must be had to posters, more time for a given operation, and most important, quality control. This last starts with the dealer pipeline which funnels in product information reports (PIRs) on manufacturing and design failures. Dealers would soon lose interest in PIRs if they were not acted upon immediately, so they are—religiously. These spot the workman at fault, and if it lies with his methods or machine (and not a chronic Monday hangover), this operation becomes subject to statistical quality control which ranges from a sampling to inspection of every part produced. Cadillac was not the first to do this, but they probably developed the system to a greater degree than any of their competitors. Every machine tool operator in the plant has his production charted. Posted by the machine, these show if he goofed, when, and how often.

CONTINUED FROM PAGE 59
Brougham from nosing down during fast stops.

The Brougham has a four headlamp lighting system like that pioneered by its original prototype, the 1955 GM Motorama show car.

This system uses outer lamps with both high and low beams; these lamps are for city driving. Low beam has more wattage than standard single lamps.

Thus, improved low beam illumination is provided. High beam of the outer lamps gives a soft, general lighting.

Inner lamps have a high beam only; actually, they furnish a kind of spotlight effect. They are used along with high beam of the outer lamps for highway and country driving.

Combined wattage of these four lamps is much greater than two-lamp systems and furnishes better illumination. In addition, the light is so directed that a driver gets maximum vision without creating a glare to blind drivers of oncoming cars.

The Brougham's power train is similar to standard Cadillacs. The Hydra-Matic transmission is mounted conventionally right behind the engine.

There are no center pillars in the Brougham. Instead, locking plates, 14 inches from the floor, provide latching points for rotary-type door locks.

Gadget lovers will have a field day with this new Cadillac. Just about everything that can be power-operated is! This includes seats, all windows (including vents), trunk lid, etc.

Power steering, power brakes and air conditioning are standard equipment. There are special heaters for both front and rear seats and Broughams all will have all-transistorized radios. (Radio antennas are power-operated—naturally—and rise automatically to "city height" when the radio is turned on. They can be raised to full height for maximum range by means of an overriding switch for country driving. The antennas automatically retract into fender wells when radio or ignition is turned off!)

Brougham styling shows its Cadillac relationship very clearly. Such typical identification features as the grille and rear fenders are retained.

An interesting construction note, however, is the one-piece front end. Fenders are made of one piece which is continuous across the front of the car above the grille. It is to this crossover panel that the forward-hinged hood is attached.

The huge compound curved windshield rakes back sharply to the roof line. Both windshield and backlight are made of tinted E-Z Eye glass to cut glare.

The price tag for the Brougham had not been announced at the time this report was written. However, it very likely will exceed $10,000. And, even at these unusual figures, Cadillac undoubtedly will be able to sell all it can make, and will no doubt give Continental a rough time for "Prestige Car" honors in 1957. ●

CADILLACS for the coming year have striking styling features, notably the "rocket" tail and dummy rear grille seen on the series 62 coupé below, and the massive frontal treatment and the curved pillars flanking a huge wraparound and wrapover screen seen in the four-door sedan on the right.

AMERICANS for 1959

CADILLAC

MORE power is provided for buyers of 1959-model Cadillacs, a new V-8 engine having the swept volume enlarged from 5,980 c.c. to 6,375 c.c. by a ¼-in. increase in piston stroke. Running with a 10½/1 compression ratio, in place of the 10¼/1 used last year, this bigger engine is catalogued as giving 325 b.h.p. in normal form with one four-choke carburetter, whilst a "Q" engine with three twin-choke carburetters provides another 20 b.h.p. and a slight torque increase. The extra engine displacement has allowed a 2.94/1 top gear to be standardized, in place of the 3.07 ratio used last year, so that there should be little increase in fuel consumption.

Use of an X-type chassis continues, as does the optional self-trimming air suspension which is an alternative to four coil springs. More consistent riding is claimed to result from use of non-foaming hydraulic shock absorbers of telescopic pattern, in which Freon-12 trapped inside a plastic sleeve replaces air as the expansion medium. Detail improvements have been made in the power steering, power brakes and automatic choke, all designed to make driving easier.

Pictures show the shape of these 1959 Cadillacs, which are produced as the simplest "60 series," a more luxurious "62 series" which includes the Eldorado models, and a "Fleetwood 75 series" of formal 8-seaters on long-wheelbase chassis. More glass area is featured by all models, and the optional heating and air-conditioning (refrigeration) systems are improved to give greater rear-seat comfort in extremes of weather. Cruise Control which will govern the car's cruising speed at any desired level on motorways is optional, as are electric door locks and an electrically lifted boot lid.

1959 CADILLAC SPECIFICATION

Cylinders	.. .. .. V-8	Wheelbase 10 ft. 10 in. (limousine,	
Bore..	.. .. 101.6 mm.		12 ft. 5¾ in.)
Stroke ..	.. .. 98.4 mm.	Overall length 18 ft. 9 in. (limousine,	
Cubic capacity	.. 6,375 c.c.		20 ft. 4¾ in.)
Piston area	.. 100.5 sq. in.	Overall height 4 ft. 5¾ in. to 4 ft.	
Valves ..	.. Pushrod o.h.v.		11¼ in.
Compression ratio	.. 10.5	Turning circle.. 47 ft. (limousine,	
Max. power (gross) 325 or 345 b.h.p.			49¼ ft.)
at	.. .. 4,800 r.p.m.	Brake lining area .. 210.3 sq. in.	
Max b.m.e.p. .. 167 lb./sq. in. at		Tyre size .. 8.00-15 (Eldorado,	
	3,100 r.p.m. or 169		8.20-15)
	lb./sq. in. at 3,400	Top gear m.p.h. at 1,000 r.p.m. 28.7	
	r.p.m.	(with 2.94 axle ratio)	
Top Gear ratio	2.94/1 (3.21 on	Top gear m.p.h. at 1,000 ft./min.	
	Eldorado, 3.36 or	piston speed 44.5	
	3.77 on limousines)		

DE SOTO face lifting for 1959 is the first new season's programme to be announced from the Chrysler group of companies. An innovation which will be welcome on such low-built cars is the use of seats which swivel through 40° to facilitate entry or exit, and the push-button control fashion is extended from the automatic transmission to the interior heater. Also standardized is an oval steering wheel, power steering being optional. On the technical side, there is a new combination of the existing torsion-bar front suspension with pneumatic rear springs which are self-adjusting to suit whatever load is being carried. Most powerful of a range of alternative engines is the Adventurer V-8 developing a gross power output of 350 b.h.p.

Determined to retain top spot in the luxury car field, Cadillac has made major appearance and technical changes in its cars for 1959. Styling especially is more different than in recent years and engineering modifications are aimed at improving already approved factors.

THE 1959 CADILLAC

STYLING

NO SECOND look will be necessary to identify Cadillacs for 1959 as completely new cars. They retain some basic styling resemblance to earlier models, but to much less a degree than has been true for some years. The process of evolutionary change hasn't been discarded completely but it definitely has been accelerated.

One familiar Cadillac trademark now missing is the "Dagmar" front bumper with its rubber-tipped, bullet-shaped guards. The new design, slightly less massive in appearance, is set low across the front of the car and has parking and turn signal lights set deeply in oval recesses.

The grille has a texture somewhat reminiscent of the egg-crate types long used by Cadillac but fender and hood changes make its shape completely different.

The hood now extends to the fender crown; the dividing line parallels the crown molding on the fender.

The greenhouse, or roof and window area, has been changed considerably. Front corner posts are more upright, do not have the reverse angle slope that has characterized past models. Rear roof pillars flow back and down to the deck, no longer slant forward sharply to the leading edge of the rear fenders.

Glass area has been greatly increased —the most ever used by Cadillac. There is more than 450 square inches more glass area in the 62 series sedan than in the same 1958 model, for example.

Rear view of new Cadillacs is dominated by pronounced fins. Pods mounted on each side of these fins contain stop, turn signals and taillights. Large back-up lights are mounted in chrome housings at the outer edges of the huge rear bumper. A small grille section, similar to the one at front, is set above the bumper.

All models again this year are hardtops, without a center roof pillar, but a new four-window sedan body style has been added in two series.

The four-window sedan has four side windows with a large wraparound rear window. The standard sedan has six side windows, including two small ones at rear, and a normal rear window.

The 1959 Cadillac line consists of six series of cars: five standard series (60, 62, 63, 64 and 67) which feature 12 body styles and the Eldorado Brougham series with just the one custom sedan body style.

There is more standardization of dimensions between series than in the past. Except for Brougham and eight-passenger Fleetwood models, all have a 130-inch wheelbase and overall length of 225 inches. Overall height varies according to body style, but is much lower than last year in all cases.

The 62 sedan is just 56.2 inches high, compared to 59.1 inches for the same model last year. The 62 four-window sedan is even lower—53.7 inches! Fleetwood 60 Specials are down from 59.1 to 56.2 inches also and Eldorado Biarritz models have dropped a full four inches— from 58.4 to 54.4.

Despite these decreases in overall height, interior dimensions have not changed greatly from last year. In 62 sedans, for example, front headroom is 34.8 inches compared to 35 inches last year; rear headroom has been decreased from 34.9 to 33.2 inches. Front legroom has gone up from 45 to 45.6 inches and rear legroom is 45.3 inches compared to 45.2 in 1958.

ENGINEERING

Engineering changes by Cadillac for 1959 include more powerful engines; a new shock absorber design and other sus-

PRONOUNCED FINS dominate rear view. Pods mounted on each side of fins contain stop, turn signal and taillights. Small grille section, similar to front, sits above bumper.

pension modifications aimed at smoother, more stable ride; improved power brake and steering systems, and a number of alterations made necessary by the new body design.

Cadillac's V-8 is basically similar to the 365-cubic-inch powerplant used in 1958 but displacement has been increased to 390 inches by lengthening its stroke from 3.625 to 3.875 inches. Stroke remains four inches. Compression ratio has been raised from 10.25-to-1 to 10.5-to-1.

These changes have upped horsepower ratings from 310 at 4800 rpm to 325 at 4800. (Torque has gone from 405 to 440 foot pounds at 3100 rpm.) This is for standard engines equipped with four-barrel carburetors.

Another version of this V-8, using three two-barrel carburetors, is again being offered. It is rated at 345 hp at 4800 rpm. This "Q" engine is standard for all Eldorados, optional for all other models.

Automatic choke control has been moved into the exhaust area of the intake manifold for quicker response and an automatic temperature compensator incorporated for improved idle operation. Intake manifolds have been redesigned with larger passages and exhaust valve shape has been streamlined for improved fuel flow.

Cadillac engineers are enthusiastic about their new shock absorbers for 1959. They are unique in that they have enclosed plastic bags of Freon-12 replacing the air normally used in conventional shocks!

The bags of Freon-12 fit in the chamber above the shock absorber piston. The captive gas can't escape to mingle with shock absorber fluid—as sometimes happens with conventional units—and thus hinder efficient shock absorber action.

Otherwise, Cadillac's standard steel suspension is similar to that used in 1958 models. Coil springs are used at all four wheels, with four-link trailing arms at rear. One arm on each side attaches to frame outriggers and runs back to the axle, positioning it laterally. A control yoke attaches to the differential cage and is hinged to a rear frame crossmember.

This design permits ready installation of optional air suspension (air springing is standard only for Broughams) at the factory. This suspension system is essentially the same as in 1958, but new valving and other refinements have been incorporated as a result of a year's experience. The accumulator tank design has also been changed from a long slim shape mounted horizontally to a short, squat type mounted vertically.

Only important brake change is a new direct-acting power brake booster of larger capacity than last year. A new rotary valve giving improved response and a larger capacity pump are used in Cadillac's power steering system; this results in an overall steering ratio of 19.1-to-1 and faster steering. Turn circle diameter, however, has increased on most models from 43.4 to 47 feet.

Standard rear axle ratios have been lowered numerically from 3.07 to 2.94-to-1. (Air conditioned cars and those with "Q" engines will use 3.21 axles.) This should help economy but will probably cancel out any performance advantages of the bigger, higher torque V-8. Axle gear teeth design has been changed to quiet gear noise.

Just how the changes for 1959, par-

ROOF AREA of the two-door Cadillac is kept to an absolute minimum. Sweeping front and rear windows cut the top to dimensions not much larger than a card table.

DASH AND CONTROL area still bespeaks the quality that has made GM's big production the coin of the luxury realm. Appointments are plush, interior comfort is high.

ticularly the styling, will affect sales will be interesting to follow. Whether the more abrupt break with the past will make more owners feel their earlier models are obsolete and spur them to buy new Cadillacs, or whether they will rebel at the less conservative approach remains to be seen. ●

CADILLAC

By JIM WHIPPLE

THE LONG, low, sleek lines of the 1959 Cadillac not only tell you that it's a brand-new body but may also give a clue to the fact that it's a much changed car in all respects. Don't worry, it still has all the quality of material and perfection of assembly and finish that have pretty much made it the standard against which other cars are measured. But, the '59 Caddy is quite a bit different from the solid, high-crowned models of years past.

It looks lower and *is* lower. Sedans have dropped from 58 and 59 inches to 56 inches in overall height, while some of the hardtops are down to 54 inches—as low as any car in the industry, barring the Corvette and Thunderbird. Headroom has been shaved a little too—from a roomy 34 and 35 inches down to 33 and 34 inches.

Seat-cushion heights have dropped, too—in some models as much as three inches. The front seat on the Sixty Special sedan, for example, is 9½ inches above the floor. A seat as low as this would have seemed out of place in anything but a sports car just a few years back.

Rear cushions have been dropped less in relation to the floor in sedans due to the fact that designers have been able to lower the floor without interference from the wasp-waisted, X-type frame.

The transmission housing and driveshaft tunnel take up just a bit more of the passenger compartment than in '57 and '58 models and have limited the size and comfort of the center-of-the-seat areas somewhat. Seating positions—particularly in the front compartment—require more stretch-out and less sit-up than the higher seats. For driver-comfort I found the six-way power seat a real boon.

In the Coupe DeVille test-car I was able to maneuver into a very comfortable position by powering the seat all the way to the rear of its travel, elevating it for proper vision and tilting it forward to find the most comfortable reach. Cadillac's designers have left no surface uncushioned and made all details work for passenger comfort.

PERSONALITY

The new, lower bodies have helped change Cadillac's road personality as well as make it one of the sleekest looking jobs that ever came down the pike. The center of gravity is lower and as a result—even though little change has been made in the suspension—the car is more stable and handles better than last year's model. And the '58 handled very well indeed. Now that Cadillac's weight has been brought as close to the road as that of its competition, it turns out to be a very stable, road-hugging car.

I took the Coupe DeVille out into a favorite test area of mine, an almost deserted and forgotten stretch of sadly beat-up and broken concrete. It's a road on which almost no engineering

Cadillac is the car for you

if... You want the most desired car in the U.S.

if... You want the inner satisfaction of knowing that you own the best all-around engineering job to come out of a U.S. auto plant.

if... You like the idea of a really luxurious car that does not sacrifice anything in roadability or ease of handling.

if... You're interested in getting all the quality and fine workmanship you're paying for.

CADILLAC SPECIFICATIONS

ENGINE	V-8	"Q" V-8
Bore and stroke	4 in. x 3.875 in.	4 in. x 3.875 in.
Displacement	390 cu. in.	390 cu. in.
Compression ratio	10.5:1	10.5:1
Max. brake horsepower	325 @ 4800 rpm	345 @ 4800 rpm
Max. torque	430 @ 3100 rpm	435 @ 3400 rpm
DIMENSIONS		
Wheelbase	130 in.	
Overall length	225 in.	
Overall width	80.3 in.	
Overall height	53.7 in.-56.2 in.	
TRANSMISSIONS Hydra-Matic		

At $13,075 factory A.D.P., there is no optional equipment on this Eldorado Brougham—everything is standard. Only 4-door hardtop is available.

Distinctive high fins of '59 set off the Cadillac on any street. Thin roof overhangs huge rear window.

Distinctive front end of Cadillac balances twin headlights with dual parking lights. Hood is extra wide for easy engine access.

skill at all was wasted when it was built some 35 years ago. There are four solid miles of serpentine curves of varying radius—most of 'em tight—all of which are banked in the wrong direction. When this road is lightly powdered with snow or sleeted over, it takes everything you've got to keep out of the ditches at 20 mph.

I took the Caddy over this stretch —happily dry at the time—at 40 to 55 mph, holding the transmission in third gear at all times. The tires screamed 'till it sounded like the zoo at feeding time, but 5000 lbs of well-balanced Cadillac stayed right where my fingertips put it. The initial response when swinging from a left-hand curve to a sharp right was the mushy beginning of a dive—or plowing—when the rapid transfer of weight from one side of the car to the other squashed the soft tires and caused a slight roll effect until the tire was compressed enough to resist. Raising the pressure from an underinflation of 24 (26 is recommended) to 28 lbs. sq. in. not only cured it, but gave the car an amazing feeling of rock-solid stability.

This trip over the serpentine gave me a great deal of respect for Cadillac's power steering—improved this year with a rotary valve. It's the best

power steering in the business today. The engineers at GM's Saginaw Division have managed to overcome all power-steering problems. The touch on the wheel is feather-light, yet not so delicately responsive that you feel in danger of swerving when you apply sudden pressure. There is good feedback of road feel in that you can pretty well gauge how much you need to increase the turn-angle of the front wheels to overcome the understeer tendencies. There is also good self-centering action—a function of front-end geometry sometimes blotted out by power steering.

In short, Cadillac power steering gives perfect two-way communication between driver and road—never interfering, and helping the driver just as much as he needs and no more.

RIDING QUALITIES

Cadillac's ride has been good in most recent years—especially in the area of control of dip and bounce. When the new coil-spring rear suspension first came out, the resultant riding qualities weren't up to those provided by the long leaf springs of earlier models. This year however, they've really hit the mark. The car

rode as level as any I've ever driven, including the fabulous Citroen DS-19. Bumps in the road displace the wheels most of their length of travel before the body begins to rise gently for a short distance.

Without a detailed analysis, let me simply say that I feel Cadillac's ride is now the best in the luxury—or any other—price field. The competition is terrific and comes very close, but this year, for the first time in recent years, Cadillac is the best.

The '59 engine is somewhat larger, displacing 390 inches instead of 365. Horsepower is up only 15—now rated at 325—but torque, the real measure of working power in the mid-speed ranges, has been increased. This has enabled Cadillac engineers to lower the numerical ratio of the rear axle to 2.9 so that the engine turns over more slowly. As a result, the engine ticks over lazily at 35 or 40—giving surprisingly high mileage and making no audible sound.

Hydra-Matic transmission, standard on all Cads, is the best of the automatics, for my money. It has positive action in four well-spaced ratios, yet the changes between them are butter-smooth and can only be noticed under full-throttle acceleration.

The big, smooth-running Cad engine

At left is the Fleetwood Sixty Special hardtop sedan, stylized by convex scoop on rear side panel.

Instrument panel features cruise control at upper left, driver can select desired speed and maintain it without any accelerator pressure.

is the other half of a perfect power team. Its high ratio provides easy, quiet, economical cruising, yet can be dropped into third for rocketlike acceleration either by flooring the throttle at any speed below 65, or by moving the selector lever to third position at part-throttle. This move provides a nice boost in power for hill-climbing without wasteful, over-powering full-throttle operation.

Driver vision is excellent over the smooth, flat hood, providing you have adjusted the power seat properly. Instrument layout has been improved and somebody up there at Cadillac listened to our previous pleas and toned down the chrome around the dials, which had proved annoyingly dazzling in past years.

The workmanship throughout the Cadillac, whether it be paint finish, fit of trim or upholstery, is the best currently available on a production automobile this side of the Atlantic, and after all, what more can you say than that?

SUMMING UP

Cadillac is a large, superbly engineered and beautifully built automobile that's hard to fault in any respect. ●

CADILLAC CHECK LIST

5 CHECKS MEAN TOP RATING IN ITS PRICE CLASS

PERFORMANCE	Although Cadillac does not top its class in acceleration or all-out power, its exceptionally smooth-running and quiet engine gives smooth, powerful and flexible performance in all speed ranges.	✔✔ / ✔✔ (4)
STYLING	Personal opinion is everything in this category. We feel that the sweeping contours and mercifully chrome-free surfaces of Cadillac make it one of the most beautiful cars we've ever seen—but we have our doubts about those fins and the "ice-tray" grilles.	✔✔ / ✔✔ (4)
RIDING COMFORT	By a narrow but discernible margin, Cadillac has the best ride in its class and in the industry. It is extremely soft yet not overly mushy, it is very well-controlled yet not harsh, and vibration is nearly non-existent.	✔✔✔ / ✔✔ (5)
ROADABILITY	Cadillac has improved roadability, coming very close to the best in its class. Its behavior is precise and predictably safe at all times.	✔✔ / ✔✔ (4)
INTERIOR DESIGN	The questionable advantages of a lower silhouette and the undoubted benefits of a lower center of gravity are the result of space taken from the important vertical dimensions that have made exit and entry more difficult than before. Body width and legroom leave nothing to be desired for all but center of seat passengers.	✔✔ / ✔✔ (4)
EASE OF CONTROL	Top-notch power steering, easy-acting power brakes and a well-balanced suspension system, plus flexible Hydra-Matic make the Cadillac surprisingly light and easy to handle for a 5000-lb car.	✔✔✔ / ✔✔ (5)
ECONOMY	Hydra-Matic and a well-engineered power plant will give the conservative driver surprisingly good mileage per gallon of premium fuel. Mileage will not quite equal the fabulous 17 and 18 miles-per-gallon performance of some earlier models.	✔✔ / ✔✔ (4)
SERVICEABILITY	The Cadillac isn't a particularly easy car to service and service will not be cheap if it's properly done, however, the amount of servicing required has been lower than average in recent years.	✔✔ / ✔✔ (4)
WORKMANSHIP	There is hardly an area throughout the car, be it upholstery, paint, trim or operation of hardware and controls, which cannot be described simply as "The Best."	✔✔✔ / ✔✔ (5)
VALUE PER DOLLAR	Cadillac has had the lowest depreciation in its field for years. There are waiting lists for used Cadillacs. This year's models live up to the quality of past years in every way. For those who can afford it, the Cadillac is a top transportation buy.	✔✔✔ / ✔✔ (5)

CADILLAC OVERALL RATING... 4.4 CHECKS

1959
ROAD TEST

WHERE there once was a wide range of choice in upper bracket American-made luxury cars, the field in recent years has been reduced to just three names: Cadillac, Lincoln and Imperial. This trio is likely to remain unchallenged by any domestic newcomer, at least in significant volume, and each make seems to have a promising future.

The chief objective in this limited class, aside from the prestige of driving a more costly vehicle, is massive luxury, supported by a higher degree of quality. On the massive luxury point there is some threat from the middle priced cars which have constantly been raising their stand-

1959 it has undergone major changes that accompany a new design. Only unaltered components are the engine, which has been carefully refined over a 10-year period, and the pioneer Hydramatic transmission.

The rest of the chassis was new in 1958 and its principal distinguishing feature is the cruciform or "hourglass"-type frame. Although air springing is available, the test car had the traditional coil and A-arm in front, matched by coils with trailing links at the rear.

In a straight line at moderate speeds, or in city cruising, the Cadillac is masterfully smooth. Flaws are noted only at high speeds, when some swaying motion sets in, and in fast corners when the tires protest loudly as the heavyweight goes through a bend. Under certain conditions on rough roads it appeared that the frame was actually flexing, as the car developed an overall quiver. During hard acceleration runs there was no wheel spin.

Fuel consumption was creditable for a car of this size. While the average for all driving was 11.7 mpg, with cautious operation during one phase of the testing a top of 22 mpg was registered for 150 miles from the center of a metropolitan area.

Cadillac's strongest claim to superiority is its unmatched feeling of luxury and quality. When riding in this car, the almost soundless operation coupled with rich materials and fine assembly produce the desired effect: you know that this is an expensive and luxurious automobile. One is never in doubt.

The interior is Cadillac's best to date. The instruments are the most legible of any GM car, deeply recessed in padded cavities. Electric latches, not an exclusive feature, permit locking of all doors with one switch, which is surprisingly handy and convenient.

Imperial in its 1959 model has some advantages. The major one is better handling qualities, although not as good as some of the lighter Chrysler Corporation

CADILLAC AND IMPERIAL

ards. As yet, however, the prestige trio is more secure in its position than any other category of U.S. cars.

The real differences between these cars are often subtle and slight. Performance is relatively adequate by today's averages, with no apparent effort at outstanding accelerating ability in keeping with the conservative requirements of dignity. Distinctive features are largely on the surface, a matter of styling and appointments rather than extreme basic design.

Two of these luxury cars, a Cadillac four-door hardtop of the most popular series, and the rarer Imperial convertible, were recently tested. While two such body types were certain to produce different results, they do make an interesting study.

Cadillac is the more noteworthy this year, not only because it still is the undisputed leader in this class, but because in

CADILLAC FRONT AND REAR is massive as ever, but sleeker. The flamboyant fins are as controversial as they were 10 years ago.

IMPERIAL LOOKS GOOD but needs greater distinction from the Chrysler line in order to match its rivals in the luxury class.

One is nearly all-new—and one is not. But the differences that count are not revolutionary features. Solid luxury is the word

a heavy steel plate X-member assembly for the convertible body type. It is this and similar strengthening elsewhere that adds to the car's weight.

The Imperial's handicap in its field is not that it is a lesser car, which it positively is not, but that it is a comparatively new name alongside Cadillac and Lincoln. Some years will be required to develop its personality. Another limiting factor is Imperial's close relationship with Chrysler —much closer than, say, Cadillac is to Buick or Lincoln is to Mercury. A greater separation is necessary for prestige and distinction.

Cadillac, in 1959, unquestionably remains the leader in this exclusive class and it has earned the right again through production quality and engineering of details. Imperial may be more roadable and may even possess some advantages in style, and in performance potential, but these are almost secondary factors. Magnificent massive luxury is the mark. ●

vehicles. Nonetheless it corners well, travels at high speeds with a surer degree of control.

The acceleration figures for the test convertible do not reflect the normal ability of the Imperial, which in lighter body types would be a second or two quicker.

The Imperial, of course, is much the same car it was in 1958. The minor facelift included lowering of the headlights and locating them in the dual chromed pods which project forward of the front fender. The grille has been dressed up so that it no longer consists of the simple patterns of straight bars. In general, the alterations have not improved the appearance of the car, and it might have been better left as it was in the preceding year.

The instrument panel is definitely less desirable than 1958, when it was a more logical arrangement. Night reading of dials is easier than by daylight.

Frame of the Imperial is conventional boxed outside frame rails, universal in Chrysler products, with the addition of

Test Data

Test Car: 1959 Imperial
Body Type: Convertible
Basic Price: $5773
Engine: V-8
Carburetion: Single four-barrel
Displacement: 413 cubic inches
Bore & Stroke: 4.18 x 3.75
Compression Ratio: 10.1-to-1
Horsepower: 350
Horsepower per cubic inch: .84
Torque: 470 lb.-ft @ 2800 rpm
Engine speed: 2000 rpm @ 60 mph
Test Weight: 4910 lbs. without driver
Weight Distribution: 55 per cent on front wheels
Power-Weight Ratio: 14.02 lbs. per horsepower
Transmission: Torqueflite
Rear Axle Ratio: 2.93
Steering: 3½ turns lock-to-lock
Dimensions: overall length 226 inches, width 81, height 57, wheelbase 129
Springs: Torsion-bar front, leaf rear
Gas Mileage: 11.5
Speedometer Error: Indicated 30, 45 and 60 mph are actual 32, 46½ and 61 mph, respectively
Acceleration: 0-30 mph in 4.0 seconds, 0-45 in 7.2 and 0-60 in 12.2

Test Data

Test Car: 1959 Cadillac
Body Type: Four-door sedan
Basic Price: $5498
Engine: V-8
Carburetion: Single four-barrel
Displacement: 390 cubic inches
Bore & Stroke: 4 x 3.875
Compression Ratio: 10.5-to-1
Horsepower: 325 @ 4800 rpm
Horsepower per cubic inch: .83
Torque: 430 lb.-ft @ 3100 rpm
Engine speed: 2200 rpm @ 60 mph
Test Weight: 5160 lbs. without driver
Weight Distribution: 52 per cent on front wheels
Power-Weight Ratio: 15.8 lbs. per horsepower
Transmission: Dual Range Hydramatic
Rear Axle Ratio: 2.94
Steering: 4 turns lock-to-lock
Dimensions: overall length 225 inches, width 81, height 56, wheelbase 130
Springs: Coil
Gas Mileage: 11.7
Speedometer Error: Indicated 30, 45 and 60 mph are actual 26½, 39 and 52 mph, respectively
Acceleration: 0-30 mph in 3.8 seconds, 0-45 mph in 6.4 and 0-60 mph in 10.3

"Quiet elegance" is the way Cadillac describes the instrument panel of the Eldorado Brougham. Instruments are well clustered, recessed, raised closer to eye level. All equipment is powered and is standard, including windows, ventipanes, steering, brakes, seats and door locks. Other standard features include "cruise control" and air conditioning.

ELEGANT

Custom-designed and custom-built, Cadillac's Eldorado Brougham continues as a limited production car—for the "not-so-limited" few.

A new (and necessary) innovation is in the rear quarter panel window. As the rear door is opened, the window slides into a recess for easier passenger entry. As the door is closed, it returns to its original position. The window can also be operated in the normal manner from the inside.

Interior appointments of the Brougham shout quality, from the mouton carpeting, to the broadcloth upholstery, to the courtesy lights, to the way that the car is finished. Extra storage for small, valuable items is possible in two lockable compartments in the package shelf behind the rear seat. (It's a safety feature, too.)

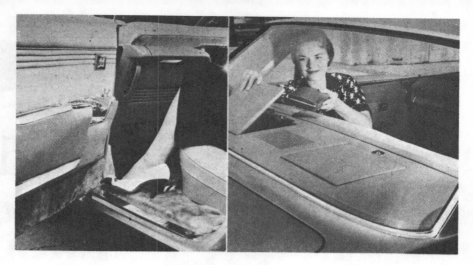

ELDORADO

IN **STYLING, CRAFTSMANSHIP,** interior luxury and attention to every detail, the Brougham has no peer. It is the true monarch in Cadillac's realm of motoring majesty for 1959." So said James M. Roche, general manager of Cadillac, when this GM division introduced the car at the Chicago International Auto Show in January of this year.

Until recently, we had to take him at his word, for these $13,075 luxury cars were as scarce as the proverbial hen's teeth. Now, however, we have been able to look over a virtual bevy of them that were being prepared for customers in the special shop set aside for this purpose in Detroit. And we'll have to admit: styling, craftsmanship and interior luxury are all far better than on most any car we've seen.

The cars get their beginning at Cadillac, where the parts are built, pre-assembled, crated and shipped off to Italy. There, Pinin Farina drops on the body he has built for it, installs the interior, finishes it off and sends it back to Detroit. Final touch-up, including finish painting, polishing and tune, is given to the cars and then they're whisked away to dealers for delivery to lucky customers.

The entire trunk of the Eldorado Brougham is covered with a nylon frieze material, including the decklid, the spare tire (laid horizontally) and the fold-down cover over the battery. Though the trunk is not as great in cubic space as some cars, it still holds ample luggage.

Cadillac's
ELDORADO
BROUGHAM

AMERICA'S COSTLIEST CAR, the Cadillac Eldorado Brougham has never before been subjected to impartial analysis. Though it has 345 hp, weight of special equipment slows its performance.

TWO STORAGE COMPARTMENTS, recessed into the shelf behind the rear seat, typify the details to be found in the Brougham. Each holds almost a cubic foot and can be individually locked.

by John Lawlor

FABULOUSLY expensive automobiles are not only interesting in themselves, they provide exacting standards by which lesser vehicles can be judged. Thus, MOTOR LIFE has published reports on such cars as the Continental Mark II, the Rolls-Royce Silver Cloud and, now, the Cadillac Eldorado Brougham.

The Brougham was made available by George Barris, the well-known customizing and paint expert, who had just given it a beautiful pearlescent green finish for the new owner. Time did not permit a full road test but the car was driven over as many road surfaces as possible and basic performance figures were recorded.

Essentially, the Brougham is a regular Cadillac with a custom-built body and most every known item of special equipment included as standard.

The body is a Cadillac design with a Fleetwood label but is actually built by Italy's Pinin Farina.

Barris pointed out several details of Farina's workmanship to the test crew. Seams are hammer welded without the use of solder, potential rust spots have been filled with sealer, the chrome trim is made from brass castings and protective flanges

TRIPLE CARBURETOR ENGINE, also used in Eldorado coupe and convertible, is buried under plumbing for accessories. Small two-cylinder motor at lower left is air suspension compressor.

under the car prevent the rocker panel scraping on steep driveways.

As one would expect, the hood, trunk and doors all fit perfectly. Tolerances along the panel edges do not vary a fraction of an inch.

The trunk, though smaller than usual, is fully carpeted with matching covers for the spare tire and battery, which balance each other at opposite sides of the compartment.

When a rear door is opened, the quarter window slides back a couple of inches to allow more room for entry and exit. The usefulness of this feature was proven on the test car when one of the windows jammed and made it noticeably more difficult to pass through the narrow door opening.

The windshield design revives conventional pillars, anticipating a feature that will be seen on many '60 and '61 cars. Arched well into the roof, it measures a full three feet at the center.

From the front seat, this massive expanse of glass loses much of its glamour. There are annoying reflections in the upper corners and the sun warms the legs of occupants even with the air conditioner going full blast.

The interior, upholstered in a soft broadcloth, is full of mysterious little storage compartments and warning lights. The instrument panel is stock, supplemented by a dazzling array of controls for all the accessories.

Some of the earlier Brougham's most elaborate features, such as the power-operated hood and deck lids, have been abandoned on the new model.

The Eldorado engine is a triple carburetor version of the familiar Cadillac V-8, producing 345 hp at 4800 rpm, and the rear axle ratio is 3.21-to-1. The only chassis modification has been the substitution of air bags for the coil springs.

Despite 20 added horsepower and lower gearing, the weight of the Brougham's custom body with all its power equipment resulted in a 0-to-60 time of 11.7 seconds, 1.4 seconds slower than the standard 62 sedan tested earlier this year.

It was interesting to note a difference in performance with the air conditioner on, 0-to-30 in 4.7 seconds against 4.5 with it off, an indication of the power it takes to keep cool.

The ride was extremely smooth. The air suspension took the roughness out of just about any surface at any speed. When the car crossed railroad tracks, for example, they were heard more than felt.

There was a slight floating sensation at cruising speeds, but a much milder one than on softly-sprung conventional car.

At no time was there the frame quiver that has been experienced on other Cadillac test cars, though a slight rumble was noticed at about 50 mph, possibly due to inadequate undercoating.

Otherwise, the noise level was quite low. Aside from the air conditioning blower, the hum of the tires on the pavement was about the loudest thing to be heard.

In general, the car felt like what it was, a refined Cadillac. Would it be worth the $13,075 asking price? To those who appreciate extremely fine workmanship and the prestige of exclusive styling, yes. These are the Brougham's prime advantages over a regular Cadillac, since the latter can be almost as lavishly equipped.

More than anything else, the Brougham pointed out the value to be had in today's lower priced cars. There is simply not the difference that once existed between the cheapest models and the most expensive. •

ELEGANT INTERIOR features luxurious broadcloth upholstery, has extra clock mounted behind front seat, red warning lights to indicate door is open. Instrument panel is stock Cadillac.

DISTINCTIVE BROUGHAM STYLING, enhanced by a special Barris paint finish, was created in Detroit though body construction is by Italy's Pinin Farina. Non-wraparound windshield design, easing front seat access, is sure to be seen on other cars in near future. Mounted on standard 130-inch Cadillac wheelbase, car measures same 225 inches overall length as stock 62 sedan.

photo by Arch Brown

1959 CADILLAC ELDORADO BIARRITZ

NOTHING SUCCEEDS LIKE EXCESS

by Arch Brown
photos by Dave Brown

MENTION the Cadillac Eldorado convertible and most people will immediately call to mind the big, front-wheel-drive job of the 1970s — the one that was promoted, toward the end of its production run, as GM's "last convertible," which, of course, it was not.

Cadillac enthusiasts recall, however, that for 14 years — 1953 through 1966 — there was another Eldorado convertible. This one, basically an uptown version of the Series Sixty-Two ragtop, employed the conventional rear drive. Always lavishly equipped, at times it featured some really dazzling styling innovations, and for six years it came with a more powerful engine than the lesser Cadillacs.

And from 1956 through 1963 it was known as the Biarritz, or to give its complete title, the Cadillac Eldorado Biarritz.

The first of the Eldorado convertibles, back in 1953, pioneered the use of a dogleg-style, wraparound windshield. This — in combination with cut-down, dipped-profile doors, a flush-fitting metal boot to cover the top when it was lowered, and a gleaming set of chromed

wire wheels — gave the Eldorado a smart, distinctive look. Heavily influenced by Cadillac's 1952 Motorama show car, it was an eye-catching machine. As it should have been; for its $7,750 price tag was nearly half again as high as that of the Series 62 convertible. Production was limited to only 532 cars.

For 1954 the Eldorado's price was slashed to $5,738, but the car was downgraded to such an extent that apart from those gorgeous chromed wires and some brightwork applied to the lower rear fenders and quarter panels, it could easily be mistaken for the Series 62.

No one, however, could mistake the 1955 model for anything but an Eldorado. Cast aluminum and steel "Sabre-Spoke" wheels replaced the earlier wires, and the car received a pair of "rocketship" rear fenders, inspired — like the wheels — by an experimental

show car displayed the year before. Twin four-barrel carburetors boosted the Eldorado's horsepower to 270, 20 more than other Cadillac models.

By this time, sales of the upscale convertible were good — very good, considering its premium price, which, though much lower than that of the 1953 model, was still some $1,700 higher than Cadillac's base ragtop. For 1955 3,950 Eldorados were produced, more than seven times as many as the 1953 model!

The Biarritz name was adopted in 1956 to distinguish the Eldorado convertible from its newly introduced hardtop counterpart, the Seville. Changes from 1955 were minimal, although a smart (if hazardous) twin-bladed hood ornament was added. Horsepower by this time had been increased to 305 on both Eldorados — again, 20 more than the less expensive Cadillacs.

The entire Cadillac line was completely restyled for 1957. Abandoning the little "fishtails" that had been featured since 1948, Cadillac stylists adopted what the flacks were pleased to call "stabilizer-type" rear fenders — in effect, a modified version of the Eldorado's "rocketship" fins. A three-inch reduction in the height of the automobile was made possible in part by the adoption of a tubular-center, X-type frame, a configuration that would be outlawed today because of its total lack of side-impact protection.

Overall, the 1957 Cadillac was distinctly new in appearance from every angle, yet it was instantly recognizable as a Cadillac. And at the top of the line that year was a magnificent new luxury sedan, the Eldorado Brougham (see *SIA* #2). Evidently conceived in response to Lincoln's Continental Mark II (see *SIA* #2), at $13,074 it was by far the most expensive car then being built in the United States. And its long list of standard equipment included, in addition to the expected amenities, a complex system of air suspension.

But the Brougham's market was a limited one; only 400 were produced for the 1957 model year. Much more numerous were the Seville and Biarritz, whose respective totals came to 2,100 and 1,800. Both featured rear-quarter styling that was distinct from any other Cadillac: Softly rounded rear fenders, reflecting the downward slope of the trunk, sprouted a pair of very smart, sharply pointed tail fins. Beautifully proportioned, these fins gave the Biarritz and Seville models a more balanced, sleeker appearance than that of the corresponding Series 62 cars.

The Biarritz, along with the Seville, was little changed in appearance for 1958, though a number of styling modifications were made to the rest of the Cadillac line. Quad headlamps and a wider grille made up of several rows of metallic studs constituted the principal distinctions from the previous year's Biarritz. More important changes took place under the hood, where the use of three two-barrel carburetors helped to boost the horsepower from a more-than-adequate 300 in the 1957 version to a neck-snapping 335. The Brougham's air suspension system was made optionally available, but even without that feature the price of the Biarritz (and the Seville as well) shot from $6,648 to $7,500. In combination with the recession that year, the increase led to a sharp reduction in sales.

And then came 1959. It was a pivotal year in terms of General Motors' corporate design policy, because for the first time the basic body styling was the same for all GM marques. Each division would thereafter have to depend upon differences in such details as the grille, fenders and assorted trim items to distinguish its product from those of its sister divisions. If the reader will visualize the 1957 models of, say, Chevrolet, Oldsmobile and Cadillac, it's easy to see that the three of them — while bearing some design relationship to one another — represented three dis-

tinct styling developments. The same cannot be said of the 1959 models of those three marques. There's some difference in size, of course, but mainly the distinctions among them have to do with their frontal appearance, and the configuration of the rear fenders. That was the year of Chevrolet's "gull wings," a variation on the then-popular "fin" motif. Oldsmobile, alone among GM divisions, eschewed sizeable fins in any form, in favor of a rather tailored appearance at the rear. And Cadillac went totally bonkers!

Perhaps it was appropriate that Cadillac was the one to carry the fender-fin idea to the point of absurdity, for it was Cadillac that had started the craze in the first place. As Stephen Bayley recounts the story, it was the Lockheed P-38, the twin-fuselage fighter plane of World War II, that supplied the inspiration. Because the P-38 was powered by

engines from GM's Allison Division, corporate executives were privileged to see it — at some distance, to be sure — prior to its public unveiling. And at the preview the attention of Harley Earl, General Motors' vice president for styling, was riveted upon the airplane's twin tail booms.

When the 1948 Cadillac appeared (see *SIA* #11) — the first, along with the Olds Ninety-Eight, of the corporation's true postwar cars — it featured what the public initially referred to as "fishtails." Sprouting from each of the Cadillac's rear fenders was an elevated taillamp, suitably modest in size but clearly modeled after those Lockheed tail booms.

There was nothing modest about the tail fins on Cadillac's 1959 model, however, and their enormous height was accentuated by the very low profile of the car; for three inches had been chopped from the 1958 model's already modest elevation. Company publicity spoke glowingly of "the sweeping lines of beauty (which) culminate in gracefully tapered, chrome-edged rear fender fins with twin, nacelle-like contours containing the projectile-shaped red lenses of the tail, stop and turn signal lamps...." But Walter M.P. McCall was probably closer to the mark when he wrote, "Their towering, dagger-tipped tail fins with podded, dual-bullet taillights became synonymous with the automotive styling excesses of the 1950s. Cadillac, which had started the tail fin styling craze a decade earlier, carried them to ludicrous heights in the 1959 model year." Indeed. But at least in 1959 the designers put a stop to the insane practice of running the exhaust pipes out through the rear bumper!

The Biarritz lost a good deal of its individuality that year. For the first time since the Eldorado convertible of 1954, the top-of-the-line convertible's body contours were identical to those of the base Cadillac ragtop. Even the gorgeous

Right: Eldo rides on 10-foot, 10-inch wheelbase with 95 more inches of overhang. *Below:* From certain angles the fins can be positively graceful. *Bottom left:* Traditional Caddy crest and "v" ride up front. *Bottom center:* Eldo i.d. is subtly spelled out at bottom of front fenders. *Bottom right:* Gas filler rides smack in middle above rear bumper accents.

1959 CADILLAC

Sabre-Spoke wheels were gone, their place taken by a set of attractive, though undistinguished deep-dish wheel covers. There was a special grille at the rear, echoing the car's frontal appearance. But the principal styling distinction of the Biarritz was a long, chromed spear, extending from the rear bumper up over the quarter panel and — gradually narrowing — across the door. And just to make sure that everyone would recognize Cadillac's premium convertible, the word *Eldorado* was spelled out in chromed block letters along the lower edge of each front fender.

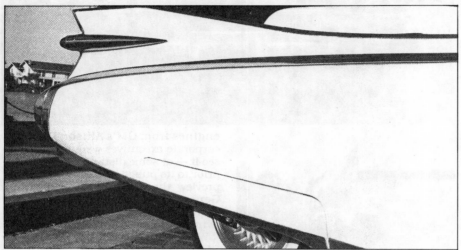

1959 Cadillac Price and Production Table

	Price*	Production
Series 62 (130-inch w.b.)		
Coupe	$ 4,892	21,947
Sedan, 4-window	$ 5,080	14,138
Sedan, 6-window	$ 5,080	23,461
Convertible Coupe	$ 5,455	11,130
Export Sedan, CKD	N/a	60
Series 63 (130-inch w.b.)		
Coupe de Ville	$ 5,252	21,924
Sedan de Ville, 4-window	$ 5,498	12,308
Sedan de Ville, 6-window	$ 5,498	19,158
Series 60-Special (130-inch w.b.)		
Sedan, Fleetwood	$ 6,233	12,250
Series 64 (130-inch w.b.)		
Eldorado Seville Coupe	$ 7,401	975
Eldorado Biarritz Convertible	$ 7,401	1,320
Series 67 (149.8-inch w.b.)		
Sedan, Fleetwood	$ 8,750	710
Limousine, Fleetwood	$ 9,748	690
Series 69 (130-inch w.b.)		
Eldorado Brougham	$13,074	99
Series 68 (156-inch w.b.)		
Commercial Chassis	N/a	2,102
Total Model Year Production		142,272
* Including federal excise tax		

But if the appearance of the Biarritz was less distinctive than before, its list of standard equipment was more impressive than ever. To the power seat, power windows and power vent wings, the radio, heater and a whole galaxy of auxiliary lights — not to mention the HydraMatic transmission, power steering and brakes — was added air suspension, introduced a year earlier on the Eldorado Brougham. Bucket seats, available for the first time, were a no-cost option; and the horsepower went up again, this time to 345. Overall length was increased by 1½ inches to 225 inches, but the low profile combined with the sweeping lines of the car to make it appear even longer.

And moving against the trend of the times, the price of the Biarritz was reduced just a trifle, from $7,500 to $7,401.

The 1960 Cadillacs, including the Biarritz, reflected the public's negative reaction to 1959's styling excesses. The fins were trimmed down to manageable size, resulting in a much more attractive automobile, though other changes were minor in nature.

1961, however, was another matter. Both the Seville and the ultra-expensive Brougham were dropped, leaving the Biarritz as the only remaining Eldorado model. Air suspension, plagued from the start with persistent leaks, was eliminated, as was the six-barrel carburetion. Nearly a thousand dollars was shaved from the price of the Biarritz, reflecting its new, reduced status; and the downward trend in that respect continued. By 1964 even the Biarritz name was eliminated. Thereafter, until the end of its production life in 1966, Cadillac's most expensive convertible was known as the Fleetwood Eldorado.

Cadillac Eldorado Convertibles: 1953-1966

Year	Price	Production	Horsepower	Compression ratio	Carburetion
1953	$7,750	532	210	8.25:1	1 4-bbl
1954	$5,738	2,150	230	8.25:1	1 4-bbl
1955	$5,814	3,950	270	9.10:1	2 4-bbl
1956	$6,014	2,150	305	9.75:1	2 4-bbl
1957	$6,648	1,800	300*	10.0:1	1 4-bbl
1958	$7,500	815	335	10.25:1	3 2-bbl
1959	$7,401	1,320	345	10.50:1	3 2-bbl
1960	$7,401	1,285	345	10.50:1	3 2-bbl
1961	$6,477	1,450	325	10.50:1	1 4-bbl
1962	$6,610	1,450	325	10.50:1	1 4-bbl
1963	$6,608	1,828	325	10.50:1	1 4-bbl
1964	$6,608	1,870	340	10.50:1	1 4-bbl
1965	$6,738	2,125	340	10.50:1	1 4-bbl
1966	$6,631	2,250	340	10.50:1	1 4-bbl

* a 325-horsepower version with two 4-barrel carburetion was available at extra cost.

Note: Only the 1956-1963 models carried the Biarritz name. From 1964 through 1966 this model was known as the Fleetwood Eldorado.

Left: There will never, ever be a car built to match the '59 Eldorado in sheer audacity of styling. Below: If you have two head-lamps on each side, you've just got to have two parking/directional lamps to match. After all, the '58 Impala had the same arrangement and the flagship of the GM fleet's not to be outdone.

Driving Impressions

We found our driveReport car in Canyon Dam, a community located on the shores of beautiful Lake Almanor, high in the Sierra Nevada mountains of northern California. It is part of a fleet of 23 vintage Cadillacs belonging to Dick Dimick, a retired general contractor. (See sidebar, page 98.)

Two modifications have been made to this car, one visual, the other mechanical. In company with nearly all the Eldorados of this era, Dimick's '59 Biarritz has undergone transplant surgery to replace its troublesome air bags with conventional coil springs. And as a matter of personal preference — one in which we heartily concur — Dick has substituted a set of Sabre-Spoke wheels, robbed from an earlier Eldorado, for the less distinctive wheels that were furnished with the '59 Biarritz.

Dick located this car some five years ago, through an ad in the *San Francisco Chronicle*. He restored it himself, as he has a number of other vintage Cadillacs. Plating and upholstery were farmed out to specialists; otherwise the entire

The Things They Said
1959 Cadillac Eldorado

Tom McCahill, *Mechanix Illustrated*, November 1958
"This year the engine is up to 390 cubic inches, though remaining basically the same as in previous years.... Air suspension is on all four wheels, tied up with new Freon 12 shock absorbers which give 'an amazingly soft ride.' "

Motor Life, May 1959
"When riding in this car, the almost soundless operation coupled with rich materials and fine assembly produce the desired effect: You know that this is an expensive and luxurious automobile. One is never in doubt."

Arthur R. Railton, *Popular Mechanics 1959 Fact Book*
"The smaller steering wheel gives a more sporty feel. Handling has been improved markedly. There is less 'load' on the power steering, and this, plus the lower center of gravity, makes it feel better."

Compiled by R. Perry Zavitz

specifications

Illustrations by Russell von Sauers, The Graphic Automobile Studio

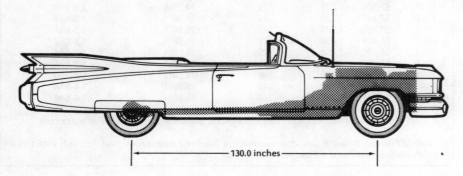

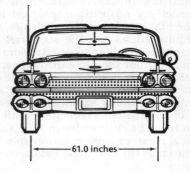

|← 130.0 inches →| |← 61.0 inches →|

1959 Cadillac Eldorado Biarritz

Price	$7,401 f.o.b. factory, with standard equipment. Federal excise tax included
Standard equipment	HydraMatic transmission, power steering, power brakes, air suspension, electric door locks, 2-way power seat, driver's side only, power windows, power vent regulators, "Q" engine (3 2-bbl carburetors), heater, radio, remote-control trunk lid lock, fog lamps, fluted wheel discs, electric clock, 4 cigarette lighters (2 front, 2 rear), dual back-up lights, courtesy and map lights, front and rear, 3-way, E-Z-Eye rearview mirror, whitewall tires, windshield washer (partial list)
Options on dR car	Air conditioner, tinted glass, cruise control, automatic headlight dimmer
Non-standard equip. on dR car	Sabre-Spoke wheels (from 1958 Biarritz)

ENGINE

Type	90-degree V-8, cast-iron block
Bore/stroke	4 inches x 3⅞ inches
Displacement	390.0 cubic inches
Valve config.	Ohv
Max bhp @ rpm	345 @ 4,800
Max torque @ rpm	435 @ 3,400
Compression ratio	10.5:1
Number main brgs	5
Lubrication system	Pressure
Induction system	3 2-bbl carbs, camshaft pump
Exhaust system	Dual
Electrical system	12-volt
Valve lifters	Hydraulic

TRANSMISSION

Type	HydraMatic, fully automatic planetary gearset
Ratios: 1st	3.97:1
2nd	2.55:1
3rd	1.55:1
Reverse	3.74:1

DIFFERENTIAL

Type	Hypoid
Ratio	3.21:1
Drive axles	Semi-floating

STEERING

Type	Saginaw ball nut sector, hydraulic power
Turns lock-to-lock	3½
Ratios	Gear, 17.5:1; Overall, 18.9:1
Turning radius	24 feet 2 inches

BRAKES

Type	Hydraulic drum, self-adjusting, power assisted
Drum diameter	12 inches
Total swept area	210.32 square inches

CHASSIS & BODY

Frame	Tubular-center "X" type
Body construction	All steel
Body style	Convertible coupe

SUSPENSION

Front	Independent, direct-action coil springs with torsion rod stabilizer
Rear	Conventional, helical coil springs*
Tires	8.20/15 4-ply
Wheels	Sabre-Spoke (standard: pressed steel)

*Replacing original air suspension

CAPACITIES

Crankcase	6 quarts (including filter)
Cooling system	19.7 quarts with heater and air conditioner
Fuel tank	21 gallons
Transmission	23 pints

WEIGHTS AND MEASURES

Wheelbase	130 inches
Overall length	225.0 inches
Overall height	54.4 inches
Overall width	81.1 inches
Front tread	61 inches
Rear tread	61 inches
Ground clearance	6.6 inches
Shipping weight	5,060 pounds

INTERIOR DIMENSIONS

Head room	33.7 inches front; 33.6 inches rear
Shoulder room	60.5 inches front; 51.8 inches rear
Hip room	66.3 inches front; 52.7 inches rear
Leg room	45.7 inches front; 38.7 inches rear
Seat height	8.6 inches front; 11.5 inches rear

It's massive, all right, but in its day it was surpassed in length by the rival Continental convertible, which was two inches longer!

1959 CADILLAC

project represents Dick's own handiwork. "I've always enjoyed messing with cars, ever since I was a kid," he explains. "And when I retired I had the time."

The Dimicks, Dick and his wife Jody, enjoy displaying the '59 Biarritz at Cadillac-LaSalle Club meets. But it is not a "show" car; it's a driver! Dick and Jody have made a number of trips to Oregon in it, and even drove it to Texas on one occasion. "We could have sold it four or five times before we got home from that one," Jody recalls. Remarkably enough, the big convertible covers about 17 miles on a gallon of gasoline. Leaded premium is required, of course.

The term "fully equipped" has suffered a lot of abuse in recent years. But this automobile is *loaded*! In addition to the long list of standard goodies with which every '59 Biarritz left the factory, Dimick's car has air-conditioning, tinted glass, cruise control and the "Autronic Eye" automatic headlight dimmer.

A few of these cars — reportedly 99, out of a production run of 1,320 — were outfitted with what the factory was pleased to call "bucket" seats. The term is pure hype. *Individual* front seats they are, *buckets* they're not. Dick's car is one of the 99, and we found little to recommend this seating arrangement. Lateral support is no better than the regular bench seat, and the too-erect angle of the backrests is downright uncomfortable. The six-way power seat

Above: *Eldo's outsized air cleaner has been removed to show the three two-barrel carbs, a sight which would gladden OPEC immensely if they appeared on new Cadillacs today.* **Left:** *Instrument layout didn't differ from less costly series Cadillacs.* **Below:** *How would you like to be impaled on one of those rear fenders?*

Puttin' on the (Biar)Ritz

When the decision was made to augment the Eldorado convertible with a hardtop version for the 1956 season, corporate planners decided that each of the cars should have its own distinctive name. And being Cadillacs — top-of-the-line Cadillacs at that — the names should (and indeed *must*) be evocative of status, of class, of panache.

They called the coupe the Seville, after the historic town in southern Spain. The name, still in use today, has a nice ring to it. But for the convertible Cadillac went all-out, naming it the Biarritz. No doubt that last syllable, *Ritz*, had something to do with the selection. But to the *cognoscenti* it meant something more, for Biarritz, located on the Bay of Biscay in southwestern France, is a favorite resort of the very rich. Frequented in earlier times by the likes of Napoleon III and his Spanish empress, Eugenie — not to mention Queen Victoria and Kings Edward VII of England and Alfonso XIII of Spain — Biarritz became known as "the queen of resorts and the resort of kings."

What better name, then, to suggest wealth, position — and yes, power!

One Takes the Bitter with the Sweet

The editor keeps wanting to know what we like and what we don't like about the subjects of our various driveReports. In this case it's easy, for we have strong feelings in both directions.

We like:
- The silken ride, smooth as cream. Doubtless it would be even better if the original air suspension were still intact.
- The silence. For a convertible, it's incredibly quiet.
- The nearly flawless level of fit and finish.
- The brisk performance.
- The relative economy of operation, for a car of its size and power.
- The excellent, seemingly fade-free brakes.

But there's a downside:
- The highly touted air suspension gave so much trouble that today it's nearly impossible to find one of these cars that hasn't been converted to conventional coil springs.
- Seats are too low, and they're much less confortable than those of earlier Cadillacs.
- Nor is handling on a par with the '57 and '58 models.
- Body structure, while generally satisfactory, doesn't seem quite as sturdy as the earlier cars.
- The gears that operate the power vent wings tend to strip rather readily. Were they made of pot metal?
- And those garish fins, whatever they do for — or to — the styling, are unquestionably hazardous.

We have to agree with Dick Dimick: This is a *good* car, but not a *great* one. In too many respects it falls short of the standards of its predecessors.

1959 CADILLAC

Above and right: Tim Cashin's '59 Eldo demonstrates what the cars look like with factory stock wheel covers; driveReport car uses unauthentic but handsome "Sabre-Spoke" wheels which were supplied on 1955-58 Eldos.

adjustment that was standard with the bench seat is replaced, in this instance, by two-way power on the driver's side only. And in company with all General Motors cars in 1959, the seating position is very low. Four inches lower, in fact, than the corresponding 1957 model. Obviously the change was made in the interest of providing the car with a lower profile. In our view it was a poor trade; seating in the earlier cars is much more comfortable.

Leg room, however, is ample. Knee room to the rear is more than adequate, too, although the seat is so low and so erect that those of us with long legs can almost look straight ahead at our knees!

But of course the ride is very, very smooth — and very quiet. Acceleration is good. Not really flashy; perhaps the 4,500-foot elevation at Lake Almanor takes a little of the edge off it. But it's a fast car — faster, Dimick reports, than his '57 Biarritz, and more economical as well. Presumably this felicitous combination is due to the use of three two-barrel carburetors in 1959, in lieu of 1957's dual four-barrels.

Typically of HydraMatic transmis-

The Man Who Likes Cadillacs

Some people collect teddy bears; others acquire old hooch bottles. Still others accumulate antique furniture, but Dick Dimick likes Cadillacs. Old Cadillacs. At latest count he has 23 of them — 16 of which are licensed, running and used more or less regularly. The others are either under restoration or awaiting their turn.

A small barn situated on a lot adjacent to the Dimicks' home shelters a few of the cars, while others are hidden under an assortment of lean-tos which Dick has improvised here and there. Exposed to the elements are several parts cars, not included among the official count of 23.

Most of the Cadillacs date from the late fifties; none is later than a 1964 model — and the Dimicks don't even own a modern car. There's really no reason why they should!

SIA asked Dick Dimick how he happened to acquire so many of these fine old cars.

Dimick: I guess I've always enjoyed Cadillacs, from when I was a kid. And I liked the '57 Eldorados the best, so that's what I looked for when I started to collect Cadillacs. I particularly wanted to restore convertibles — cars that I thought would be worth my effort, so when I got through they'd at least be worth the time and the money that I had in them. So all of my cars are convertibles. And the Eldorado Biarritzes always caught my eye because they were something different.

SIA: What do you have in your collection now — the ones that are restored and running, that is?

Dimick: Well, we've got two '57 Biarritzes and a '57 Series 62 convertible. Then there

are four '58s, all Biarritzes. And four '59s, two Biarritzes and two 62 convertibles. I bought another '59 Biarritz just recently. It's a mess, but we'll be restoring it pretty soon.

Then there's a '60 Biarritz and a regular 1960 convertible, and a 1962 Series 62. And two '64 Eldorados. How many does that make?

SIA: Sixteen.

Dimick: When you get this many you have a hard time keeping track! My wife tallies them up now and then. I just don't pay much

attention, you see.

SIA: When did you get started in this hobby?

Dimick: Oh, about eight, nine years ago. When I retired. Because you just don't have time to do anything when you're in business for yourself.

SIA: How much time do you devote to these cars?

Dimick: Oh, all my spare time! We hunt and we travel around, but when I'm home this gives me something to do. If I'm here all week I'll put in 40 hours. But if I'm not — well, I don't intend to be a slave to it!

SIA: Do we understand that all 16 of these cars are driven regularly?

Dimick: We try and drive them at least once every two weeks. Sometimes this isn't possible, when there's snow on the ground. Then they'll set till the road gets better. But then let a good day come and I'll take one out and use it. I go and have coffee almost every morning in Chester. That's a 30-mile round trip, and I take a different car every day. And if my wife goes into town in the afternoon, she'll generally take another one. Because I think the worst thing for the cars is not to exercise them!

SIA: Are there other cars that you'd like to own?

Dimick: No, not really. These are the ones I enjoy. I like some of the older cars, but we prefer the ones we can drive. The Cadillac Club is having a meet in Palm Springs pretty soon, so we'll drive one down there.

SIA: Which one?

Dimick: The green '57 Biarritz, probably. I think it's my favorite.

Comparison Table: 1959 Luxury Convertibles

	Cadillac Biarritz	Lincoln Continental
Price (f.o.b. factory)*	$7,401	$7,056
Engine	90-degree V-8, ohv	90-degree V-8, ohv
Bore and stroke	4 inches x $3\frac{7}{8}$ inches	4.297 inches x 3.7 inches
Displacement	390.0 cubic inches	430.0 cubic inches
Horsepower @ rpm	345 @ 4,800	350 @ 4,400
Torque @ rpm	435 @ 3,400	490 @ 2,800
Compression ratio	10.5:1	10.0:1
Carburetion	3 2-bbl	1 4-bbl
Transmission	HydraMatic	Turbo-Drive
Gear ratios	3.97/2.55/1.55/1.00	2.37/1.48/1.00
Torque conv. ratio at stall	None	2.10
Differential	Hypoid	Hypoid
Ratio	3.21:1	2.89:1
Steering (power)	Ball nut sector	Recirculating ball
Ratios (gear/overall)	17.5/18.9	17.0/19.5
Brakes (power)	Hydraulic drum	Hydraulic drum
Drum diameter	12 inches	11 inches
Effective area	210.3 square inches	262.0 square inches
Suspension (factory)	Air	Coil springs
Tire size	8.20/15	9.50/14
Shipping weight	5,060 pounds	5,169 pounds
Measurements: wheelbase	130 inches	131 inches
Overall length	225 inches	227.1 inches
Overall width	81.1 inches	80.1 inches
Overall height	54.4 inches	58.0 inches
Tread, front/rear	61 inches/61 inches	61 inches/61 inches
Production (this model)	1,320**	2,195
Horsepower/c.i.d.	.885	.814
Pounds per horsepower	14.7	14.8
Pounds per c.i.d.	13.0	12.0

* Including federal taxes
** Cadillac's total convertible sales, including the Series 62, came to 12,450. (The Continental was Lincoln's only convertible)

sions of this vintage, shifts produce a pronounced surge — especially in the upshift from second to third gear. It's not bothersome, once one gets used to it.

Steering is fairly quick — 3½ turns, lock-to-lock — but we found it a little numb. As softly sprung as it is, we expected the big Cadillac to heel over sharply in the turns, but it behaved better than we anticipated. And the

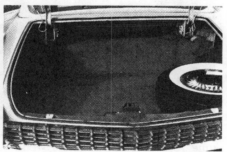

Above left: Although the mass of sheet metal gives car a slab-sided appearance the body actually is gracefully curved. *Left:* With a car this size there had better be generous trunk space! *Below left:* Rear of seat has decoration molded in. *Below:* Fiberglass boot adds to massive look of car when top's down.

1959 CADILLAC

brakes are excellent — powerful, yet smooth.

Down the road, the Biarritz fairly begs to be turned loose. At 60 it seems to be loafing. But there is just a little tendency to wander at high speeds. We questioned Dick Dimick about that, and he replied that all four of his 1959 Cadillacs display the same characteristic. This, he explains, is why he prefers to drive the '57 and '58 models. And so, at Dick's invitation we took the wheel of a '57 Biarritz and found ourselves in total agreement. Not only is the seat much more supportive than that of the later car, but the handling is distinctly superior. Son Dave, our photographer on this assignment, gave a similar report upon driving a '58 model.

Those big fins, which frankly have always seemed a bit grotesque to us, at least have the virtue of locating precisely the rear corners of the car — a real advantage in parallel parking. They also turn the heads of passers-by. Whether or not one likes the extreme styling of this model, the '59 Biarritz attracts a lot of attention!

Hidden under the broad expanse of the rear deck is a trunk so huge that Dick Dimick has hauled a full set of five wheels and tires in it. He's disinclined to be quite so utilitarian with it now, however, having recently lined the luggage compartment with carpeting that represents a distinct improvement over the original.

In sum, then, we found the '59 Biarritz to be a powerful, beautifully appointed convertible with many virtues and not a few drawbacks (see sidebar, page 19). Equipped with virtually every creature comfort that the state of the art permitted in 1959, it's a car that really pampers its passengers — which is more than one can say about most automobiles nowadays! Its styling is unique, but you'd better not own and drive one unless you like lots of attention! □

This page, above: Unlike the Lincoln of that year, there's hardly a straight line on the Caddy. **Right:** Buck Rogers would have loved the Eldo. *Below:* Depending on how you look at it, the car represents either the ultimate development of the automotive tailfin or proclaims that Cadillac stylists had a great sense of humor back in 1959.

Acknowledgements and Bibliography
Automobile Industries, *March 15, 1959; Stephen Bayley*, Harley Earl and the Dream Machine; *Cadillac factory literature; Jeffrey I. Godshall*, "A Fifties Fantasy," Automobile Quarterly, *Volume 16, Number 4; Maurice Hendry*, Cadillac: The Complete History; *Richard M. Langworth*, Encyclopedia of American Cars, 1940-1970; *John Lawlor*, "Cadillac's Eldorado Brougham," Motor Life, *October 1959; Walter M.P. McCall*, Eighty Years of Cadillac-LaSalle; *Roy A. Schneider*, Automobile Heritage's Illustrated Guide to Cadillac, 1950-1959; *Jim Whipple*, "Cadillac," Car Life, *May 1959; "Cadillac and Imperial Road Test," Motor Life, May 1959; "Testing the Luxury Cars," Motor Life, August 1960.*
Our thanks to Ray Borges and Linda Huntsman, Harrah Automobile Foundation, Reno, Nevada; Dave Brown, Durham, California; Tim Cashin, Stockton, California; Ralph Dunwoodie, Sun Valley, Nevada; Bob Weiss, Stockton, California. Special thanks to Dick and Jody Dimick, Canyon Dam, California.

REPRINTED WITH PERMISSION FROM
Special Interest Autos #88, August 1985
Box 196, Bennington, Vermont 05201

A Publication from Hemmings Motor News